THE JUSTICE BROKER

THE JUSTICE BROKER
Lawyers and Ordinary Litigation

HERBERT M. KRITZER

New York   Oxford
OXFORD UNIVERSITY PRESS
1990

Oxford University Press

Oxford New York Toronto
Delhi Bombay Calcutta Madras Karachi
Petaling Jaya Singapore Hong Kong Tokyo
Nairobi Dar es Salaam Cape Town
Melbourne Auckland

and associated companies in
Berlin Ibadan

Copyright © 1990 by Herbert M. Kritzer

Published by Oxford University Press, Inc.,
200 Madison Avenue, New York, New York 10016

Oxford is a registered trademark of Oxford University Press

Excerpts from "Fee Arrangement and Negotiation: A Research
Note," "The Impact of Fee Arrangement on Lawyer Effort," and
"Studying Disputes: Learning from the CLRP Experience" which
originally appeared in LAW AND SOCIETY REVIEW 21:4, 19:2,
and 15:3-4 are reprinted by permission of the Law and Society
Association.

Library of Congress Cataloging-in-Publication Data
Kritzer, Herbert M., 1947–
The justice broker : lawyers and
ordinary litigation / Herbert M. Kritzer.
p. cm. Includes bibliographical references.
ISBN 0-19-506142-X
1. Justice, Administration of—United States.
2. Lawyers—United States. I. Title.
KF8700.K77 1990
347.73—dc20 [347.307] 89-49455

2 4 6 8 9 7 5 3 1

Printed in the United States of America
on acid-free paper

To Amy

Preface

The data that form the basis of the analysis described in this book were collected by the Civil Litigation Research Project (CLRP) during 1979–1980. CLRP was a unique undertaking, both in purpose and in scale. The funding for the project came initially from the Office for Improvements in the Administration of Justice in the U.S. Department of Justice (Contract No. JAOIA-79-C-0040); after the political winds shifted in 1981, responsibility for the project was transferred to the National Institute of Justice (Contract No. J-LEAA-003-82). Over the years since funding from the Department of Justice came to an end, support for specific pieces of work and analysis were provided by the National Institute for Dispute Resolution (NIDR) and the National Science Foundation (Grant No. SES-8320129). Substantial supplemental support has been forthcoming from the University of Wisconsin Graduate School and the University of Wisconsin Law School. With additional support from the National Science Foundation (Grant No. SES-8511622) data collected by the project (and on which this book is based) have been archived for use by other researchers; data and accompanying documentation are available from the Interuniversity Consortium for Political and Social Research (ICPSR), University of Michigan, P.O. Box 1248, Ann Arbor, Michigan, 48106.

Bits and pieces of the work in this book appeared previously in a variety of sources, and I would like to thank those sources, and my original coauthors, for permission to use those materials.

Herbert M. Kritzer, Austin Sarat, David M. Trubek, Kristin Bumiller, and Elizabeth McNichol, "Understanding the Costs of Litigation: The Case of the Hourly-Fee Lawyer," *American Bar Foundation Research Journal*, 1985, pp. 559–604.

Joel Grossman, Herbert M. Kritzer, Kristin Bumiller, Austin Sarat, Stephen Mc-Dougal, and Richard E. Miller, "Dimensions of Institutional Participation: Who Uses the Courts and How?," *Journal of Politics, 44*, February 1982, pp. 86–114 (Table 3, p. 99; Table 4, p. 102; and Table 5, p. 102). Reprinted by permission of the University of Texas Press.

Herbert M. Kritzer, "Fee Arrangements and Negotiation: A Research Note," *Law & Society Review, 21,* 1987, pp. 341–348. Reprinted by permission of the Law & Society Association.

Herbert M. Kritzer, William L. F. Felstiner, Austin Sarat, and David M. Trubek, "The Impact of Fee Arrangement on Lawyer Effort," *Law & Society Review, 19,* 1985, pp. 251–278. Reprinted by permission of the Law & Society Association.

Herbert M. Kritzer, "Adjudication to Settlement: Shading in the Gray," *Judicature, 70,* October-November 1986, pp. 161–165.

Joel B. Grossman, Herbert M. Kritzer, Kristin Bumiller, and Stephen McDougal, "Measuring the Pace of Litigation in Federal and State Trial Courts," *Judicature, 65,* August 1981, pp. 86–113.

Herbert M. Kritzer, "Studying Disputes: Learning from the CLRP Experience," *Law & Society Review, 15,* 1980–1981, pp. 503–524. Reprinted by permission of the Law & Society Association.

Herbert M. Kritzer, Austin Sarat, David M. Trubek, and William L. F. Felstiner, "Winners and Losers in Litigation: Does Anyone Come Out Ahead?," Paper presented at the 1985 Annual Meeting of the Midwest Political Science Association, Chicago, Illinois.

The work that I describe in this book reflects substantial contributions by a number of people. David M. Trubek (professor of law, University of Wisconsin, and director of the Institute for Legal Studies) served as project director, taking on the burden of the day-to-day administration of the project during the years when so many people were involved on a daily basis. Along with David Trubek, William L. F. Felstiner (American Bar Foundation), Joel Grossman (professor of political science, University of Wisconsin), and Austin Sarat (professor of political science, Amherst College) collaborated in thinking through the design of the research and planning the data collection and the early analyses. I regret that for various reasons the exciting collaboration of the early years of the project could not be continued to the completion of this book. The intellectual debt that I owe to Dave, Bill, Austin, and Joel is deep, and they will influence my future work.

Most of the survey data were collected on our behalf by Mathematica Policy Research in Princeton, New Jersey. The work of Lois Blanchard and Joey Cerf insured that the data collected would meet our requirements; Paul Planchon supervised the work in Princeton. The court records data were coded by the law students working under the direct supervision of Stephen McDougal and Judith Hansen; additional aspects of work in the field were researched by Jill Anderson. In Madison, Laura Guy, Richard Miller, Kristin Bumiller, Elizabeth McNichol, Mary Pfister, George Brown, and Dan Krymkowski carried out much of the processing and management of the large data set that we assembled. More recently, I have had excellent assistance from several other graduate students: Karen Holtz, Tom Schmeling, and Jung Il Gill.

Many other persons, both students and nonstudents, worked on the project over the years. I appreciate the hard work of all of them. Finally, Jeanette Holz saw that people got paid, plane tickets got purchased, and reports got prepared for distribution. No project of the scale of CLRP could possibly succeed without the tireless efforts of someone like Jeanette.

The first complete draft of this manuscript was finished while I was enjoying the benefits of a sabbatical leave from the University of Wisconsin (which allowed me to escape from committees, students, and telephone calls long enough to complete the analysis and writing that went into that draft); during that leave, University College, London, and the Institute of Advanced Legal Studies, London, provided me with library resources and facilities that permitted me to complete the work. I benefited from comments by Herbert Jacob and Stuart Scheingold on portions of that draft. Comments and direction from John Flood at several important junctures helped clarify the focus on brokerage.

My family—Amy, Naomi, Abigail, and Than—has lived with this project much longer than any of us ever expected. Their tolerance, support, and good humor have helped us all survive it.

While my debts to colleagues, collaborators, and funding sources are great, as always the responsibility for what is said in the book rests solely with me.

Madison, Wisconsin   H.M.K.

Contents

I

INTRODUCTION

1

Brokers and Professionals: The Roles of Lawyers in Ordinary Litigation

Lawyers are intermediaries between the American public and the judiciary, the third independent branch of government in the United States. In this role lawyers find themselves in a love–hate relationship with the citizenry; they are cursed as troublemakers while remaining the dominant choice of the public for key elective positions in the legislative and executive branches of state and national government.[1] In recent years, we have come to know a great deal about the role of lawyers in the operation of the criminal justice system.[2] However, while most people think first about the criminal courts—when they think about the courts at all—a much greater proportion of the resources of our justice system is devoted to processing the noncriminal, or civil, side of the courts' dockets.[3] We know remarkably little about what lawyers actually do in this larger judicial arena.

If we are to understand the role of courts in American society (Council on the Role of Courts, 1984) and if we are to seek systematic improvement in the functioning of our courts, we must understand how lawyers perform their functions in our civil courts. The goal of this book is twofold. First, I describe the realities of lawyering in civil litigation: the backgrounds and experiences lawyers bring to their work, and how they go about their daily work. Second, I show that we need to go beyond traditional images of professionalism if we are to understand why lawyers do what they do and why they achieve the results that they achieve.

In pursuing these themes, I am not concerned with the big, newsworthy case such as that growing out of the Buffalo Creek disaster (Stern, 1976) or with the work of the "kings" of the tort bar (Jennings, 1989; Grescoe, 1978; Jenkins, 1988) or the "megalawyers" (Galanter, 1983b) of Wall Street (Steven, 1987; Stewart, 1983; Smigel, 1964), Washington (Laumann et al., 1985; Green, 1975; Goulden, 1972), and big firms generally (Nelson, 1988). Instead, I look at the lawyers who deal with the bread-and-butter work of America's civil courts—the ordinary, modest cases, such as a lawsuit over injuries suffered in an auto accident, a dispute over the failure of a remodeling contractor to complete the job to specifications, litigation over who has title to a piece of property, an allegation of unlawful discrimination in hiring or promotion, the fallout from a denial of a rezoning request, or a lawsuit that comes in the wake of a denial of an application for disability payments.[4] The kind of case I am concerned about is the one that usually involves $25,000 or less—what I call "ordinary litigation." Thus, this book is about "ordinary lawyering" in "ordinary cases."

Lawyers have attracted considerable attention from scholars in recent years:

- Heinz and Laumann (1982) have examined stratification in the large city bar.
- Nelson (1988) has described recent developments in the world of the corporate law firm.
- Landon (1982, 1985, 1988) has brought attention to the world of lawyers practicing in small towns and rural settings.
- Eisenstein (1978) and Horowitz (1977) have looked at lawyers employed by the federal government.
- Kessler (1987), Katz (1982), and Johnson (1978) have looked at lawyers working for government-funded legal services programs, and Erlanger (1978) and Rabin (1976) have looked at public interest lawyers.
- Spangler (1986) has focused on the situation of lawyers working as employees (in law firms, corporations, the federal government, and legal services organizations), and Rosen (1988–1989) has examined the specific situation of lawyers employed by corporations.
- Slovak (1979, 1980, 1981a) has studied lawyers working on behalf of the elite in the business, social, and cultural worlds of one large city.
- Halliday (1987), Foster (1986), and Powell (1988) have analyzed the efforts of leaders of the profession to extend and enhance the profession's power, regarding both its own economic interests and its role in the larger sociopolitical system.
- Abel (1986b, 1988a, 1989a) has painted a broad portrait of the development of the American legal profession (and the profession in England and Wales as well—1987, 1988b[5]), with a specific concern on the profession's efforts to "control the production of producers" and to "control the production by producers"—that is, to control in most, if not all, dimensions the marketplace for legal services.

The theoretical issues motivating most of this research come from the area of inquiry called the "sociology of the professions" and reflect both general themes in sociology (e.g., stratification and social hierarchies) and themes specific to analyzing professions (market control and professional training and socialization). By and large this has led to a focus on the macro sociology of the profession: the relationship of the profession to the larger social system (how the profession as a corporate body has sought political power, economic control, and social influence) and the internal structure of the profession (practice structures, stratification and divisions, socialization, and self-regulation).

The ideas underlying the work come from diverse theoretical traditions, including Weber, Durkheim, and Marx, as well as from contemporary theorists who have interpreted and extended those ideas, such as Parsons (1939, 1954, 1968), Johnson (1972), and Larson (1977). Research and analysis in that tradition have been more concerned with the *profession* (i.e., the *institutional* aspects of the lawyer's existence) than with the actual *work* of lawyers,[6] although frequently scholars have discussed the implications of the institutionalized profession for the work lawyers do (e.g., Heinz and Laumann, 1982; Spangler, 1986; Landon, 1982, 1985, 1988; Nelson, 1988).

This book reverses the focus. I examine the work of lawyers in one specific realm (ordinary civil litigation) and draw from the resulting analysis the implications for both the profession and the larger society. I argue that one must move beyond ideas associated with the sociology of the professions to understand the work of lawyers in ordinary litigation, and that an enlarged framework brings both the work of lawyers and the litigation process into clearer focus. I do not discard the insights suggested by the *professionalism* framework, but propose that one must overlay this sociological tradition with a theory of *brokerage* that is more typically associated with political analysis. The resulting dual framework highlights aspects of the litigator's work overlooked by either of the approaches taken singly, and it makes clear some of the tensions and contradictions that are a pervasive part of the litigator's existence. In the balance of this chapter, I discuss the professionalism and brokerage frameworks as they can be applied to understanding litigators and litigation. In subsequent chapters I discuss in detail lawyering in ordinary litigation.

The Professionalism Perspective

Lawyers are members of one of the three archetypical "learned" professions (physicians and the clergy comprise the other two). Much of what we know about the legal profession comes from the work of sociologists who take "the professions" as the focus of their study. The body of research on this subject is substantial[7] and reflects many different specific topics of study. As is true with most areas of the study of human affairs, there is substantial disagreement over definitions and boundaries (i.e., what is the definition of a "profession"?), yet many of the themes in this literature form the framework for the way we think about the legal profession, its work, and its role in society.[8] In fact, while scholars disagree on what constitutes a profession (see Freidson, 1983), and even on whether or not one should seek to define this concept (Freidson, 1983; Johnson, 1972: 24–25),[9] the common themes found in efforts at definition have provided a focus for much of the empirical research on professions in general and the legal profession in particular.

The characteristics typically used to define a profession include (but are not necessarily limited to):

1. "Possession of esoteric but useful knowledge and skills, based on specialized training or education" (Moore, 1970: 6).[10]

2. An orientation toward service in the interest of an identifiable client.
3. Autonomy of action, with regard both to the specific action (i.e., the professional is in control of the relationship with the client) and to the definition and enforcement of standards of professional behavior.
4. The existence of one or more organizations to serve the internal and external needs of the profession.[11]

In one sense, the concept of professionalism as applied to the legal profession is a normative concept that provides an ideal that lawyers should strive to meet (Nelson, 1988: 18); in the words of one recent commentary on the legal profession, "legal practice is . . . idealized as a self-directed calling, informed by the spirit of a public service" (Rhode, 1985; 592, quoting in part Pound, 1953: 14).[12]

But professionalism is more than a goal for practitioners (American Bar Association, 1986; Morgan, 1985). The conceptual elements comprising it guide and frame much of the empirical research on lawyers (Rueschemeyer, 1986; 442; see also Simon, 1985). This can easily be seen in the importance in much of the research on the legal profession of the definitional themes just listed; in addition to the broad issues referred to previously, we have specific studies of:

- The ways in which new lawyers come to be socialized to the profession through law school and the early years of practice (Abel, 1979a; Rathjens, 1976; Zemans and Rosenblum, 1981; Erlanger and Klegon, 1978; Stover, 1989).
- The relationship of lawyers to the social and political structure of their local and larger communities (Podmore, 1980; Szanton, 1973; Eulau and Sprague, 1964).
- The ways in which lawyers as professionals serve their clients and communities (Handler, 1967; Kagan and Rosen, 1985; Cain, 1979; Mungham and Thomas, 1983; Etheridge, 1973; Hosticka, 1979; Moore, 1970: 97–102; Reed, 1969; Sarat and Felstiner, 1986, 1988).
- The relationship of lawyers to the various work settings in which they find themselves (Smigel, 1964; Carlin, 1962; Johnson, 1974; Handler, Hollingsworth, and Erlanger, 1978; Spangler, 1986; Katz, 1982, 1985; Johnson, 1978; Menkel-Meadow and Meadow, 1982; Landon, 1982, 1985, 1988).
- The role of professional organizations in the adoption and enforcement of standards of behavior (Carlin, 1966; Schneyer, 1989).
- The nature and impact of stratification within the profession (Heinz and Laumann, 1982; Galanter, 1983b).

Recently, students of the legal profession have devoted substantial attention to the key concept of autonomy (Cain, 1979; Heinz and Laumann, 1982; Kagan and Rosen, 1985; Heinz, 1983; Nelson, 1988). This research has raised questions about whether lawyers in fact enjoy autonomy of action, particularly with regard to work specifically requested by a client. Concern about this question is central to the analytic concept of the professions because of the way the expected autonomy is derived from the other components of the definition of what constitutes a professional, and because it is this autonomy that differentiates the work situation of the professional from that of other members of the labor force (Daniels, 1973; Rueschemeyer, 1983; Johnson, 1972; Freidson, 1960, 1970: 23–46; Moore, 1970: 87–108); in Freidson's words, "autonomy of technique is at the core of what is unique about the profession" (1970: 44–45). While other workers have significant amounts of autonomy, that autonomy typically derives from employment status (i.e., self-employment) rather than from the nature of the tasks to be completed. Many workers have relatively little autonomy; the extreme example is the person working on an assembly line. Thus, what sets the professional's work situation apart from that of other workers is both the existence of autonomy of action and the basis of that autonomy.

The autonomy of the professional derives from two sources. First, it reflects the specialized, abstract knowledge of the professional, obtained through a formal process of higher education. That specialized knowledge is often accompanied by a technical language. The unique knowledge and language establish a particular kind of relationship between the professional and the consumer of the professional's services; the consumer, or client, is not in a position to instruct the professional on the services to be delivered but, instead, depends on the professional to determine what services (and how much of those services) will be rendered. Obviously, this dependence creates a situation that might easily lead to abuse if professionals were to take advantage of their *superior* position vis-à-vis the client.

Such abuse is avoided, at least in theory, because of the second reason that the professional is granted autonomy. A person working in a professional capacity is seen as engaging in that work not primarily for personal gain; the primary motivations are a combination of a commitment to service for the client and a love of the work in which the professional is engaged. This combination leads to an image of the professional as the clients' dispassionate "alter ego" — doing for clients what the clients would choose to do if they had the professional's expertise and were able to look "objectively" at their own situations. In the words of James Boswell (quoted in Megarry, 1962: 53), "A lawyer is to do for his client all his client might fairly do for himself if he could." Furthermore, according to Roscoe Pound, while "gaining of a livelihood is involved in all callings, in a profession [such as law] it is incidental" (Pound, 1953: 6); in fact, "the best service of the professional man is often rendered for no equivalent [i.e., fee] or for a trifling equivalent and it is his pride to do what he does in a way worthy of his profession even if done with no expectation of reward" (Pound, 1953: 10). As Richard Abel (1989a: 27) notes, this leads to "the widespread convention that lawyers and physicians do not discuss fees in advance."

This rejection of a profit motive for the lawyer as a professional can be observed historically in several ways. First, entering a profession was linked to the religious idea of a "calling" for which recompense was almost an insult;

naturally, some compromise was necessary to secure a livelihood, and various devices, such as the hood worn by academics into which students at medieval universities placed fees paid to their professors (Abel, 1989a: 27), bridged the gap between ideal and actual. Second, the tradition for barristers in England (the "senior" branch of the legal profession in that country) and for *avocats* in France was that they were not paid fees but received honorariums in appreciation for their work (see Abel-Smith and Stevens, 1968: 43; Le, 1982: 68–79;[13] that is, the payments received for "intellectual activities . . . were considered to be manifestations of the client's gratitude, since no price could be set on such intellectual services" (Le, 1982: 69). One implication of this is the rules in England and France that bar the English barrister and the French *avocat* from suing clients who fail to pay for the lawyer's services.[14]

Obviously, the preceding description is a "model," an abstraction from the real world. While much of what I have stated concerning the professional could easily be applied to occupations not usually considered by those who study the professions—the auto mechanic is a good example—the focus on autonomy arising from the combination of specialized knowledge, selfless motivation, and a particular type of relationship between professional and client is central to perceptions of how lawyers are supposed to go about their work. However, there is substantial research that calls into question all three of these components—autonomy in client relations, the reliance on abstract, specialized knowledge derived from formal training, and motivations unrelated to personal financial gain—especially as they relate to the work of lawyers in ordinary litigation. This research comes at a time when the premier institution of the profession, the American Bar Association (1986; see also Rotunda, 1987; Moore, 1987), has been voicing much concern about professionalism. An examination of the research challenging explicit and implicit assumptions in the professionalism framework will show us how the brokerage framework places into perspective many of the apparent inconsistencies and contradictions.

Autonomy

The literature dealing with the autonomy of the lawyer as a professional examines the implications of that autonomy and/or the variations in autonomy, often relating those variations to stratification within the legal profession. Heinz and Laumann's study, *The Chicago Bar* (1982), is an important examination of these related questions. A central dimension of stratification in Chicago distinguishes between lawyers who provide services to large corporations (the "corporate services" lawyers) from those who serve the needs of individuals and small businesses ("personal services" lawyers).[15] According to the portrait drawn by Heinz and Laumann, the corporate services lawyer is typically a person who attended an elite law school (and performed well academically there) and has a social background that parallels that of the dominant elite. The personal services lawyer is more likely to have attended a local law school (perhaps part time) and to be a member of an identifiable ethnic group. Corporate services lawyers, by definition, serve high-status clients and are paid substantial fees by those clients. The clients of personal services lawyers are able to pay only modest fees (except for the occasional large contingent fee case). The work of the corporate services lawyer is highly prestigious, often requiring specialized legal research and offering the opportunity to draft creative and unique documents, even though the "legal needs" of the corporate world include lots of relatively ordinary materials (see Kagan and Rosen, 1985: 422; but see Nelson, 1988: 26). One thinks of the personal services lawyer as carrying out repetitive tasks (drafting routine wills, filing routine lawsuits arising from auto accidents, etc.).

This picture suggests that the corporate services lawyer is the "real" professional, while the personal services lawyer is at best striving to meet the professional ideal. Heinz and Laumann find, however, that if professionalism is defined in terms of autonomy, the personal services lawyer, not the corporate services lawyer, best corresponds to this image. The explanation for this reversal is straightforward: personal services lawyers have many clients and are not dependent on any one client for a substantial portion of their livelihood; moreover, the clients of the personal services lawyers tend to be relatively unsophisticated vis-à-vis the legal system—"one-shot" players, in Galanter's terminology (1974). For corporate services lawyers, on the other hand, the client base is much narrower, and a single major corporate client can account for 10 to 20 percent of a firm's annual billings; furthermore, many large corporations are sophisticated users of the legal system ("repeat players"), frequently employing in-house lawyers to advise corporate executives and to serve as liaisons with outside lawyers. Heinz and Laumann conclude that the result of the differences, in terms of both client sophistication and economic independence, is that the personal services lawyer has a more autonomous professional life than the corporate services lawyer, who is highly dependent on the large corporate client as a "patron."[16] While the personal services practitioner may have more autonomy of action than a lawyer in a corporate law firm, other research (Cain, 1979) has found that even the work of the personal services lawyer is often best described as simply carrying out the instructions of the client, requiring little, if any, autonomous thought or action on the part of the lawyer. Thus, autonomy in the working world of the lawyer is more problematic than posited by the theoretical core of the sociology of the professions.

Specialized Knowledge

There is no doubt that lawyers handling civil litigation must draw on specialized knowledge, but is this *abstract* knowledge that is based on *formal* training? One sketchy description of lawyers' day-to-day handling of ordinary civil litigation is in Carlin's study of lawyers working in solo practice in Chicago (1962: 71–91). Carlin downplays the formal, legal aspects of the work, emphasizing instead practical experience and skill—such as knowing what needs to be in the lawyer's case file (doctor's reports, witness accounts, etc.) in order to persuade the adjuster, and negotiating with the tortfeasor's insurance company. Some lawyers may routinely file suit, but this is not so much a legal step as a way of showing the other side that the lawyer is serious about the case. Lower-level practitioners are described as "read[ing] nothing in the way of legal materials and engag[ing] in no research" (p. 75); or as "rarely [being] in court except to file a complaint in the clerk's office" (p. 76). Upper-level practitioners spend more time on trial work and in reading legal materials, but the emphasis for them is still on obtaining effective settlements rather than on the formalities of the litigation process.

Even when one turns to more complex litigation, in most cases much of the work is routine. An extreme example of this is when one party provides documents to a second party ("document production"). This involves a great deal of attention to detail but, for the most part, requires little specific legal expertise. In fact, in very large cases, most of the work of document production is carried out by paraprofessionals working under the supervision of a lawyer.[17]

The Lawyer's Financial Self-Interest

In the discussion of the "hemispheres" of the bar, the dependent position of the corporate segment was partly attributed to a relatively small client base. Specifically, it is very much in the financial interest of the corporate law firm to keep its large clients happy; if such a client were to leave it would have a major impact on the income of the firm. When one turns to the personal services sector of the profession, there are again some important questions about the ability of lawyers to distance themselves from their own financial interests. Most often, these questions have to do with the use of contingent fees, whereby a lawyer is paid a percentage of what is ultimately recovered (which means that no fee is paid if nothing is recovered).[18]

Some practitioners and scholars argue that the contingent fee creates too much of a commonality of interest between the lawyer and client (see MacKinnon, 1964; Ross, 1980: 86). By obtaining a financial stake in the claim through the contingent fee agreement, the lawyer is seen as losing the ability to provide dispassionate advice to the client. Other researchers point out that the contingent fee creates a clear conflict of interest between the lawyer and the client (see Schwartz and Mitchell, 1970; Rosenthal, 1974; Clermont and Currivan, 1978; Johnson, 1980–1981) in many cases. Given that the lawyer's interest is best served by obtaining the highest possible per hour return for the time devoted to the case, it is often the situation that a relatively low but quickly obtained recovery will produce a much higher per hour return than a higher recovery obtained after substantial effort. In the personal injury arena, plaintiffs' lawyers often have a number of cases against a single insurance company; in this situation the lawyer may try to negotiate settlements for several cases at the same time. Given the lawyer's interest in maximizing the return from the complete set of cases, it may be expedient to forego a maximum return in any single case in order to achieve the best aggregrate result (see Ross, 1980: 82). Thus, in crude terms, it is often in the lawyer's financial interest to "sell out" the individual client's interest.

But even when the lawyer is not retained on a contingent fee basis, there may be a conflict of interest. First, consider the situation of a lawyer paid on a flat fee basis — a frequent form of payment in divorce cases; once the fee is set, the less time that is spent on the case, the better the return for the lawyer because the lawyer can then "sell" the time not spent on the case to another client. When the third common form of payment is used, charging by the hour, there is a clear motivation to put in more time than absolutely necessary — presuming the lawyer does not have other uses for the time that could be spent on the case — because the more time spent, the greater the fee (see Wessel, 1976; Johnson, 1980–1981). In reality, the contrast of the flat and hourly fee is nothing more than the ever present conflict between paying on a piecework basis (which creates a motivation for speedy, but shortcut, production) or on a time-wage basis (which may improve quality by reducing time pressure while creating an incentive for loafing).

Discussion

This discussion indicates the need to consider alternative images of what it means to work as a lawyer in ordinary litigation. The beginnings of such an alternative can be found in an exploratory study of the relationships between corporations and their outside lawyers (see Kritzer, 1984a). Based on a series of semistructured interviews, I concluded that the relationships between lawyers and clients were more complex than what was reflected in standard discussions of how lawyers and clients interact. My analysis suggested that those relationships should be described in terms of a series of distinct dimensions. I suspect that there are a number of ways that these dimensions could be broken out,[19] but the following conceptualization is indicative of the framework I will propose in the next section.

1. An expertise dimension, where professionals use their special training and knowledge on behalf of clients.
2. An autonomy dimension, which captures the degree to which the client structures the work to be done or the service provider structures the work.
3. A business dimension, which describes the relative dependence of the professional and client on one another for each side to derive a livelihood. (Is there a continuing relationship or is the relationship a one-time affair? On what basis will the professional be compensated?, etc.).
4. A personal dimension, which reflects the presence of familial or friendship relationships that might impinge on the other three dimensions.

This formulation of lawyer–client relations involves additions to the categories traditionally derived from the sociology of professions (dimensions 1 and 2 just listed) and suggests how alternatives to the professionalism image might further our understanding of the lawyer's work in litigation.[20] It is necessary to consider dimensions of the litigator's working context that are not taken into account by the professionalism tradition. Some of the dimensions complement the professionalism core (autonomy, expertise, and other regardingness), and others are in tension with that core. The brokerage framework provides a basis of analysis that includes many of the elements missing from the professionalism core.

The Brokerage Perspective

The work of lawyers in ordinary litigation has many of the characteristics of what is commonly called *brokerage*.[21] I define a broker as "a person hired to act as an intermediary." This suggests a distinction between the idea of acting as an alter ego, which is the notion typically used when talking about the professional, and the idea of acting as an *intermediary*. The former carries with it the expectation that persons acting as alter egos work solely in the interests of their clients, with no concerns or interests of their own (the "pure service" image). In its most general sense, the term intermediary carries no connotation whatever regarding the intermediary's own interests. Defining the broker as a *hired* intermediary indicates that the broker acts on behalf of the client but has a set of interests that intervenes on, or even conflicts with, the goal of pure service.[22]

While the broker and the professional differ regarding the business dimension of relationships with clients, the two images do not represent a fully contrasting dichotomy. Instead, they are alternative conceptions that combine contrasting and complementary elements; used jointly, they provide a better vehicle for understanding the work of lawyers in ordinary litigation than either one does in isolation. The two perspectives taken together reflect the tensions and contradictions that underlie the daily work of lawyers in the American civil justice system. They capture the reality of an occupation whose members have been socialized to a professional ideal but who must cope with a set of working realities that often conflict with that ideal.

Conceptualizing the Broker

The concept of the broker is not well developed in the social science literature. It has been most extensively used by anthropologists,[23] and the best conceptual treatment is to be found in the work of Boissevan (1969; 1974: 147–169). His development of the concept starts by distinguishing between two types of resources to which people need access in social, political, and economic life: first-order resources, such as land, jobs, education, and money,[24] and second-order resources consisting of "strategic contacts with . . . people who control resources directly or have access to such persons (1974, 147)." A person who specializes in dispensing second-order resources for personal profit or gain is a broker. Central to this role is the interactional nature of the work within a stable context that extends beyond any single transaction; in Boissevan's terms these contexts involve networks, action-sets, and cliques. Thus, a broker is someone who serves as an intermediary between persons seeking and dispensing first-order resources within a set context and who engages in this activity for personal gain.[25]

Political scientists have used the brokerage concept as a way of describing the essential aspects of machine politics: a transactional relationship between the constituents and the "local" politicians (Carty, 1981: 53). The politician as broker is one who secures constituent loyalty through transactions (i.e., snow removal in return for votes), as contrasted to the politician as partisan leader, who secures constituent loyalty through common identification with a party or ideology (Carty, 1981: 53). While the transactional relationship is central to machine politics, brokerage relationships in politics are not limited to political machines. A number of studies of politics in developing countries have drawn on the broker image (Perry, 1973; Silver, 1981; De Jongh, 1982). For example, De Jongh describes the role of a city councillor in Port Elizabeth as that of an "urban broker" who "could give a township resident certain benefits and services" (1982: 341) in return for "respect (with the implication of status), a promised or implied promise of a vote, public prominence and regular opportunities to confront directly the 'powers that be'" (1982: 342).[26] Bailey (1963: 101) describes the broker in Indian villages as "a person with special knowledge and special contacts who can help the villager to get in touch with or manipulate the Administration or who can perform the same service in the other direction for an official." The broker's role consists of "bridging the gap between the peasants and the administrative and political elite" in return for "a share [of the value of the transaction] for the time and trouble he takes and . . . as a return upon the expertize which is his stock-in-trade" (Bailey, 1969: 41).[27]

Surprisingly, there is virtually no social science literature on brokering in the area where the term is used in common parlance: stockbrokers, real estate brokers, and the like. One noteworthy exception, which is particularly relevant in understanding the contrast between the broker role and the professional role, focuses on status-set and role-set conflicts among stockbrokers (Evan and Levin, 1966). The study raises the question of the "professionalization of the stockbroker." Such a transformation is problematic, according to Evan and Levin, because it requires the broker to be concerned with "promoting the welfare of the customer. . . . Yet the broker is under great pressure to sell securities . . . [The broker's] recommendation to customers of particular securities may be unduly influenced . . . by a higher return to the brokerage firm [and to the broker himself]." Furthermore, a stockbroker obtains compensation only by buying or selling securities for customers, in contrast to a physician, who is paid a fee for a consultation even if that consultation does not lead to carrying out a medical procedure. Thus, the business relationship between the stockbroker and the customer makes it difficult, if not impossible, to transform the overall relationship from that of buyer–seller to that of professional-client (1966: 80–81). There is a striking similarity between the business aspects of the stockbroker's relationship with customers and the business aspects of the contingent fee lawyer's relationship with clients: in both cases, the broker/

professional has a direct interest in the "outcome" from the perspective of the client/customer (i.e., whether or not a sale is made in the case of the stockbroker, and whether or not a settlement or plaintiff's judgment is achieved in the case of the contingent fee lawyer).

This discussion highlights two of the characteristics that distinguish brokers from other kinds of actors. First, brokers serve as intermediaries; in Boissevan's terms, they bring together distributors and recipients of first-order resources. More generally, brokers aid in transfers of information, money, property, and the like between two parties; those parties can be individuals and/or organizations (including governmental institutions such as the court system). Second, in aiding these transfers, brokers extract a "tax" of some sort (whether that be a fee, a percentage, or some sort of future obligation);[28] in other words, brokers are motivated by their own interests, either long term, short term, or both,[29] rather than by altruism or some other "moral" base.[30]

With this as background, let me briefly point out the other ways in which the broker image sheds useful light on the work of lawyers in ordinary litigation. First, the image of the broker combines the expectation of specialized, expert knowledge (e.g., in the case of the real estate broker, different methods of financing) with what can be described as "insider" knowledge (the current selling prices of houses in a neighborhood, to continue the real estate broker example).[31] One can easily identify the kinds of insider knowledge that are important to lawyering in litigation: going rates for particular injuries (or, in criminal cases, for particular offenses), recent trends in jury verdicts for particular kinds of cases, the attitudes of trial judges as related to the situations of a lawyer's clients, and the style and experience of the opposing party's lawyer.

Second, central to the image of the broker is a process of regularized interaction with other "players" (other brokers, specialists, organizations, etc.) as a necessary basis for delivering the service required by the client; the image of a professional does not preclude such interaction, but nothing in that image explicitly recognizes the importance of the interaction process. Interaction of the type associated with brokering is a major part of the work of the lawyer, particularly litigation work. The lawyer must interact with other lawyers and with court personnel, including judges, magistrates, commissioners, and clerks; as I will discuss shortly, research on the criminal justice system has shown that this regularized interaction results in the creation of a "courtroom workgroup" that defines the day-to-day operation of the system (Eisenstein and Jacob, 1977).

Third, while the image of the professional is grounded in the assumption that the client plays a secondary role in the decision-making process, usually following the advice and/or instructions of the professional (this is clearest in the doctor–patient relationship), the broker image portrays the broker as being specifically instructed by the client and then carrying out those instructions in the best way possible. Much of what both corporate services lawyers (see Kagan and Rosen, 1985: 411) and personal services lawyers (see Cain, 1979) do falls in the category of carrying out the instructions of the client, whether that be reviewing the papers for a $100 million securities offering or preparing a

TABLE 1-1. The Professional and the Broker

Dimension	Professional	Broker
Centrality of fee-paying relation-ship	Low	High
Nature of expertise	Technical/formal	Insider/informal
Position occupied by professional/broker vis-à-vis other actors	[unspecified]	Intermediary between client and other actors
Autonomy/client control	Professional controls	Client instructs/broker responds

simple will. Expert knowledge may be required to construct the documents so that they meet legal requirements, but the goal is usually defined fairly explicitly by the client. Lawyers involved in litigation, particularly where the lawyer is being paid on a percentage basis, may in fact be less bound by explicit instructions from a client than are lawyers carrying out other kinds of work.

Table 1-1 provides a capsule contrast of the two images along four dimensions: (1) the centrality of the fee-paying aspects of the relationship with the client; (2) the relative importance of expertise based on insider (what I will later refer to as "informal legal") versus technical (what I will term "formal legal") knowledge; (3) the positioning of the professional/broker as an intermediary between the client and other actors in the process;[32] and (4) the autonomy of the professional/broker vis-à-vis the client.

The Criminal Lawyer as Broker

The usefulness of the broker framework can readily be seen by applying it to several major analyses of the work of lawyers in the criminal side of the justice system. First let us consider Blumberg's "The Practice of Law as a Confidence Game" (1967a). Blumberg described the defense lawyer as an "agent-mediator" who has close ties to other actors in the process, including judges, prosecutors, clerks, probation officials, and the press (1967: 20). While normally there is relatively little that can be done in aid of the defendant-client, the lawyer, particularly the private defense lawyer, finds it necessary to convince the client that the services delivered were of some value in order to insure that the client actually pays the lawyer's fee. To account for the willingness of the client to pay for something of relatively little benefit, Blumberg used the analogy of the confidence game, describing a process of "cooling out" clients in order to convince them to pay the lawyers' fees after it had become clear that the lawyers' efforts had been less than a complete success from the clients' perspective (1967: 27). Whether or not one accepts the confidence game analogy, the impact of fee for service on the processing of cases and on the relationship between lawyers and clients raises problems for the professional ideal of selfless application of technical knowledge on behalf of a client. In contrast, fee for service is consistent with the image of the broker—in the case of the lawyer, easing the client's passage through the criminal justice system in much the same way that a customs broker eases the passage of goods through the customs system.

Second, let us look at the idea, mentioned briefly previously, of the courtroom workgroup discussed at length in Eisenstein and Jacob's book *Felony Justice*. This workgroup picture of the felony justice system is predicated on there being a relatively stable group of players in the system who interact on a repeated and ongoing basis across a number of cases. That is, clients come and go, but the courtroom workgroup lives on (see also Rosset and Cressey, 1976; Blumberg, 1967a). There is concern for the needs of the defendants who come into the system, but what happens to a defendant often depends less on the relationship between defendant and lawyer than on that between the defense lawyer and the other members of the courtroom elite—the prosecutor and the judge (Nardulli, 1978). That is, the lawyer is the link between the ongoing system and the outsider who comes into that system (i.e., an "agent–mediator," to use Blumberg's terminology), and this insider/outsider distinction, not the technical knowledge and professional training of the lawyer, dominates the relationship between lawyer and client.

Finally, consider the common perception of the American criminal justice system as being dominated by a process called "plea bargaining." Plea bargaining is usually presented in one of two ways: it is seen as coercing defendants into entering guilty pleas with a promise of a sentence substantially below the maximum out of fear of receiving a much more severe penalty, or it is seen as allowing guilty defendants to obtain unwarranted reductions in charges and/or sentences by threatening an overworked system with requiring a time-consuming and pointless trial. The first image represents the current system as one that sacrifices the adversarial search for truth in favor of efficiency (Alschuler, 1968, 1975, 1976); the latter represents it as sacrificing the proper punishment of criminals in the name of efficiency (van den Haag, 1975; Fine, 1986). Some literature on the system (Feeley, 1982; Utz, 1978; Rosset and Cressey, 1976; Nardulli, Flemming, and Eisenstein, 1985; Nardulli, Eisenstein, and Flemming, 1988; Eisenstein, Flemming, and Nardulli, 1988) uses the same evidence to paint a picture of an advocacy process that tries to identify the appropriate sanction for a criminal defendant by agreeing on where the offender and the offense fit into a vague notion of going rates (cf. Sudnow's notion of "normal crimes," 1965). The advocacy carried out by the defense attorney is one that fits well with the broker image: the advocate seeks to represent the client in the best possible light given the "facts" and utilizing knowledge of the "going rates." The interaction between defense and prosecution is primarily aimed at resolving factual as opposed to technical legal questions, although some routine technical questions (e.g., the admissibility of evidence) may arise; this process has been described by Utz (1978) as *Settling the Facts*.

The common feature of all three sets of analyses is the limited concern for the "professional" aspects of the lawyer's work in the criminal justice system. In fact, the general literature on lawyers in the criminal justice system is strikingly devoid of a concern with professionalism as that notion is generally used in studies of the sociology of the professions.[33] As the preceding discussion suggests, this reflects the fact that the criminal lawyer, particularly the defense lawyer, functions less as a professional, serving as the alter ego of the client, and more as a broker, seeking to assist the client's passage through the system by using a great deal of insider knowledge and a relatively small amount of specific, routine technical knowledge.

Lawyering in Civil Litigation as a Brokerage Function

In the previous discussion, I identified four dimensions that distinguish between the activities of the professional and those of the broker. To set the stage for the analysis that follows in later chapters, this section briefly discusses what the brokerage image would lead one to expect with regard to lawyering in ordinary civil litigation. I will draw on prior research concerned with ordinary civil litigation.

Concerning the nature of the expertise required for day-to-day civil litigation, I have already noted Carlin's findings that solo practitioners handling injury cases devote relatively little of their time to activities that draw on their formal legal knowledge (i.e., the technical use of the law and the skills learned in law school). Carlin's report of how lawyers handle personal injury cases is consistent with Ross's analysis of the claims adjusters on the other side of the relationship (1980), where the emphasis is again on the kind of knowledge that insiders have (necessary documents, "building up specials," etc.) and not on expertise based on formal training. Ross, in summarizing Carlin's analysis of the work of the solo practitioner, characterizes much of that work as brokerage (1980: 75) and, in reference to negligence work, says that it "may be easily regarded as brokerage rather than the profession of law" (Ross, 1980: 77). Ross implicitly draws a distinction between the professional and the broker, but never really develops that distinction beyond the simple statement of its existence.

A second concern in the analysis to follow will be the role of the fee-paying relationship between the lawyer and the client and how that impinges on the lawyer's work. I already noted the argument that the interests of lawyer and client frequently clash, and how, in the case of the contingent fee lawyer, this may lead to a less than zealous advocacy. More than half of Carlin's account of the personal injury work of lawyers revolve around the nature of referrals and the question of payment for such referrals (1962: 80f);[34] one very common feature was the dependence on recommendations from past clients. Much of the rest of Carlin's discussion concerns the dependence of the clients on their lawyers; for example, the lawyer is often in a position to make loans to clients to tide them over until a settlement is reached, or to insure that bills incurred by the client (e.g., for medical expenses) are paid, either promptly or eventually (Carlin, 1962: 79–80). This dependence is institutionalized in the norm that the settlement payment is made in the form of a check payable jointly to the lawyer and client and sent directly to the lawyer; the lawyer then deducts the fee, expenses, and any "loans," paying the balance to the client (Carlin, 1962: 74).

The fee-paying relationship is most evident when the lawyer is paid on a contingency basis, but it may also be evident for hourly fee lawyers who take cases from regular clients on a routine basis with little regard for the particulars of the individual case.

The issue of control is central in Rosenthal's analysis of the underlying conflicts in relations between contingent fee lawyers and their clients (1974). The problem for clients, in Rosenthal's view, is to insure that their interests dominate the work of the lawyers; for the client with a contingent fee lawyer, this means insuring that the lawyer does not shortchange the client's case. As Wessel points out (1976; see also Johnson, 1980–1981: 569–584), the exact opposite may be true for the hourly fee lawyer, where the short-term incentives may provide a motivation to overwork the case in order to build up the amount of time billed to the client. The answer to these problems is for the client to control at least the quantity, if not the specific content, of what the lawyer does on the client's behalf. On the other hand, the common assumption among those directly involved in the litigation process is that lawyers should control the clients so that the lawyers may exercise their professional judgment in an autonomous fashion.[35] Where the client is financially dependent on the attorney, such as when the fee is to be paid on a percentage (contingency) basis, this dimension may be problematic for the brokerage argument. It will be interesting to see what differences, if any, emerge in the domain of client control/autonomy between lawyers paid on hourly versus contingent fees.

The discussion of the intermediary role of the criminal defense lawyer can be easily extended to the lawyer in civil litigation. In both contexts, the lawyer serves as the intermediary between client and justice system, broadly defined. Where the criminal defense lawyer stands between the client and prosecutors, judges, and other court personnel, the lawyer in civil litigation stands between the client and representatives of the opposing party (lawyers, claims adjusters, etc.), and between the client and other litigation participants, such as experts (e.g., doctors and engineers), judges, and other court personnel.[36] As with the criminal lawyer, it is the ongoing involvement with a broadly defined workgroup that shapes the day-to-day activities of litigation. In his study of lawyers in nonurban Missouri, Landon (1985: 95) reported that one lawyer told prospective clients at their first meeting that "You can hire me to fight your case, but you can't hire me to hate the opposing attorney!" The need to maintain cordial relationships among actors who frequently interact is not limited to rural settings; it arises from the natural desire to have a relatively pleasant and harmonious work environment. Maintaining such an environment often can work to the benefit of the client, at least in terms of convenience and time (e.g., scheduling or minimizing court sessions), if not in terms of eventual outcomes.

Ross points out important workgroup components in the relationship between personal injury plaintiffs' lawyers and insurance adjusters. First, he notes that these two actors share a common interest in the quick disposal of cases and that they share the insider knowledge of the going rates associated with various kinds of injuries (1980: 86). Second, in his discussion of the pressures that might come to bear on an attorney to agree to a lower settlement for a particular case than might be achievable by holding out, Ross notes the difficulties that a refusal by the lawyer to accept such a settlement might create for obtaining desirable settlements in future cases (1980: 82).

Summary

This discussion indicates some of the themes to be pursued in more detail in the chapters that follow. I will use the images I have described under the labels professional and broker to highlight and explicate the patterns revealed in the analyses that I will present, and I will return regularly to the categories laid out in Table 1-1; however, instead of developing each of those categories in a separate analysis, I will weave them into a broad portrait of what is involved in ordinary civil litigation. As the results will show, in some ways the broker image is better for explaining the work of lawyers in ordinary litigation, while in other ways the professional image is better.[37] The tensions inherent in the two images suffuse the working context of lawyers handling ordinary litigation, and one of the dilemmas that lawyers must cope with is how to deal with these tensions. The distinction also suggests important questions about the monopoly lawyers possess for handling certain kinds of disputes in the United States; I will discuss those questions and their implications in Chapter 10.

Chapter 2 describes the data set used in the analyses and descriptions that follow. Part II (Chapters 3 and 4) describes the cases that comprise ordinary litigation and provides a portrait of the lawyers in the study, their training, experience, expertise, and attitudes. Part III (Chapters 5 and 6) looks at relationships, both between lawyer and client and between the lawyer and other players in the system. Part IV (Chapters 7, 8, and 9) focuses on the litigation process itself. Chapter 7 describes the work of the lawyer in ordinary cases, primarily focusing on the amount of time lawyers spend on cases and what their work entails; Chapter 8 examines the impact of the lawyer–client relationship, particularly the effect of fee arrangement, on both the amount and nature of the effort that lawyers put into their cases; and Chapter 9 examines outcomes, both in terms of the results of the cases and how those results influence the evaluations of the experiences by the lawyers' clients. The book concludes in Chapter 10 with a reexamination of the role of the lawyer in the civil justice process and a discussion of the implications of the analysis for reform and regulation.

2

The Data

The Civil Litigation Research Project

In 1979, the Office for Improvements in the Administration of Justice (OIAJ) of the U.S. Justice Department commissioned a major study of civil litigation in the United States. The two goals of those who developed the initial plans for the study were to obtain baseline information on the civil justice process in the United States, particularly with regard to costs, and to create an information base that would be useful for understanding the civil justice system in order that proposals for reforms of the system could be rationally considered (see Rosenberg, 1980–1981; Sarat, 1981). The contract for the research was awarded to a consortium consisting of the University of Wisconsin, the University of Southern California, and Mathematica Policy Research.[1] The research effort, which became known as the Civil Litigation Research Project (CLRP), involved the design and implementation of a complex data collection effort,[2] with most of the fieldwork and data collection having been carried out during 1980. This chapter summarizes the data collection procedures that were used to obtain information on litigation in the United States.

Data Sources

The Research Sites

The data collected by CLRP come from samples of state and federal court cases terminated during 1978 in 5 selected federal judicial districts: Eastern Wisconsin, Eastern Pennsylvania, South Carolina, New Mexico, and Central California. While a set of 5 federal judicial districts cannot be said to be strictly representative of the 90 districts that cover the entire country (excluding the federal judicial districts that serve nonstates such as Puerto Rico, the Virgin Islands, and Guam), these 5 were selected to be broadly representative of the variations that exist in the country. Table 2–1 shows a number of selected

TABLE 2-1. Characteristics of the Five Federal Judicial Districts[a]

Characteristic	Central Calif.	N.Mex.	Eastern Pa.	S.C.	Eastern Wis.
Population 1975 (in 1,000s)	10,759	1,144	5,092	2,816	2,831
Population change 1970–1975 (%)	3.9	12.5	−0.5	8.7	2.3
Net migration 1970–1975 (%)	−0.5	5.8	−2.6	3.4	−0.2
Population 1970 (in 1,000s)	10,343	1,016	5,112	2,591	2,768
Population growth 1960–1970 (%)	29.3	6.8	7.7	8.7	12.2
Black population, 1970 (in 1,000s)	838	18	767	788	119
Population of Spanish heritage 1970 (in 1,000s)	1,768	407	nil	nil	nil
Urban population 1970 (in 1,000s)	9,990	711	4,287	1,232	2,128
Median years of education 1970	11.9	11.8	11.4	10.0	11.6
Number of farms over 10 acres 1969	8,568	10,563	12,845	27,080	34,648
Percent of land area on farms	25.1	60.2	42.0	37.1	53.6
Percent of labor force in blue-collar occupations	43.9	27.4	53.1	58.8	54.3
State court organization[b]	Multitiered	Unified	Overlapping multitiered	Multitiered	Multitiered
State court use of federal rules of civil procedure[c]	No	Yes	No	No	Yes
Number of federal judges 1975[d]	16	3	19	5	5
Weighted federal caseload per judge, 1975[d]	414	385	242	520	383
Civil only	270	264	193	402	282
Median disposition times federal civil cases (in months)[e] with no court action	6	4	5	5	7
During or after pretrial but before trial	16	10	13	12	21
All civil cases	6	7	9	7	11
Number of lawyers[f]	190,360	13,190	90,420	23,790	48,120

[a]Unless otherwise indicated, data compiled by the author. Versions of this table previously appeared in Kritzer (1980–1981: 514) and Grossman et al. (1981: 99).

[b]From *National Survey of Court Organization* (LEAA, 1973), and supplements. In both South Carolina and Wisconsin, the lower court was abolished in the late 1970s, so that the systems in those two states are now essentially unified in nature.

[c]From personal inquiries.

[d]From Report of the Administrative Office of the U.S. Courts, 1975, Table X-1.

[e]From Report of the Administrative Office of the U.S. Courts, 1978, Table C-5.

[f]From data collected by Carroll Seron and Wolf Heydebrand.

characteristics of the districts included in the sample; there is no reason to believe that this sample of districts is systematically unrepresentative of the country as a whole, and for that reason the analyses in this and the following chapters are probably generalizable, with inevitable specific exceptions, to ordinary litigation in the United States.

Samples, Cases, and Data Collection

In each of the five federal judicial districts, samples totaling approximately 300 cases were selected, half from the federal court and half from the state courts.[3] In three of the districts (South Carolina, New Mexico, and Central California) state cases were selected from a single court, the court serving the county in which the federal district court was based.[4] In the remaining two, approximately 120 state cases were selected from the court serving the urban center, with the remaining 30 state cases chosen from an outlying rural or suburban county.[5] For the federal courts, a list of cases terminated in 1978 was obtained from the Administrative Office of the United States Courts, and a random sample of cases was chosen for each district from the list; the sampling method used in each state court varied, depending on the information available on cases terminated.[6] Certain types of cases were excluded from the sample, or otherwise included selectively in some way. Excluded cases involved uncontested collections (where the defendant made no appearance and a default judgment was entered), prisoner petitions, one governmental unit suing another governmental unit, probate, bankruptcy, judicial review of administrative agency decisions except if the case involved a trial de novo or involved federal court reviews under the Administrative Procedure Act, deportations, Narcotic Addiction Recovery Act (NARA) Title II cases, and labor law cases that arose out of grievance procedures normally covered by collective bargaining agreements (e.g., appeals from the decisions of arbitrators). Also excluded were "small claims" cases, which were defined as cases involving only a monetary claim of less than $1,000, and cases that were clearly "nonordinary" as shown by the magnitude of the court file (a total of 36 nonordinary cases were ultimately excluded, all but 4 from the federal courts). In addition, domestic relations cases were arbitrarily limited to no more than 20 percent of the sample of cases in any state court and were excluded entirely in Pennsylvania, where they were maintained on a docket entirely separate from the primary civil docket.

Two different kinds of data were collected. The first kind consisted of information extracted from the documents on file with the court for each of the cases in the sample; these data were coded in the field by law students supervised by project staff members. The information collected included names, addresses, dates of filings, cause of action, pleadings and motions filed, discovery, judicial actions, and appeals. Court record information was collected for a total of 1,649 cases. With this information in hand, telephone interviews were conducted with all of the primary participants (lawyers and litigants) who could be identified and located. Not all of the cases in the records sample were included in the interview sample (either because after examination the case was found to fall into one of the excluded categories, because it was unclear whether or not the case had actually terminated, or because funds for conducting interviews had run out). The interviews were conducted by Mathematica Policy Research from Princeton, New Jersey. The typical, full interview ran about 1 hour in length. All of the participant interviews focused on the specific court case in the sample, including information about the background of the case, what was at stake or issue in the case, time and money spent on the case, relationships with other case participants, negotiations among the parties, outcome of the case, and the participant's evaluation of how well the court had handled the case. Additional background and attitudinal questions were asked of each participant as well.

The Interviews

The primary interview data used in the analysis come from 1,382 lawyers;[7] supplemental information is drawn from interviews with 224 individual litigants and representatives of 307 organizational litigants. As these figures suggest, less success was obtained in locating and contacting litigants than was the case with lawyers; this is attributable to several factors. First, the court records provided good information for contacting the lawyers involved in the case; much less information was available on the litigants themselves. Second, locating a person to speak to when the litigant is an organization is often difficult, particularly if the organization is large and deals with a lot of litigation (this might be characterized as the problem of "institutional memory" or lack thereof). Third, individual litigants, as with the rest of the American population, are highly mobile, and 2 years or more after a case has ended there is a substantial chance that address or telephone information in the court documents or obtained from lawyers who had represented the individual will be obsolete. While I will make use of some data from the litigant surveys, I will use them with caution because of the potential problem of lack of representativeness.

The 1,382 lawyer interviews fall short of the total number of lawyer interviews that might have been carried out given that interviews were actually sought for 1,423 cases (out of the original sample of 1,649). One problem encountered was that some lawyers were involved in two or more cases in the sample. Since it was unreasonable to ask an individual to go through an entire 1-hour interview more than once, multiple-case lawyers were interviewed only about one of their cases, with some brief questions about the additional cases. These brief sets of questions constitute another 430 short interviews that are not used in the analysis. An entirely separate survey was conducted with government lawyers involved in the court cases; these represent another 96 interviews that I will draw on for one or two specific points in the analysis (another 136 short interviews, which will not be used in the analysis, were conducted with government lawyers). Of the lawyers that should have been interviewed but were not, some refused outright, but more begged off, claiming to have been only minimally involved in the case or to have no recollection of the case; I suspect that many of these latter cases had been handled through fairly routine office procedures with relatively little specific involvement by the attorney of record. This is borne out by comparisons between the cases for which lawyer interviews were obtained and those for which no interviews were obtained. On average, the cases without interviews involved fewer docket entries and took less time (date of filing to date of termination) to dispose of and were more likely to have involved domestic relations issues (see Trubek et al., 1983a: I–120). Thus, if anything, the lawyers interviewed tended to be involved in longer, more involved, less routine cases than those who were not interviewed and, therefore, any bias will be in the direction of overstating the amount of work and activity involved in ordinary litigation. Given that one of the major thrusts of the analysis is that ordinary litigation is a relatively low-intensity activity, the likely bias in the data would be toward an understatement of that trend rather than to have created a pattern that does not exist.

II

CASES AND LAWYERS[1]

To understand how ordinary civil cases are handled in the courts and the role(s) that lawyers play in processing those cases, we need to know something about the cases and the lawyers. In this part, I present sketches of both. With regard to the cases, I have focused on the questions and amounts in controversy and the litigants involved; I leave to Part IV discussion of what happened as the cases went through the system.[2] Concerning the lawyers, I go into considerable detail on the lawyers' training, experience, and legal practices.

3

The World of Ordinary Litigation

In this chapter I describe the ordinary, everyday cases that are the focus of the analyses in Chapters 5 through 9 and that make up the bulk of the work of courts of general jurisdiction. In the following discussion, I focus on three descriptive dimensions.

- The kinds of issues presented for resolution.
- The "size" of the cases (i.e., what's at "stake").
- The nature of the parties.

I leave to Chapters 7, 8, and 9 discussions of what actually occurred as the cases proceeded through the justice system and the outcomes of the cases.

What Are the Cases About?

A wide variety of issues can be raised in a lawsuit, and categorizing those issues involves a great deal of ambiguity. In many jurisdictions, lawyers filing a lawsuit are required to indicate on a standard form the legal category into which the case falls.[1] While one could use this information to describe the kinds of issues that are dealt with in the cases, the category chosen by the lawyer may have more to do with jurisdictional rules and litigation strategy than with the substance of the case.

Because of this problem, the law students who coded the court records made their own judgments regarding the kinds of issues raised by each case;[2] the coders were permitted to identify up to four different types of legal issues raised by the case.[3] For purposes of discussion, I will employ eight broad categories:

Real property.

Contracts/commercial.

Torts.

Business regulation.

Domestic relations (primarily divorce).[4]

Discrimination/civil rights.

Government benefits (disability, social security, black lung, welfare).

Government action (taxation, zoning, political process, governmental financial obligations, freedom of information, voting rights, immigration/ naturalization, and abuse of governmental authority).[5]

Table 3-1 shows the variation, by court and by location, in the kinds of issues in ordinary litigation.[6] Probably the most striking difference is the relative concentration of tort (injury) cases within the state courts (with the exception of New Mexico) compared to the lack of any similar such concentration in the federal courts. At the extreme, 98 percent of the sampled cases in the Pennsylvania state courts involved tort issues, compared to only 16 percent of the cases in the Wisconsin federal court; interestingly, the Pennsylvania federal court was also dominated by cases involving tort issues (77 percent).[7] The modal category of cases in the federal courts varies from district to district: it is torts for Pennsylvania and South Carolina, contract/commercial for Wisconsin, California, and New Mexico. Four of the categories found in the federal court—business regulation, discrimination, government benefits, and government action—are virtually nonexistent in most of the state courts in the study; real property is an important category in state courts (except possibly for Pennsylvania), but is of much less importance for the caseload of the federal courts. None of these trends should be particularly surprising, since they tend to follow jurisdictional rules. What does stand out is the dominance of torts in the state courts and the greater diversity of issues in the federal courts.

A second interesting comparison that can be discerned from Table 3-1 is the number of issues raised in the two groups of courts. At the bottom of the table, I show both the number of cases and the number of issues raised in the cases, plus the average number of issues per case (i.e., the number of issues divided by the number of cases); this average ranges from 1.16 to 1.43 for state cases compared to 1.39 to 1.56 for federal cases. There is relatively little overlap in the ranges for state and federal courts, and for all five state-by-state comparisons of the federal versus the state courts, the cases in the federal court involve more issues than do the cases in the state court. This suggests, not surprisingly, that federal cases may be somewhat more complex, at least regarding the raising of multiple issues, than are state cases.

What's at Stake in the Ordinary Case?

One of the first questions that is likely to be asked about a case is, "How much is at stake?" This apparently simple question starts to become complicated as soon as one tries to define what one means by "stakes." First, let me clarify

TABLE 3-1.[a] Kinds of Cases (Area of Law) in Federal and State Courts (Percent of Cases Involving Each Area)

Area of Law	Federal Courts					State Courts				
	Eastern Wisc.	Eastern Pa.	S.C.	N.Mex.	Central Calif.	Eastern Wisc.	Eastern Pa.	S.C.	N.Mex.	Central Calif.
Torts	16%	77%	55%	40%	35%	70%	98%	70%	45%	95%
Contracts/commercial	50	32	46	49	39	40	26	20	55	29
Real property	13	5	8	8	3	24	5	23	12	12
Business regulation	34	17	6	12	29	1	<1	5	1	2
Discrimination/civil rights	16	9	10	19	22	<1	0	1	<1	<1
Government actions	13	4	3	9	8	1	0	3	<1	2
Government benefits	13	5	10	12	10	0	0	<1	0	0
Other	5	0	1	7	3	<1	<1	2	1	2
Number of cases	177	151	155	172	155	149	147	140	157	128
Number of issues	277	225	216	266	229	207	192	175	182	183
Issues per case	1.56	1.49	1.39	1.48	1.48	1.39	1.31	1.25	1.16	1.43

[a]A version of this table, using a different set of categories, appeared in Grossman et al. (1982: 102).

what I do not mean. Newspaper reports of cases being filed usually talk of a lawsuit for X thousands (if not millions) of dollars. These reports refer to the amount of damages requested by lawyers at the time they initiate formal court action. The formal demand made at the time of filing is usually the outside figure of what might be recovered and may, in fact, bear little resemblance to the actual amount in controversy.[8] Consequently, I do not mean by stakes the amount formally demanded by the plaintiff. Likewise, I do not mean the amount that is ultimately recovered by the plaintiff. This amount may be substantially less than the stakes in the case. At the extreme, the case may ultimately go to a jury that finds for the defendant, awarding nothing to the plaintiff; this does not mean that the amount at stake was zero. Finally, the amount at stake is not equal to figures that might be mentioned in the course of negotiation; offers and demands may reflect negotiating strategy as much as the amount at issue.

I define stakes in terms of what the party is prepared to accept or give to resolve a case. For example, a person who has been injured in an auto accident might file a lawsuit demanding $100,000 in damages. The plaintiff's lawyer might believe that, based on prior cases, the injured party has a moderate to good chance of winning a jury verdict in the amount of $50,000. However, the lawyer might advise the client to accept a settlement of $20,000 because (1) that settlement can be obtained immediately and it would take 2 years or more to get the case to trial, and/or (2) a jury might return a much smaller verdict (or even return a verdict in favor of the defendant), and it is better to have the certainty of the $20,000 settlement rather than risk obtaining much less (or nothing at all). As I have defined stakes, the stakes in this example would be $20,000, because that is what the lawyer believed the client should accept to settle the case.[9]

Using this conception of stakes, lawyers involved in the individual cases were asked the following sequence of questions.

> Now I'd like to ask some questions about what you thought your client(s) should take or do to settle the case. In these questions we are interested in *your view of the stakes in the case*, not in actual negotiations, which we will get to in a few minutes. Did you ever form an opinion about what the case was worth *in terms of what your client(s) would be willing to take or do to settle the case*?

If the response to this was *yes*, the lawyer was asked, "Based on that opinion, what did you think at the time should have been done to settle the problem?" The lawyers whose responses involved something other than or in addition to money were then asked, "Suppose there could have been a settlement at that time which involved only a lump sum payment of money. What would you think it should have been?" Of the 1,382 lawyers interviewed, 859 were able to describe the stakes entirely in monetary terms; of the remaining 523 respondents, 331 said that they had never formed an opinion about what the case was worth, and 192 had an opinion but it involved a significant nonmonetary component that could not be translated into monetary terms.[10]

Table 3–2 provides a summary of the stakes involved in the cases in the sample. The largest estimate of stakes was $2,500,000,[11] which is quite consis-

TABLE 3-2.[a] Distribution of Lawyers' Perceptions
of Stakes

	All Cases	State	Federal
$0–5,000	40%	55%	26%
$5,000–10,000	16	18	15
$10,001–25,000	20	16	23
$25,001–50,000	12	7	17
$50,001 and up	12	4	19
n	859	411	448
Median		$4,500	$15,000

[a]Part of this table previously appeared in Kritzer (1984b: 32).

tent with the popular image of the dockets of our courts being dominated by big cases. However, this case was not only the largest, but it was also atypical. Most state cases are quite small, involving less than $5,000; if the median is used as a measure of typicality (the median is the middle case, when the cases are sorted from smallest to largest), the typical case in state court involves $4,500.[12] Very few cases in state court (4 percent) exceed the "moderate" level of $50,000. In federal court the cases are larger, as one would expect given the jurisdictional minimums in those courts: the median case involves $15,000, and 19 percent of the caseload involves more than $50,000.[13] If one is interested in the characteristics of most cases in American courts, the state figures provide a pretty good picture,[14] because over 97 percent of the civil cases (of the type we are interested in) filed in the United States are litigated in the state courts;[15] the "all cases" column in Table 3-2 is included primarily to give an overall picture of the data I will be using as the discussion proceeds.

What about cases where the lawyers were not able to monetize the stakes, or where they were unable to describe what their clients were willing to take or do to settle the case? What were those cases about? For the "nonmonetized" cases, I looked at the lawyers' description of that nonmonetary element, and for the cases where there was no idea regarding "what to take or do," the lawyers were asked, "What was at stake from the viewpoint of your client?" Information regarding the nonmonetized stakes and regarding what was at stake is summarized in Table 3-3.

As is evident from the table, money was at stake in most of the cases where the lawyers had not formed an idea of exactly what their clients should take or do to settle the case (the first column in the table). The first three categories relate directly to money and constitute 69 percent of the responses. Even the ostensibly nonmonetary stakes (shown in the second column in the table) tend to reflect money (if one assumes that cases where the lawyer described the stakes as "getting the case dismissed or getting my client dismissed from the case" were primarily about money); 47 percent (204 of 437) of the responses fell into the first three categories. Thus, while lawsuits can raise questions that are not easily expressed in dollars and cents, the vast majority of lawsuits are about money, but *not* about large sums of money.

TABLE 3–3. What Was at Stake? (For Those Cases in Which Stakes Were Not Entirely Monetized or the Lawyer Had No Opinion Regarding What Should Be Done to Settle the Case)

	"No Opinion" Regarding Settlement	Nonmonetary Components
Money[a]	233	62
Get case or client dismissed	33	121
Divorce: support/property	6	21
Divorce: custody/visitation	5	17
Interpretation of law, contract, or insurance policy	21	4
Vindication	28	0
Obtain compromise or agreement	0	33
Stop or prevent action or practice	10	2
Continue action or practice	0	8
Obtain action (or permission for action)	16	48
Restore status quo ante (e.g., reinstate job)	10	26
Modify action or practice	0	45
Give up property/reclaim goods/enforce decision	0	20
Nothing/do not recall	19	15
Other	13	15

[a]This category includes things such as "deny liability" or "pay as little as possible," which were given in response to the stakes questions in the interview.

What kinds of systematic variations are there in stakes? Here let us look first at variations by location, and then at variations by area of law. The variation in monetary stakes by judicial district is summarized in Table 3–4. Perhaps the most striking aspect of this table is the relatively small amount of variation in the median, particularly in the federal cases. The ratio of the largest median to smallest median for federal cases in 1.66. For federal cases this should not be particularly surprising, since the jurisdictional rules govern-

TABLE 3–4. Monetary Stakes by Location

Location	State Court(s)		Federal Court	
	Median	Maximum	Median	Maximum
Eastern Wisconsin	$5,004	$75,000	$13,072	$675,000
n		97		57
Eastern Pennsylvania	$3,001	$450,000	$20,010	$500,000
n		107		100
South Carolina	$4,517	$150,000	$12,017	$2,500,000
n		67		111
New Mexico	$5,993	$165,000	$14,994	$800,000
n		57		111
Central California	$6,000	$108,500	$17,516	$2,000,000
n		83		80

ing the federal courts are uniform throughout the country. There is somewhat more variation in the state cases, with a largest to smallest ratio of almost 2.00. At least part of this variation is probably attributable to the presence in some of the jurisdictions in the study of limited jurisdiction courts that process moderate-sized cases (as distinct from small claims) involving claims under a specified amount (e.g., $5,000 or $2,000).[16] However, the specific variations in stakes do not track with the variations in the jurisdictional maximums in the lower-level courts. For example, the Wisconsin limited jurisdiction court handled cases up to $2,000 but the median stakes in the general jurisdiction courts in Eastern Wisconsin exceeded that for South Carolina where the limited jurisdiction court could hear cases involving up to $15,000.[17] Furthermore, the Wisconsin median was only slightly smaller than the California median, even though California's limited jurisdiction court heard cases involving as much as $5,000 at the time the research was carried out.[18]

What kind of variation is there in the amount at stake depending on the area of law involved in a case? Since cases can raise several different areas, one cannot unambiguously separate cases into substantive areas. One can look at the median stakes for cases that raise a particular type of issue although doing this makes it unavoidable that some cases will be included more than once. At this juncture, I will include in the discussion domestic relations cases, even though one cannot compare state and federal cases for this area of law. Note that some types of cases (e.g., government action, business regulation) are less likely to involve monetary stakes than are others; specifically, the discussion that follows applies only to the cases for which lawyers were willing and able to express the stakes in monetary terms.

Figure 3–1 shows the median stakes by area of law for state and federal cases. As one would expect, for most substantive areas there is a substantial gap in the amount at stake for federal and state cases. The biggest gap seems to be for the property area, but one should keep in mind that a relatively small number of federal cases raised property issues, and the median stakes figure for federal property cases is less reliable than most of the others. Nonetheless, the biggest gaps are in the areas where federal jurisdiction is likely to be based on diversity of citizenship and cases are thus ostensibly required to involve at least $10,000.[19] In the regulatory area, one field in which the federal courts have jurisdiction largely under federal law rather than under the constitutional provisions regarding diversity of citizenship, the federal/state gap is much smaller, primarily because the federal median is substantially lower (as opposed to the state medians being higher).

The relatively large amount of variation in the federal medians (from about $60,000 for property cases to about $5,000 for civil rights/discrimination cases) reflects in large part this presence or absence of jurisdictional minimums. In contrast, the state medians, with one exception, typically show less variation; except for domestic relations, they are all in the $2,500 to $5,000 range. Domestic relations is clearly the outlier (i.e., a category with an extreme value) for state cases, and this probably reflects the fact that monetized domestic relations cases, in which there is no dispute over custody, are likely to involve the

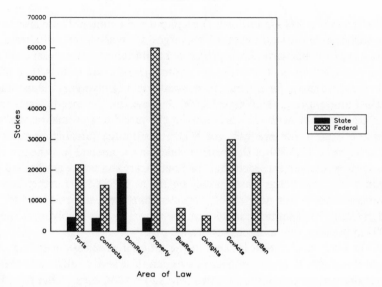

FIGURE 3–1. Stakes by area of law and court.

division of substantial pieces of real property (e.g., a house); the presence of such assets drives up the stakes figures for these cases.

Who Goes to Court?

There are three kinds of "popular" images of who is involved in the cases entering our courts. One image suggests that the typical case involves a large powerful organization ("the haves") suing a helpless individual ("have nots"), with the organization "coming out ahead" (Wanner, 1973, 1974; Galanter, 1974). A contrasting image presents the picture of a greedy, ambulance-chasing lawyer representing an individual (or group of individuals) who has suffered some imagined or dubious injury suing a wealthy professional or corporation; the "victim" defendant is often depicted as settling what is a "frivolous" lawsuit because the cost of fighting the case in court exceeds the amount at stake.[20] A third image is that of two Goliaths (or one large Goliath and one small Goliath) slugging it out in court to see who will control a market or technology (e.g., MCI's antitrust case against AT&T). While cases that fit all of these images do occur, these data suggest a very different image for the ordinary, everyday, garden-variety case.

When one looks at the parties named as plaintiffs and defendants in the court records of the sampled cases,[21] a clear picture emerges concerning plaintiffs: they are overwhelmingly individuals (with the possible exception of state courts in New Mexico, where organizations place a close second). As shown in Table 3–5, the picture for defendants is less clear. In the federal courts, there are relatively few cases in which the defendant is an individual standing alone. In

TABLE 3–5. Nature of Plaintiffs and Defendants in Federal and State Courts

	Federal Courts					State Courts				
	Eastern Wisc.	Central Calif.	Eastern Pa.	S.C.	N.Mex.	Eastern Wisc.	Central Calif.	Eastern Pa.	S.C.	N.Mex.
Plaintiffs										
Individuals	42%	57%	60%	63%	64%	68%	75%	83%	72%	46%
Organizations	28	27	28	24	24	24	20	16	21	37
Government	18	12	6	10	6	2	2	1	2	10
Mixed[a]	5	4	5	1	5	4	3	–	<1	6
Other	7	<1	1	1	1	3	–	–	3	7
Defendants										
Individuals	13	8	18	27	17	20	52	48	52	48
Organizations	32	45	56	45	37	20	23	35	22	32
Government	18	20	7	17	22	2	2	3	8	4
Mixed[a]	23	26	18	11	22	53	23	14	18	15
Other	13	–	–	–	2	5	–	–	1	<1
Number of cases	152	157	151	155	172	132	128	147	143	157

Source: Reprinted, with rounding, from the *Journal of Politics* 44(February 1982), p. 99 by permission of the University of Texas Press.

[a]This is a residual category for cases with different types of plaintiffs and defendants—mostly individuals combined with financial institutions and insurance companies.

the state courts, however, with the exception of Wisconsin, a plurality of cases seem to involve individuals as defendants. On the other hand, there are very few cases in the state courts where the defendant is a government agency, while in the federal courts (with the exception of Pennsylvania), government agencies appear as defendants in 15 to 20 percent of cases; this difference largely reflects lawsuits in the federal courts over government benefits such as social security payments and the like.

The most striking figure in Table 3–5 is the absence of individuals alone as defendants in state cases in Wisconsin; this anomaly leads to a major caveat in drawing conclusions about who is involved in court cases. In injury cases where the defendant's liability is covered by insurance, it is usually the insurance company that hires and instructs the defense attorney; effectively, it is the insurance company that is being sued because it is the insurance company that is at risk. However, in most jurisdictions, the fiction that it is the tort-feasor (the party responsible for the injury) who is being sued is maintained, and often neither party is permitted to reveal whether or not the alleged liability is covered by insurance. In Wisconsin, however, an injured party may file suit directly against the insurance company of the tort-feasor, with the case listing both the insurer and the tort-feasor as defendants.[22] Thus, in Wisconsin, the court record more accurately reflects the actual parties in interest, and one finds a small number of individual defendants but a large number of "mixed" defendants. This suggests the need to be cautious in estimating the role played by individuals as defendants in civil litigation, at least if one is basing those estimates on information contained in court records. This conclusion is reinforced by examining the configuration of parties by location and type of court.

Table 3–6 shows the configuration of the parties (according to the court records) in each case in the sample. In four of the state courts, the largest single category seems to consist of disputes between individuals; again, Wisconsin stands out as the exception (although in New Mexico, while individual versus individual suits constitute a plurality, it is a very thin plurality), and this again reflects the practice of listing the insurance company as a defendant in tort actions. In the federal courts, there is no single dominant pattern. What is most striking in the table is the relatively small number of cases where organizations sue individuals.[23]

Summary: The Ordinary Case

While there is, strictly speaking, no such thing as the "typical" case in civil litigation, the preceding discussion provides a good composite picture of ordinary litigation. Most civil litigation takes place in state courts and involves modest sums of money. Cases most often involve an individual plaintiff suing an organizational defendant; the major exceptions to this are domestic relations cases, pitting two individuals against one another, and debt collection cases, where an organization usually sues an individual (resulting, in a very high proportion of cases, in default judgments in favor of the plaintiffs be-

Table 3–6. Configuration of Parties, Selected Groups:[a] State and Federal Courts

	Federal Courts					State Courts				
Plaintiff-Defendant	Eastern Wisc.	Central Calif.	Eastern Pa.	S.C.	N.Mex.	Eastern Wisc.	Central Calif.	Eastern Pa.	S.C.	N.Mex.
Ind-ind	8%[b]	45%	41%	45%	19%	4%	4%	12%	17%	12%
Ind-org	14	12	27	14	17	10	20	32	26	20
Ind-org	2	2	3	6	2	14	20	6	16	21
Ind-mix	41	15	12	7	7	9	13	11	4	10
Org-ind	8	5	7	4	15	3	2	3	4	2
Org-org	5	8	8	7	13	12	17	18	16	12
Org-mix	8	7	1	8	7	8	7	5	4	8
Gov-ind	2	<1	<1	<1	11	7	2	1	6	2
Number of cases	132	128	147	144	158	152	157	151	155	172

Source: Reprinted, with rounding, from the Journal of Politics 44 (February 1982), p. 102 by permission of the University of Texas Press.

[a]Reported are the most frequent out of 25 possible combinations of individual (ind), organization (org), government (gov), and mixed (mix); note that, as mentioned in the discussion of the sample design, cases of government versus government (gov-gov) were excluded from the study.

[b]Percentages do not add to 100 because only selected categories have been included.

cause the case is uncontested by the defendants). The vast bulk of litigation involves routine issues arising from accidental injury, contracts, and the dissolution of marriages; in the more esoteric world of the federal courts, cases involving business regulation, civil rights/discrimination, government benefits, and government action can also be found.

It is very important to keep this portrait in mind as I turn to look at the lawyers handling ordinary civil litigation and the work involved in those cases. The image of the civil justice system found in newspaper stories and other popular accounts, whether those accounts describe the big case or the silly case (a case almost always has to be either big or silly to capture popular attention[24]), differs sharply from the more mundane world in which lawyers go about their work on a daily basis. It is in this mundane, albeit very important, world that the two images, the professional and the broker, are to be applied.

APPENDIX 3A

Area of Law Codes and Groups

Real Property
  Land use/land development
  Land use restrictions/zoning
  Torts to land
  Condemnation of land
  Land title transfer
  Foreclosure
  Real estate contracts
  Owner–tenant
  Building permits
  Boundary lines
  Mortgage
  Other real property

Contract/Commercial
  Contract for goods
  Contract for services
  Restitution for goods
  Restitution for services
  Lending and credit transactions
  Contracts for employment or wage and
    hour practices
  Insurance
  Employee benefit/retirement funds
  Government procurement contracts
  Marine
  Indemnity in admiralty cases
  Torts in business relationships
  Consumer major purchases

Home builder and repair problems
Other contract
Mismanagement
Organizational control/ownership
Corporate finance
Stockholder/bondholder claims
Mergers and acquisitions
Partnership agreements
Bankruptcy/receivership/reorganization
Government claims, including taxes
Other business and corporation law
Enforcement of arbitration under
  contract

Torts
  Personal injury
    Motor vehicle
    Railroad
    Marine
    Airline
    Other transport
    Product liability
    Malpractice
    Worker's compensation
    Workplace accident
    Other accident
    Animal
    Negligence of employee
    Wrongful death

Battery (intentional infliction of
  emotional harm)
Other personal injury tort
Property damage
  Motor vehicle
  Railroad
  Marine
  Airline
  Other transport
  Product liability
  Intentional business torts
  Defamation/libel/slander
  Accident nontransport
Regulatory
  Marketing
  Business licensing
  Professional licensing
  Health and safety licensing
  Public convenience licensing
  Wage and hour practices
  Other labor/employment practices
    (nonwage and hour)
  Union rights – organizing
  Union rights – bargaining
  Union rights – strike, job action
  Workplace safety/occupational safety
  Anti-trust
  Intellectual property
  Securities/commodities exchange
  Unemployment compensation claim
  Environmental protection
  Public health and safety
  Other business regulation
Discrimination/Civil Rights
  Discrimination – racial
  Discrimination – sex
  Discrimination – age

Discrimination – other classification
Discrimination – handicapped
Racial discrimination
  (nonbusiness) – housing
Racial discrimination
  (nonbusiness) – public
  accommodations
Racial discrimination
  (nonbusiness) – other
Civil rights issue (nonracial)
Civil liberties
Government Action
  Tax assessment/collection
  Immigration/naturalization
  Political process
  Abuse of governmental authority
  Government financial obligations
  Civil commitment
  Armed forces
  Voting rights
  Freedom of Information Act
  Other public law
Government Benefits
  Welfare benefits
  Nonwelfare government benefits or
    services
  Social security benefits
  Other government benefits
Domestic Relations
  Divorce/dissolution/annulment
  Alimony
  Child custody
  Child support
  Property division
  Legal separation
  Other domestic relations

4

Lawyers Who Litigate

Who are the lawyers who litigate the kinds of ordinary cases described in Chapter 3? What kinds of training, experience, and expertise do they bring to their work? What are their attitudes toward their work? How do these characteristics reflect the lawyers' efforts to balance the often inconsistent demands of the professional and broker roles? These are the questions addressed in this chapter.

Over the years there have been a variety of demographic (and other) descriptions of the legal profession. Some of these concentrate on lawyers in particular kinds of practice situations (e.g., Smigel, 1964; Carlin, 1962; Laumann and Heinz, with Nelson and Salisbury, 1985); some focus on lawyers in particular locations (Heinz and Laumann, 1982; Handler, 1976; Landon, 1982, 1985, 1988); and some try to provide a general overview of the legal profession in the United States at a particular time (Sikes, Carson, and Gorai, 1972; Curran, 1986). The following description is of a group of lawyers engaged in a particular type of work (during a particular period of time—the late 1970s). Where appropriate I will draw comparisons to other descriptions of lawyers in the United States.[1]

There are many dimensions along which one could describe any occupational group; in this chapter, I concentrate on three general dimensions to describe the lawyers handling ordinary litigation: background (including training, experience, and expertise), "nature" and "style" of law practice, and attitudes toward law practice and litigation. By nature of practice I am referring to the social and structural settings of lawyers' practice and the type(s) of work that they engage in; by style of practice I mean the ways lawyers go about doing their work (use of standardized procedures, etc.).

Background

Law School

Virtually all of the lawyers in the sample (1,378 out of 1,382) are graduates of law schools. A total of 127 law schools were attended by these lawyers. I have divided the law schools into four groups.[2]

"Elite" law schools (Harvard, Yale, Chicago, University of Michigan, Columbia, and Stanford).

"Prestige" law schools (University of Pennsylvania, University of Virginia, University of California at Berkeley, UCLA, University of Texas, Northwestern, Cornell, Duke, and New York University).

Other state-supported law schools (usually affiliated with major state universities).

Other private, nonproprietary law schools (usually affiliated with private universities).

Not surprisingly, the largest group of lawyers (48 percent) attended state-supported law schools outside the elite and prestige groups; the second largest group (30 percent) attended private law schools outside the elite and prestige groups; only 21 percent of the lawyers attended one of the law schools in the upper echelon (8 percent to elite schools and 13 percent to prestige schools).[3]

According to their own reports, these lawyers compiled above average records in law school. Two indicators of performance are available: rank in class and membership on the law review. Seventy-four percent of the lawyers claimed ranks in the top half of their law school class (35 percent reported being in the top quarter and 16 percent in the upper decile). This high level of performance seems to be borne out by the relatively frequent reports of participation on the law review (26 percent over half of whom were officers).[4] This high level of performance may seem a bit suspicious; are the respondents puffing up their backgrounds for the benefit of the interviewers?

In fact, the performance of this group of lawyers is very similar to the overall group performance reported in a study of the impact of legal training. Zemans and Rosenblum found that 50 percent of the lawyers in their survey, all of whom were practicing in Chicago during the late 1970s, reported being in the top 20 percent of their class, and 77 percent reported being in the top 40 percent (1981: 24); 24 percent of the Chicago lawyers reported participation in law review (1981: 108). This comparison suggests that the lawyers doing ordinary litigation do not differ appreciably from practicing lawyers as a whole in terms of how well they did in law school.

Still, is there a general tendency for lawyers to exaggerate their performance in law school? There may be some puffery going on, particularly regarding class rank (which is very difficult to verify);[5] it is less likely that someone would falsely claim to have served on the staff of a law review, because this can be very easily checked. Alternately, it is likely that, for whatever reasons (see Zemans and Rosenblum, 1981: 24–25), law students in the lower half of their classes have a smaller chance of developing a career practicing law than do those in the upper half, or lower-ranking students may find themselves in practice situations that are less involved in litigation or that are less visible to researchers; as I will show, the lawyers handling ordinary civil litigation are unlikely to be in the most marginal forms of practice (i.e., solo practice) compared to lawyers in private practice as a whole.

Apprenticeship Opportunities

The early years of legal practice have been likened to an internship or apprenticeship, particularly for young lawyers working in large firms (Smigel, 1964) or in
the U.S. Department of Justice (Horowitz, 1977). To what degree do the lawyers
handling ordinary litigation enjoy this kind of early, on-the-job training? The
lawyers in the survey were asked to identify all of the types of situations in which
they worked during the first 5 years of practice (or since starting practice, for
those with less than 5 years of experience). The most common kind of experience
was working in solo practice (21 percent) or in firms with less than 10 lawyers (49
percent); only 13 percent reported working in a firm with 20 lawyers or more,
and even fewer, 10 percent, reported working for the federal government (and a
substantial portion of those probably worked as Assistant U.S. Attorneys, not in
the kinds of situations associated with apprenticeship experiences).[6] At the beginning of their careers, these lawyers were in situations where they quickly had
to learn to cope with handling their own cases. Few had an opportunity to have
an apprenticeshiplike experience where they could hone the abstract, technical
skills of lawyering, such as brief writing or legal research and analysis, under the
tutelage of an experienced practitioner.

Experience

The experience this sample of lawyers brought to their work can be assessed in
two different ways: how long the lawyer had been practicing law, and how
many "similar" cases the lawyer had handled. As is well known, starting in the
early 1970s, there was a major influx of persons into law school and then into
careers as lawyers (see Sander and Williams, 1989). This influx is clearly reflected in the group of lawyers handling ordinary litigation: 34 percent of the
lawyers in this sample had been in practice for 5 years or less; the remaining
lawyers were closely divided (20 to 24 percent) among those who had been
practicing 6 to 10 years, 11 to 20 years, and more than 20 years. This is broadly
similar to the findings of a national study that found that 42.3 percent of
lawyers in practice in 1980 had been admitted to the bar after 1970 (see Curran,
1986: 37). Overall, the lawyers handling ordinary litigation bring substantial
years of experience to their work; however, there are also substantial numbers
of younger, less experienced lawyers handling these cases as well.[7]

Regarding experience with actual cases, the lawyers were asked to identify
the field of law into which the sampled case fell. They were then asked how
many cases in that field they had handled prior to taking on the sampled case.
Most of the lawyers indicated that they had previously handled many cases in
the same substantive area. Only about 25 percent had handled 25 cases or fewer
in the area; 54 percent had handled over 100 "similar" cases. As with years of
experience, one finds that most of the lawyers had substantial amounts of
specific substantive experience, although there was definitely a group with
substantially less such experience.[8]

Expertise

Let us now turn to "expertise" as opposed to "experience," recognizing that these two ideas are closely related. In addition to information regarding the numbers of prior cases in the particular field, the lawyers were asked to assess their own expertise in that field. Specifically, they were asked whether they considered themselves to be "an expert," "somewhat of an expert," or "not an expert." Most of the lawyers viewed themselves as being an "expert" (42 percent) or "somewhat of an expert" (41 percent) in the field; very few (17 percent) described themselves as "not an expert."

These figures are consistent with the lawyers' reports of significant amounts of outside (i.e., noncase related) activity in the substantive field of the sampled case. The lawyers were asked whether, since being admitted to the bar, they had taken or taught courses or workshops in the field, written articles or books about it, or served on any bar association or government committees that dealt with the field. Five specific activities were asked about, and only 16 percent of the respondents reported no outside activities. Fifty-four percent had been involved in two or more of the activities.[9]

Background Summary

The general picture of training and experience that one sees in the preceding figures is that of a group of lawyers with sound legal training from well-regarded law schools, who have gained substantial expertise in the legal fields that comprise ordinary litigation. They have strong formal backgrounds, as indicated by their generally above average performance in law school, but they did not have the opportunity to develop that formal training substantially in the years immediately after law school. Clearly, they have been educated as professionals and were successful during their professional training. In the years after completing their formal professional training, most have built up solid records of experience; they are insiders in the litigation system, handling large numbers of cases and taking opportunities to improve their ability to work within specific substantive areas. In terms of training and experience, these litigators combine the formal background of the professional and the insider experiences of the broker.

Nature and Style of Practice

In this section I will look at the type of practice situation these lawyers are in and then at some general factors describing how they go about conducting their practices. Recall that lawyers directly employed by government agencies were excluded from this primary survey (a separate survey was conducted of those persons); consequently, most of the lawyers (95 percent) in the sample are in private practice. The exceptions to this are those who work as direct employees or organizations that are not law firms (i.e., "house counsel"), for some sort of prepaid legal services plan (including legal aid), or in some other kind of situation (e.g., as a volunteer).[10]

Of those lawyers in private practice, only 18 percent were working solo (i.e., outside of a multimember law firm). This differs strikingly from the situation for all lawyers working in private practice in the United States, which is reported by Curran (1986: 28) as involving almost 49 percent of the lawyers in solo practice.[11] Another 30 percent of the lawyers handling ordinary litigation were in firms with two, three, or four lawyers. Table 4–1 shows the complete distribution for lawyers in ordinary litigation (based on the CLRP survey) and for all lawyers in private practice (based on Curran's data).[12] As the table shows, the other kind of private practice situation that was underrepresented among lawyers in the sample was the large firm with 50 lawyers or more. In some ways this latter figure is less surprising, because ordinary cases are not the usual work of the larger law firms. The low percentage of solo practitioners suggests that ordinary civil litigation does not usually go to the most marginal practitioners (commonly found in solo practice). This is less surprising than it might first seem because it probably means that institutional defendants (e.g., insurance companies) turn to established firms for their representation, and that individual plaintiffs, particularly those seeking to hire a lawyer on a contingency basis, need not seek out the lowest-cost alternatives (as might be the case for those individuals seeking divorce counsel or counsel to handle probate or

TABLE 4–1. Size of Law Firm of Lawyers in Private Practice

Size of Firm	Percent
Litigators Only[a]	
1 (solo)	18
2	10
3–4	20
5–9	24
10–19	13
20–49	10
50 and up	5
n	1,347
All[b]	
1 (solo)	49
2–5	22
6–10	9
11–20	7
21–50	6
51 and up	7
n	370,111

[a]From the Civil Litigation Research Project data set.
[b]From Curran (1986: 28), percentages rounded.

property-related matters).[13] The relative absence of solo practitioners may also mean that the most marginal practitioners avoid formally initiating lawsuits (see Carlin, 1962), either because they get the most marginal cases where uncertainties or low stakes make formal litigation unattractive or because the lawyers do not have the expertise or experience to pursue formal litigation.

A lawyer handling an ordinary case in the civil courts is likely to have a practice that is heavily weighted toward litigation. About two thirds of the lawyers spent more than half of their time working on court cases, and 45 percent reported spending more than three quarters of their time on such cases. While court cases dominated the lawyers' activities, the actual trying of cases tended to consume a small portion of their time. Only 3 percent of the lawyers reported spending as much as half of their time actually trying cases, and 81 percent spent less than a quarter of their time on trials.

Recall that most of these lawyers have had a lot of experience with cases in the substantive area of the sampled case. However, while many of the lawyers could be characterized fairly as being litigation specialists, there was not an overwhelming trend for the lawyers to specialize in one substantive area of the law for their litigation work. When asked to estimate the *percentage* of their cases that were in the same substantive area as the case in the sample, 39 percent of the lawyers reported that over half of their cases was in that area compared to 38 percent who indicated that less than a quarter of their cases fell into that area. Because they typically handle large numbers of cases, by necessity given that the potential return from any one case is relatively low, ordinary litigators can gain a lot of experience with cases in a number of different legal fields; this accounts for the apparent expertise (as described in the previous section) without any corresponding specialization in a particular field of law.

There is one last indicator of the nature of the law practice of these lawyers. As the use of the term "ordinary" suggests, much of the work of the day-to-day case may be repetitious, permitting lawyers to draw on previous work products to speed up the handling of a case. When asked to estimate the percentage of their time that is devoted to fairly unique situations or problems, requiring tailor-made responses, 64 percent reported spending no more than half of their time on such cases (35 percent reported no more than a quarter of their time), and only 19 percent spent more than three quarters of their time on these relatively unique cases.[14] As one might expect, routine cases can lead to procedures for increased efficiency. Many of the lawyers reported mechanisms for standardizing their work in litigation (cf. Engel, 1977; Spangler, 1986: 48–49, 128–130, 161–162). The lawyers were asked about their use of preprinted forms for pleadings, motions, and discovery; 57 percent used them for pleadings, 52 percent for motions, and 67 percent for discovery. Twenty-four percent of the lawyers reported not using preprinted forms for any of the three activities, and 40 percent reported using such forms for all three activities. While it would be difficult to use preprinted forms for briefs (this study was done before word processors were as ubiquitous as they are today), lawyers could simply reuse sections of previously written briefs. Only 13 percent reported that they never reused sections;[15] 60 percent said that they did this occasionally.[16]

Practice Summary

In this section one gets a broad view of the daily working situation of lawyers handling ordinary litigation. These lawyers' practices do not fall at the extremes of where private practice lawyers work; instead, they are to be found in the small (under 10 lawyers) law firm. The work of these lawyers is heavily dominated by court cases, but not by actual trial work. The litigator's practice, while being specialized in the sense of being heavily weighted toward litigation, is not substantively specialized by area of law; yet while the lawyers are not likely to specialize in a particular type of case, they have a lot of experience with such cases simply by handling many cases since starting to practice. The large number of similar cases leads to the utilization of standardized procedures through the use of preprinted forms or the reuse of materials written previously. Relatively few of the lawyers devote the majority of their time to cases that present unique issues requiring custom responses.

Attitudes Toward Legal Practice

What kinds of attitudes toward their work do lawyers bring to ordinary litigation? The lawyers were asked about four different types of attitudes. The first had to do with what was important and unimportant about their work. The second concerned what part of their work as litigators they particularly like or dislike. The third concerned qualities they believe to be important to be a successful litigator. The fourth attitudinal area asked about sought to tap the respondents' commitment to the lawyer's craft.

Lawyers rated the importance of eleven considerations related to why they were pursuing their legal practice. These eleven "goals" included things such as making money, having an enjoyable and challenging work situation, and serving people and the community.[17] The lawyers described each of the eleven goals as "very important," "somewhat important," or "not important." The responses are summarized in Table 4–2. As the table shows, very few of the goals received more than a handful of "not important" ratings. Twenty-two percent of the respondents said that "making a lot of money" was not important; the only other goals to be rated as unimportant by 10 percent or more of the respondents were the two that referred to the community, "serving the community and public" and "having a high standing in the community." The most highly rated goal, with 75 percent of the lawyers describing it as very important, was "being your own boss." Five of the other goals were rated as very important by about 67 percent of the lawyers, with two others, both having to do with the specifics of the work situation (physical surroundings and coworkers), being somewhat less important to the respondents.[18]

Lawyers were asked which of the following aspects of their litigation work they most liked and which they most disliked: negotiating, planning and research, and arguing and trying. Each respondent also indicated how intense those likes and dislikes were ("very strong," "strong," or "slight"). Responses to

TABLE 4-2. Lawyers' Attitudes Toward Their Work[a]

Aspect	Very Important	Somewhat Important	Not Important	n
Intellectual challenge	63%	35%	2%	1,361
Winning	67	31	2	1,360
Serving the community and public	39	51	10	1,360
Making a decent living	64	35	1	1,360
Helping individual people with problems	66	31	3	1,358
Being your own boss	75	22	3	1,359
Having a high standing in the community	42	42	16	1,357
Having the respect of family and friends	64	30	6	1,358
Working with pleasant and interesting people	57	38	5	1,356
Making a lot of money	16	62	22	1,356
Having comfortable work surroundings	46	50	4	1,361

[a] The wording of the question was, "Overall, in looking at your legal work, how important is each of the following considerations for you?"

the likes and dislikes are summarized in Table 4-3; by far the largest group of lawyers (53%) liked arguing and trying cases the best, with negotiating coming in a poor second; planning and research was both the least likely to be the most liked and the most likely to be the least liked. It is also noteworthy that those who most liked arguing and trying were more intense regarding that preference (somewhere between strong and very strong) than were those whose first preference was either negotiating or planning and research.[19]

The lawyers were presented with five traits that might be associated with success as a litigator.

• Being firm.
• Being fair.
• Being thorough.
• Being willing to compromise in order to resolve a problem.
• Being consistent.

TABLE 4-3. What Litigators Like and Dislike About Their Work

Aspect	Most Liked	Intensity[a]	Least Liked	Intensity
Negotiating	25%	2.0	33%	1.6
Planning and research	18	1.9	47	1.7
Arguing and trying	53	2.3	16	1.7
Combination	4	—	4	—
	100%		100%	
n	1,290		1,236	

[a] The intensity scale is computed based on a follow-up question that asked whether the preference was "very strong," "strong," or "slight." Intensity is the average of these responses, with very strong coded 3, strong coded 2, and slight coded 1.

They were asked to rate each one as "very important," "somewhat important," or "not important" (Table 4–4). Thoroughness clearly stood out in the eyes of these litigators, with 91 percent of them rating that trait as very important. At the other end of the ordering of importance was the willingness to compromise, with only 43 percent rating it very important and another 46 percent rating it somewhat important. There was strong agreement that the remaining three traits—firmness, fairness, and consistency—were very important, but the views regarding these traits did not approach the near unanimity for thoroughness.[20]

A final work-related attitude concerned commitment to the legal craft. To tap this dimension, lawyers were asked about their willingness to devote extra attention to their work.

> This question is about your work habits. Assume a client who regularly uses lawyers but is careful about that use. If you have completed several drafts of an important document for that client, how likely is it that you would spend any additional time to make slight improvements in that document?

Not surprisingly, most of the lawyers (60 percent) indicated that it was very likely that they would put in the additional time; only 12 percent said that it was unlikely they would do so. It would be interesting to know how frequently the lawyers actually found themselves confronted with the need to make such a decision; unfortunately, no question along those lines was asked.

Thus, what one finds regarding the lawyers' attitudes toward their work is a relatively high degree of agreement regarding what is important, both from the viewpoint of individual satisfactions and from the viewpoint of what is necessary to be a successful litigator. If one were constructing the typical litigator from what I have presented (assuming that all of the preferred traits could be combined into one individual), that lawyer would be someone who was thorough, firm, fair, and consistent and who wanted to make a decent living and liked being his or her own boss while helping individuals by winning disputes.

There is one intriguing contradiction in this portrait. The lawyers were almost unanimous in their belief that being thorough was very important in

TABLE 4–4. The Makings of a Good Litigator[a]

Trait	Very Important	Somewhat Important	Not Important	n
Being firm	66%	30%	4%	1,342
Being fair	75	19	6	1,345
Being thorough	91	8	1	1,350
Being willing to compromise in order to resolve a problem	43	46	11	1,342
Being consistent	61	30	9	1,325

[a] The wording of the question was, "To be a successful litigator, how important do you think it is to have a reputation for each of the following?"

order to be a successful litigator; at the same time, very few of the lawyers said that the part of their work that they liked the most was the planning and research that are required to be thorough. The lawyers said what they liked best about their work was the more glamorous aspect of arguing and trying cases. This tension between what is important and what is liked does not necessarily mean that lawyers shortchange their efforts regarding planning and research (recall that very few lawyers reported spending more than 25 percent of their time actually trying cases), but it does suggest something of the reality of the working world of the ordinary litigator.

The Ordinary Litigator: A Sketch

The various pieces I have presented provide a good sense of the background and attitudes that lawyers handling ordinary civil litigation bring to their work. The image of the lawyer–litigator one would form from this discussion differs sharply from the image of courtroom advocate popularized in various television series and movies, although it seems that the lawyers themselves may tend to aspire to that popular image.

Ordinary litigators come to their work with solid backgrounds of training and experience and with expressed commitments to serve the needs of their clients. The image of the advocate (see Simon, 1978) is not inconsistent with what I have described; ordinary litigators usually express more concern about serving their clients than about either serving the broader community or maintaining their reputations in their communities (even though neither community service nor status is seen as unimportant). At the same time, the work of these litigators might be fairly characterized as mundane. A majority of the time of these lawyers is spent on cases that do not require tailor-made responses, and the lawyers make substantial use of standardized work products of various sorts.

Broadly speaking, this general image of lawyering has been documented in previous research (e.g., Carlin, 1962; Handler, 1967), although the group of lawyers who work in the world of ordinary litigation do not seem to be as marginal in their professional life as the large portions of the bar described in the analyses of Carlin (1962) or Blumberg (1967). This difference is evident in the relatively small percentage of ordinary litigators who are solo practitioners and in the relatively comfortable (if not spectacular) incomes the lawyers reported. The median income from legal practice was $45,000 (these figures were collected in 1980). As Table 4-5 shows, only 3 percent of the lawyers reported marginal incomes (less than $15,000) and only 8 percent reported incomes over $100,000. Ordinary litigators make a comfortable living, but they are not getting rich from their legal work. While few ordinary litigators have to worry about where their next meal (or client) is coming from, most of the lawyers in the sample probably have more in common with the solo practitioners or small-city lawyers described by Carlin and Handler than with the elite lawyers described by Smigel (1964) and Nelson (1988).

TABLE 4-5. Income from Legal Practice

Income	Percent[a]
Under $15,000	3
$15,000–25,000	16
$25,000–40,000	26
$40,000–50,000	15
$50,000–75,000	20
$75,000–100,000	12
Over $100,000	8

Median = $45,000.
Mean = $52,700.
[a]Based on 1,258 respondents.

In summary, lawyers handling ordinary litigation are individuals secure in their work, even though they are probably not particularly excited by much of what they find themselves doing from day to day. They spend a lot of their time working on routine cases and trying to do things to ease the tedium that results; the part of their work that they find most stimulating and exciting is direct advocacy (arguing and trying cases); however, a small portion of their time is actually devoted to such activities.

Brokers and Professionals

How does this sketch relate to the images of the professional and the broker? How does the routinization suggested by the information on the daily work situation connect to professionalism and brokerage? Do the attitudes toward the work of the litigator comport to what one might expect of one or both of the two images?

To the degree to which technical knowledge is reducible to standardized forms or procedures, one could argue that such knowledge falls short of the kind of abstract knowledge one associates with years of professional training and experience. Clearly, some of the work that lawyers do in litigation can be reduced to a routine; whether that routine can be done by someone with much less training than that possessed by a professional is not indicated by the information I have discussed so far. The analysis presented in Chapters 7 and 8 will shed some light on that question.

But is it fair to link lack of routinization with professionalism? This is a difficult question. After all, when one seeks out a surgeon to perform open heart surgery, one ideally wants a person for whom the operation is routine rather than a surgeon for whom the operation is a new and challenging experience. At the same time, one wants a surgeon who has the training and judgment to be able to respond quickly and appropriately if something unexpected happens during the operation (i.e., something that requires deviation from the routine). But even in the medical realm there is an important distinction between the professional and the paraprofessional, with the latter more oriented toward dealing with the daily routine and the former handling the more unusual and challenging situations (e.g., the obstetrician and the midwife, or the physician and the physician's assistant). This is not to say that paraprofessionals are lacking in training to carry out their responsibilities; instead, the training is of a different order and has a somewhat different goal.

One pattern in the data that is intriguing is the clearly mixed feelings that these lawyers hold regarding "planning and research," given that this activity is likely to involve the most "technical lawyering." The lawyers almost universally recognize the importance of thoroughness as a trait of a good litigator but, at the same time, they do not particularly enjoy the planning and research that must go into thoroughness. Is this because a large portion of the planning and research is routine and mundane? Or does this simply mean that arguing and trying cases is more exciting and publicly rewarding? This apparent inconsistency may be a hint that the daily work of litigation is less the work of the abstractly trained and oriented professional and more the world of the streetwise and experienced insider, the broker.

III

LAWYERS AND
THEIR RELATIONSHIPS

Litigation is an activity that takes place within the context of a set of social relationships. In this part I explore some of the theoretically and practically interesting relationships involved in litigation: the relationship between lawyers and their clients, and the relationships between lawyers and the other regular actors (e.g., opposing lawyers, judges, and/or opposing parties) in the litigation process.

In my development of the alternative images of the professional and of the broker, the lawyer's relationships with these other actors was important. Brokers, I suggested, would be highly dependent on their sets of ongoing relationships with other regular actors (the knowledge of these actors forming a significant component of the insider knowledge on which the brokers would draw) and would have relationships with their clients that would involve substantial amounts of input and control by the clients. Furthermore, the fee-paying component of the broker/client relationship would be explicit and fairly central. In contrast, professionals would exercise the dominant role in the relationship with clients, and the fees to be paid by the clients would have only a minimal (if any) impact either on those relationships or on the work that the lawyers would do. The lawyers' motivations for the work would flow partly from a desire to act as the clients' informed, dispassionate alter egos and partly from commitments to the work itself.

Several points need to be made about this sketch before considering the everyday realities of the relationship network within which lawyers work. First, relationships between the broker and actors other than the client are *very* important. In contrast, the formally expected relationships between the American lawyer as professional and nonclients seldom go beyond what would be associated with an abstract commitment to a system of justice; the responsibility is to the client, even when that responsibility might cause damage to others, both in the civil justice system and outside of it.[1] The most recent efforts to formulate

"Model Rules of Professional Conduct" by the American Bar Association reflected the fundamental tensions between commitment to the client (particularly client confidentiality) and responsibilities to the system of justice (see Center for Professional Responsibility, 1987: 47–55, 121–127; Schneyer, 1989), and some of the recent efforts to improve the professional image of lawyers in the United States have dealt specifically with increasing the bar's role as "officers of the court" (American Bar Association, 1986: 28–30). Despite this, the general expectation is that lawyers are *first*, advocates for their clients, and *second*, officers of the court. In the end, this is largely because it is the client who hires the lawyer and pays the bill.

This leads to the second caveat. The sketches of the professional and broker present some contrasts in terms that are very black and white. In fact, the world always involves many shades of gray: no professional is entirely unconcerned about the income generated by professional practice; after all, a profession *is* a means of earning a livelihood, even if it is not first and foremost a source of income. Likewise, no broker is going to be unconcerned about ethical expectations and duties to the client, whether this reflects legally imposed responsibilities or concerns about long-term interests.

Even taking into account these cautionary notes, the two alternative images provide useful vehicles for examining and understanding the set of relationships that partially structures the work of the lawyer in ordinary litigation. In the pages that follow I will first consider the relationship between lawyer and client and then more briefly examine relationships that the lawyer has with other key actors. The discussion of lawyers and clients will begin with how and why lawyer–client relationships are formed for specific cases; it will then turn to the explicitness of the business component of the relationship and, finally, to the theoretical and actual allocation of responsibility and control within the relationship. In the discussion that follows, several potential intervening variables will be considered: the kind of case (area of law, amount at issue), the complexity of the case, and the type of litigant (individual *vs.* organization).

There are some major limitations on the discussion imposed by the original data collection design that was not specifically intended for the analysis I would ideally like to have been able to carry out. Questions were often asked only if certain conditions were met (e.g., lawyers were asked about referral of cases to the opposing lawyer only if the two lawyers had had a prior, nonbusiness relationship), and other questions that would be important to use in exploring more fully the issues I have raised (e.g., about experience opposing the other side, both lawyer and litigant, in previous cases) were not asked at all.

5

Lawyers and Their Clients

The study of the relationship between lawyers and clients has received important attention by social scientists in the last several years. Some studies (e.g., Sarat and Felstiner, 1986, 1988; Berends, 1981) have involved direct observation of lawyer–client interactions; I cannot replicate the detail and richness of those studies, and I will not try. Instead, I will outline those interactions based on the more limited information I have available. I will consider three topics.

- How the lawyer–client connection is made (i.e., how clients find lawyers, and why lawyers accept cases).
- The explicitness of the business arrangements that are made between lawyers and their clients, and the form those arrangements take.
- How the lawyers and their clients allocate and exercise responsibility with regard to the actual handling of the cases.

The first topic is primarily background, since it does not relate directly to either the professional or the broker or to the tensions between them; the other two topics do relate to the issues raised by the two images.

In this chapter, I go beyond the data from the lawyer interviews (and the court records) to include information collected from the clients themselves. As I said in Chapter 2, the client data must be treated cautiously because the representativeness of the clients interviewed is subject to some doubt. Given that a lawyer in a case can represent more than one client and that a litigant in a case can retain more than one lawyer, the unit of analysis employed in the following discussion will sometimes be the lawyer or the litigant, and sometimes the lawyer–client "dyad" (as reported by the lawyer) or the litigant–lawyer "dyad" (as reported by the litigant). I will make clear in the discussion which unit is being employed. Note, however, that while I will frequently refer to both lawyers and their clients, specific items of data will be drawn from only one respondent in the lawyer–client relationship at a time; I do not have enough information from both the lawyer and the client in lawyer–client "pairs" to use that information in the analysis.

Finding Lawyers and Taking Cases

In his study of solo practice lawyers in Chicago, Carlin (1962) devoted substantial discussion to how those lawyers obtained their clients, detailing in his discussion the kinds of referral networks that led potential clients to the lawyer. Carlin's information came entirely from the lawyers' perspective. I do not have equivalent information from the lawyers in my sample, but I do have information from the disputants on how they came to use "this" lawyer for "this" case.

As one would expect, there are sharp differences in lawyer-seeking practices for individual litigants and for organizational litigants. For most organizational litigants, choosing a lawyer presents no question because there is already an established relationship between the organization and a lawyer (or law firm): 77 percent of the organizations ($n=314$) reported that the lawyer chosen was already being used at the time the case came up or had been used in the past; the comparable figure for individual litigants ($n=219$) was only 31 percent. For individual litigants, lawyers are most often chosen (60 percent of the time) on the basis of personal acquaintance, reputation, or recommendation of friends, family, or associates; the comparable figures for organizations is 20 percent.

This difference between organizations and individuals is borne out by the lawyers (although there is some difficulty in distinguishing between organizational and individual clients[1]). Over 70 percent of the lawyers who were most likely to be representing organizations reported that prior work was at least part of the reason they took the case (and for more than 80 percent of these it was the sole reason). The same approximate percentage (over 70 percent) of those likely to have been representing individuals reported that prior work had no role in their decision to take the case; less than 15 percent of these lawyers had actually done prior work for their client.

Lawyers who reported being influenced in their decisions to accept the case by something other than prior work for the client were asked to rate the importance of ten considerations in those decisions. The distributions of responses to these considerations are shown in Table 5–1. *No specific consideration was rated as very important by even a third of the lawyers*, although some of the considerations were rated as unimportant by a majority, or substantially more, of the lawyers. The only consideration rated as "very important" by more than a quarter of the lawyers was "sympathy for the client's predicament"; as shown by the figures in Table 5–1, the consideration next in importance was "the challenge involved." One interpretation of the relatively low ratings most of the considerations received is that there was little actual thought involved in taking the case, except possibly its winnability from the viewpoint of the contingent fee lawyer—a consideration that was not included in the interview schedule; the presumption of most lawyers engaged in ordinary litigation may well be that virtually all of the cases that come in the door will be accepted, assuming that there is a reasonable chance of success and that time and other resources for handling the case are available.[2]

TABLE 5-1. Considerations Affecting Lawyers' Decisions to Take the Case

	Very Important	Important	Not Important	n
Effect the case might have on your professional standing in the community	4%	13%	84%	712
Forming a relationship with a promising new client	8	32	59	468
The intellectual interest of the case	14	35	50	756
Sympathy for the client's predicament	29	42	30	753
The challenge involved	20	39	41	754
The amount of money you expected to make on this case	8	45	47	735
The case's effect on your standing in your firm or office	4	15	81	525
Public service	11	27	63	708
Opportunity for experience in a new field of law	6	17	76	710
Obtaining publicity for your firm or office	1	7	92	714

The text of the question was: "Now I'd like to ask about some (other) factors you may have considered in deciding to take the case. I'd like you to tell me how important each of the following considerations was to you in making your decision." This question was not asked if the lawyer indicated that the only reason the case was taken was that work had been done for the client previously.

Percentages may not add to 100 (across) due to rounding.

Establishing the Business Relationship

With any fee for service activity, such as the services provided by a private practice lawyer, there must be some understanding regarding how the fee will be established, even if that understanding is implicit. Interviewers asked the litigants whether or not they had discussed fees with the lawyer before receiving an actual bill. Sixty-seven percent of the individuals and 28 percent of the organizational representatives reported such discussions; another 36% percent of the organizational representatives said that they had a standing arrangement regarding fees, so no discussion was necessary. Twenty-five percent of individuals and 33 percent of organizations reported that there was no discussion of fees in advance of receiving a bill; a few others reported that there was simply no bill.

Interestingly, while a large proportion of litigants did discuss fees with their lawyer, lawyers were more likely than clients to recall having had "discussions" of fees prior to sending their bills. Ninety percent of the lawyers likely to be representing individuals and 43 percent of those likely to be representing organizations reported having had such discussions.[3] I am not suggesting that the clients were uninterested in fees, even if they did not discuss them with the lawyer; instead, it seems that the clients were more likely to see the fee issue as peripheral to the lawyer–client relationship than were the lawyers and to respect the convention, noted by Abel in his recent book on *American Lawyers* (1989a: 27),[4] that professionals do not discuss their fees in advance.

This discrepancy between the lawyers' recall and that of their clients, particularly the large gap for individuals, probably reflects that the fee discussion was a relatively minor part of the early lawyer–client contacts (i.e., individuals were told they would only have to pay the lawyer if some recovery were obtained, and organizations viewed the fee issue as just an ordinary part of business). Nonetheless, it is interesting that it is the "professional" member of the dyad who is most concerned about the fee question; this concern is in some ways dictated by codes of "professional responsibility" (Center for Professional Responsibility, 1987: 45) and by a desire that misunderstandings about fees not sour the relationship between lawyer and client or bespeak poorly of the profession as a whole (American Bar Association, 1986: 34–36). Still, the concern about fees is less surprising within the brokerage context.

The fee discussions that did take place were likely to involve two components: the way the fee would be computed and the likely amount of the bill. Lawyers reported giving estimates to only 44 percent of the clients with whom they discussed fees. Obviously, from the viewpoint of the lawyer, the way the fee was to be computed was a more important aspect of the discussion than was the amount; this would probably reflect both the uncertainty over what the fee would be (particularly if it was to be computed as a percentage of an uncertain recovery amount) and the fact that for contingent fee clients the fee would not be paid out of pocket but from the recovery.

Probably the most striking aspect of the fee arrangement itself is how closely it is related to the kind of client represented.[5] Table 5–2a shows the fee arrangements as reported by individual litigants, organizational litigants, and lawyers (for both types of clients combined). The contingent fee arrangement is the arrangement of choice for individuals,[6] probably from both the viewpoint of the individual and the lawyer. For the individual it means that there is no out-of-pocket cost in most cases.[7] For the lawyer it means having no difficulty collecting the fee when it is due, and that if the case proves to be a "real winner," the lawyer will share in that good fortune. It is also likely that the availability of the contingent fee can be used to allay any fears the potential client may have about "what this is going to cost."

While contingent fees are thought of most frequently in relation to personal injury litigation, they actually are used in most kinds of litigation involving individual plaintiffs, other than domestic relations cases. Table 5–2b shows the fee arrangement reported by individual plaintiffs broken down by three areas of law:[8] torts, contract/commercial, and other; this miscellaneous category is necessary because of the small number of observations in each of the remaining areas of law.[9] In torts, 87 percent of the individual plaintiffs recalled retaining their lawyers on a contingency basis (90 percent if the pure contingency fees are combined with the "flat plus percentage" category); this drops to 53 percent (62 to 68 percent combining contingency and "flat plus percentage") in the other areas. With the possible exception of domestic relations (primarily

TABLE 5-2. Fee Arrangements
(a) As Reported By Each Type of Respondent

	Individual Litigants	Organizational Litigants	Lawyers
Hourly fee	10%	81%	64%
Flat fee	16	7	4
Contingent (percentage) fee	59	7	20
Flat fee plus percentage	5	1	1
Other	20	5	11
n	147	197	1,142

These figures are from client–lawyer dyads (see text); for the clients, the question of fee arrangement was asked only if the client reported discussing fees prior to receiving a bill or, in the case of organizations, if the client had a standing fee arrangement with the lawyer. Percentages may not add to 100 due to rounding.

(b) Fee Arrangement by Area of Law as Reported by Individual Plaintiffs

	Torts	Contracts	Other
Hourly fee	0%	15%	10%
Flat fee	3	15	15
Contingent (percentage) fee	87	53	53
Flat fee plus percentage	3	9	15
Other	7	9	7
n	60	34	40

divorce related), hourly fee arrangements are virtually unused by individual plaintiffs, regardless of the area of law!

From the responses of the lawyers regarding settling the business aspects of their relationship with their clients, it is clear that the lawyers saw this fee-paying component as very important, more so than did their clients. This no doubt reflects the lawyers' dependence on their clients for payment.[10] It is interesting to contrast this to the situation for physicians, who usually presume that all or most of their fee will be paid by a third-party insurer;[11] where this is not the case, medical service providers are probably as concerned as lawyers as to where payment will come from, as evidenced by newspaper exposés on what is called "patient dumping" (the refusal of private hospitals to treat emergency or walk-in patients who do not have insurance). As suggested before, the gap between the lawyers' and clients' reports of discussions of fees probably reflects the litigants' perception of what one does and does not focus on in one's relationship to a professional; that is, it may be that clients view the business aspects of their relationship to the professional providers as less seemly than do the providers themselves.

Allocating Control and Responsibility

One of the major differences between the professional and the broker concerns the question of control in the relationship between the lawyer and the client. The idea of professional autonomy suggests that it is the professional who is dominant in the relationship; the brokerage image suggests more client dominance. Sorting out this distinction may be difficult because even with the image of "professional autonomy," norms for lawyer responsibility dictate that the client be advised and consulted at important junctures and that final decisions on important matters (e.g., filing a court case, rejecting or accepting an offer of settlement) be the responsibility of the client (see Center for Professional Responsibility, 1987: 38). While this ambiguity may suggest that it will be impossible to arrive at any kind of definitive statement on who dominates the relationship, the analysis shows very clearly that control rests largely with the lawyer, particularly when the client is an individual.

From the Lawyer's Viewpoint

DETERMINING CLIENT INVOLVEMENT

Looking at client involvement and control first from the viewpoint of the lawyer, there is an ambiguity in the wording of a question asked of the lawyers that is suggestive about the control issue. Interviewers asked the lawyers:

> Did you and your client ever reach an explicit understanding about the ways in which the client would participate in the preparation of the case; did you have an ongoing understanding about what (he/she/they) would do in cases like this; or was there no such understanding?

For 50 percent of the lawyer–client dyads, the lawyers reported that they had an "ongoing understanding;" the other 50 percent was split fairly evenly between an explicit understanding (23 percent) and no understanding (27 percent). As one might expect, the existence of an ongoing understanding is related to the lawyer having done prior work for the client; in such situations, lawyers report ongoing understandings for 58 percent of the dyads. However, 35 percent of the dyads, where *no* prior work on behalf of the client was reported by the lawyer, are described as involving an "ongoing understanding."

The apparent inconsistency reflects the ambiguity of the word "you," which can be either plural or singular. In the phrase "Did you have an ongoing understanding . . . ?" some respondents must have understood this to refer to only themselves and not to the lawyer–client unit; that is, many lawyers simply made an assumption about what the role of the client would be without bothering to discuss that role with the client. One might initially think that this primarily reflected presumptions of lawyers hired on a contingency basis by individuals (recall that virtually all contingency arrangements were with individuals and all hourly arrangements with organizations). In fact, this is not the case; lawyers who had not previously done work for the client were almost equally likely (34 percent and 36 percent) to report an ongoing understanding regardless of whether they were hired on a contingency or an hourly basis. Lawyers who had previously done work for their client did differ slightly, depending on fee arrangement, with hourly fee lawyers reporting an ongoing understanding for 60 percent of the dyads and contingent fee lawyers reporting them for 49 percent of the dyads. Also, where prior work had been done, lawyers indicated reaching an explicit understanding for 18 percent of the dyads, regardless of fee arrangement, compared to 27 percent (contingent) and 34 percent (hourly) where no prior work had been done. What all this suggests is that there is relatively little effort on the part of the lawyers to deal explicitly with the lawyer–client relationship other than with regard to the business aspects (i.e., in what manner and/or how much the lawyer is to be paid).

Perhaps the general lack of discussion of the client's role reflects the lack of complexity in most of the cases: in simple, routine cases there may not be much for the client, or the lawyer, for that matter, to do. Lawyers rated the cases on a one to five scale, first on the complexity of law and fact, and second on the difficulty of trying (either actual, or potential, if no trial occurred) the case. However, neither scale related to the likelihood that the client's role would be discussed. Thus, it is unlikely that the lack of those discussions can be explained by the relative simplicity of most ordinary cases.

THE NATURE OF CLIENT INVOLVEMENT
Concerning the nature of the explicit or ongoing understandings regarding the client's role, lawyers were asked to characterize them in terms of one of the following categories.

> The client would play a major decision-making role, providing (the lawyer) with instructions on some matters.

> The client would not play a major decision-making role, but (its) approval would be required on most decisions.

> (The lawyer) and the client would discuss matters, but (the lawyer) would make most of the decisions.

> The client would pretty much turn the case over to (the lawyer).

Not surprisingly, the largest groups of lawyers placed the understanding in the two intermediate categories (35 percent and 26 percent), with 19 percent describing the content of the understanding as falling into each of the two extreme categories.

Things shift somewhat when the lawyers describe the actual role taken by their clients. The actual role taken in 90 percent or more of the dyads where there was an understanding was consistent with that understanding,[12] but when there was a discrepancy, there was a slight tendency for the actual role to be one of less involvement than called for by the understanding. Client involvement tended to be substantially lower when no agreement about that involvement was reached:

- Only 20 percent of clients having an understanding with their lawyers about their involvement played no significant role at all, while 44 percent of the clients without an understanding played no significant role.
- In 19 percent of the dyads where there was an understanding, the client's involvement fell at the high end versus only 8 percent where there was no understanding.

In general, the likely organizational clients tended to play a larger role than did the likely individual clients, regardless of whether or not there was an explicit understanding; this relationship is shown in Table 5–3.[13]

This pattern is confirmed, at least from the lawyer's viewpoint, by the responses to a second question: "To what degree was your client involved in determining case strategy other than in settlement negotiations?" Sixty-seven percent of the lawyers said that their clients had little or no role in determining case strategy, and only 13 percent said that the clients had been "very much" involved in strategic planning. Again, the level of involvement among likely individual litigants was much lower than that among likely organizational litigants, with 59 percent of the likely organizations having little or no involvement compared to 79 percent of the likely individuals.[14]

One might reasonably expect the level of client involvement to depend on the complexity of the case in regard to the complexity of law and fact, and/or in regard to the potential difficulty of trial. However, there seems to be little variation by "complexity" regarding actual client involvement—the clients simply are not very involved in most cases. For lawyers representing individuals (i.e., those paid on a contingency basis), there is a slight tendency for any explicit understanding with the client to call for *less* client involvement as complexity regarding law and fact increases; it would seem that in complex cases, lawyers may be concerned about unsophisticated individual clients "get-

TABLE 5–3. Level of Client Involvement as Reported by the Lawyer Controlling for Client Type and Presence of Understanding About the Client's Role[a]

	All Clients		Likely Organizations		Likely Individuals	
	Understanding		Understanding		Understanding	
	Yes	No	Yes	No	Yes	No
Major role[b]	19%	8%	23%	12%	10%	4%
Approval	34	25	35	29	32	21
Minimal	27	23	27	23	30	25
None	20	44	16	36	28	50
n	986	394	566	183	279	162

[a]All data in this table are taken from lawyer–client dyads (see text) from the lawyer interviews. "Likely" organizations are clients who retained their lawyers on an hourly fee basis; "likely" individuals are clients who retained their lawyers on a contingent fee basis.

[b]See the main text for the full role descriptions.

ting in the way" and may tend to use discussions of the clients' role as an opportunity to warn them off. A similar pattern exists for variations by amount at stake. Agreements call for less client involvement when more is at stake, particularly when the client is an individual. Dividing stakes into low (under $10,000), medium ($10,000 to $50,000), and high (over $50,000) agreements with organizational clients fall into the lower two categories of involvement for 39 percent in low stakes cases, 45 percent in medium stakes cases, and 54 percent in high stakes cases; the comparable figures for individuals are 44 percent, 55 percent, and 71 percent. Thus, the gap between individual clients' and organizational clients' agreed on involvement increases sharply as the amount at stake goes up. When one looks at actual involvement (the lower two categories again), there is little variation for organizational clients (42 percent, 47 percent, and 49 percent for low, medium, and high stakes, respectively), but substantial variation for individual clients (55 percent, 65 percent, and 76 percent). The most obvious, and admittedly cynical, interpretation of this pattern is that contingent fee lawyers minimize client involvement as their stake in the outcome of the case goes up!

From the Client's Viewpoint

How does the locus of control of the relationship look from the client's side? Because of the structure of the client interviews, the responses of the clients give an even sketchier view of what transpired between the lawyer and client in terms of who exercised control over whom. Litigants were asked:

> Were discussions ever held with [the] lawyer about how much responsibility [you] would take in planning and carrying out this case? [IF YES, THEN:] Did this discussion lead to an explicit agreement between [you] and [the] lawyer about how much responsibility [you] would take on this case?

In addition, litigants were asked about the reports they received from their lawyers and (where appropriate) about whether they or their lawyers made the key decisions to file a lawsuit or to take the case to trial.

ALLOCATING RESPONSIBILITY

If the picture from the lawyers' side of the relationship is described as a substantial amount of autonomy being retained by the lawyer, that picture is quite consistent with what the clients report in terms of allocation of responsibility, reporting, and decision making. First, a majority of both organizational (52 percent) and individual (78 percent) litigants report that there were *no* discussions at all concerning allocation of responsibilities between the lawyer and the litigant. At least a part of this may reflect the existence of a prior relationship between the lawyer and the client in which explicit discussions had taken place or implicit understandings had been arrived at regarding responsibilities. Ninety-five of the 141 organizational litigants who reported no discussions concerning responsibilities and 50 of the 180 individual litigants so situated had had a prior professional relationship with their lawyer. If one makes the strong (and probably unwarranted) assumption that some prior discussion or agreement about responsibilities governed the relationship if the lawyer had worked for the litigant previously (and there was no explicit discussion for this particular case), then only 15 percent of the organizations were dealing with a lawyer where allocation of responsibilities had not been brought up or previously settled; the comparable figure for individuals is much, much higher at 57 percent. In actuality, the two figures for each type of litigant (15 percent and 52 percent for organizations, and 57 percent and 78 percent for individuals), provide an upper and lower bound for the likelihood that allocation of responsibilities had been dealt with "up front".[15]

The explicit discussion of allocation of responsibilities does not necessarily mean that a clear understanding about who will do what is arrived at. Only about half of the organizational litigants that had such discussions with their lawyer arrived at an explicit understanding; 67 percent of the much smaller subgroup of individual litigants reached an understanding. For organizations, the agreement usually (about 85 percent of the time) meant that the client would participate in planning and would help in researching the case; the client was somewhat less likely to be expected to participate directly in settlement discussions (67 percent), attend depositions (52 percent), or attend pretrial conferences (40 percent). For individuals, there was little variation among the specific activities listed, with the percentage agreeing to participate in each one varying from 42 percent to 55 percent.

STAYING INVOLVED AND INFORMED

This picture of greater involvement by organizations than individuals carries over to reporting practices from the lawyer to the client. Sixty-nine percent of the organizational litigants reported receiving regular written reports from their lawyer, compared to only 50 percent of the individual litigants. For the individuals receiving such reports, only 10 percent explicitly requested them— 90 percent of the time, the reports were sent on the lawyer's own initiative; only 51 percent of the organizations said that the lawyer took the initiative in sending reports, with the rest indicating that they requested written reports or that such reports were simply part of the standard procedure.

While the level of involvement of the litigants in the major decisions in the case (filing the lawsuit, going to trial) seems to be quite high, these are the kinds of decisions that the lawyer would expect the client to be involved with. In fact, it is somewhat surprising that clients reported decisions being made entirely, or mostly, by the lawyers as often as they were; it is not surprising, given the other patterns I have described here, that lawyer dominance was greater with individual clients than with organizational clients. Seventy-six organizations reported that the suit was filed on their behalf; only 20 percent said that their lawyer (or "mostly" their lawyer) made the decisions, and another 18 percent said that their own involvement had been equal to that of their lawyer. One hundred and sixty-four individuals reported that the suit had been filed on their behalf; 29 percent said it was their lawyer's decision (or "mostly" the lawyer's decision), and 22 percent reported equal involvement by themselves and their lawyer. Thus, the litigant dominated the decision to file 62 percent of the time when that litigant was an organization, but only 49 percent of the time when it was an individual.

Since it is usually "the other guy" who will not be reasonable, forcing the suit to go to trial, there are substantially fewer observations in which respondents indicated that the decision to go to trial rested primarily with their side (38 organizations and 39 individuals, to be exact). Consequently, the response patterns regarding who dominated the decision to go to trial (the litigant or the lawyer) must be treated very cautiously. Still, both organizations and individuals were less likely to report that they themselves had made the decision to go to trial (50 percent for organizations and 44 percent for individuals) than had been the case with regard to the decision to file a lawsuit (62 percent for organizations and 49 percent for individuals), although the differences for the two decisions are not large.

It is reasonable to expect that the patterns just described would vary, depending on the kind of case (torts, contracts, and "other"). For individual litigants, the only variation by area of law is that their lawyers are more likely to dominate the filing decision in tort cases than in other areas of law. For organizations, the litigant is more likely to dominate the filing decision in "other" cases (71 percent) than in contract–commercial cases (57 percent) — organizations filed virtually none of the tort cases. Tort cases stand out, however, in discussions about allocation of responsibility, with many more involving such discussions (64 percent versus 40 to 44 percent for the other two areas); furthermore, in virtually every case (35 out of 36) where no such discussions took place there was a previous relationship between the lawyer and client. This is not surprising, since most of the organizations involved in tort cases were insurance company defendants.

Are there any other variables that might usefully be introduced as control variables to extend our understanding of client–lawyer relationships from the client's side? The one variable that might be of interest is stakes, particularly given the patterns from the lawyer interviews that I described previously. Litigants may behave differently vis-à-vis their lawyers depending on the stakes: in large cases, they might want to exercise control over the case and, hence, they may be more likely to raise the issue of responsibilities with their lawyer or have greater involvement in key decisions such as filing a lawsuit or going to trial. In fact, given the range of cases in this sample (i.e., stakes of $50,000 or more constitute a "big" case — the top 17 percent of cases for individuals and the top 9 percent for organizations), there is no apparent relationship from the client's point of view between stakes and the variables discussed.

Inconsistencies of Perspective or Inconsistencies of Data?

The apparent discrepancy between the lawyer and client perspective vis-à-vis relationships between client involvement and stakes probably reflects the specific types of involvement that were probed in the two types of interviews. The clients were generally asked about the broadest kinds of involvement, particularly in the types of decisions that one would expect most lawyers to consult their clients about. The lawyers, on the other hand, were asked to describe client involvement in terms of activities that went substantially beyond the "big questions" of filing and settling.

Discussion: Lawyers and Clients

There is some fuzziness in the overall picture described here. This partly reflects gaps in the data and partly some of the inherent ambiguities in relationships between lawyers and clients. Nonetheless, some interesting points emerge. First, to the degree that the broker/professional distinction focuses attention on the fee-paying elements in the lawyer–client relationship, the analysis indicates that lawyers are very concerned to make explicit the fee-paying element at the beginning of their relationship with their clients; the "professional" member of the lawyer–client pair seems to put more emphasis on that aspect of the relationship than does the lay member.

If the explicitness of the various aspects of the relationship is taken as an indicator of centrality, then the fee-paying component clearly stands out ahead of the other components because that is the aspect most likely to be dealt with in a fairly clear and direct manner. As noted previously, however, the rules and guidelines for legal practice emphasize reaching a clear understanding concerning fees to be charged, and one can interpret the data to indicate that lawyers simply are abiding by those guidelines. Interestingly, it may be the case that since fees are an integral part of a broker–client relationship, persons in acknowledged broker roles (stockbrokers, real estate brokers, etc.) may actually be less likely to discuss the fee issue explicitly, while the client in that situation may be more likely to raise it; I have no information that allows me to test this argument. Still, the explicitness of fee discussions by the lawyers runs counter to the *traditional* image that a lawyer (or other professional) simply renders a bill "for professional services rendered," with the expectation that a grateful client willingly pays without question and with gratitude for the professional's assistance.

If the fee-paying component of the relationship lends some support for the transactional elements in the broker image, what happens after the discussion of fees is clearly consistent with the image of autonomous professionals carrying out their work with little involvement from their clients. There is little evidence in the data I have discussed indicating that clients exert systematic or meaningful controls on the lawyer.[16] There is little consideration of allocation of responsibility and, while clients frequently report making the key decisions of filing suit or going to trial, in substantial numbers of cases these decisions are made by the lawyer with little acknowledged input from the client. Still, it may be that these decisions are really nondecisions — by the time the case gets to the lawyer, the client has decided to file suit, or we are not seeing the "real" input of the lawyer that is excluded from this data set that might come in the decision *not* to file suit. Or it may be that in the ordinary, everyday case the decisions are so routine and so clear that there is relatively little discretion to be exercised. In a sense, the key decision is to go to a lawyer, or to file suit, and once that decision is taken, much of the rest flows with relatively little need for systematic input or control.

While the control question seems to support the case for professional autonomy, the strong relationship between stakes and level of lawyer control, particularly when the lawyer is retained on a contingency basis (almost always by an individual litigant), raises questions about the motivation the lawyer has in exerting this control. If control were simply a question of professional expertise, one would not expect there to be this kind of relationship; in fact, given the professional's supposed concern for the client's interest, one might expect the professional to increase the client's level of involvement as the amount at issue went up. Instead, the relationship between control and stakes (and, to a lesser degree, perhaps, complexity) seems to raise questions about whether the control is motivated by professional expertise or agent (qua broker?) self-interest; there is no way to sort out this particular question with the data available.

Thus, at least in terms of the lawyer–client relationship, using the two alternative images helps to illuminate the ways lawyers and clients seem to interact during the litigation process: lawyers are very concerned about the manner in which they will be paid by their clients but, at the same time, the lawyers seem to possess substantial autonomy in carrying out their work. However, the reasons that that autonomy is exercised may not always be motivated by concern for the clients' interests.

6

Lawyers and Their ''Workgroup''

Several important analyses of the criminal justice process, and particularly analyses of the role of lawyers in that process, have focused on what has been variously called the courtroom workgroup (Eisenstein and Jacob, 1977) or the courtroom elite (Nardulli, 1978): the group consisting of the judge, defense counsel (particularly public defenders), and prosecuting attorney, all of whom must interact frequently and regularly to process cases through the criminal courts (see also Rosett and Cressey, 1976; Blumberg, 1967b).[1] The emphasis in these analyses has been on the important role played by the group process generally, and on the specific need to maintain the relationships at the core of that process. The need to insure good working relationships among the regular players in the criminal justice process is often a more important goal to one or more of the actors than is achieving a desirable outcome for a specific case.

Hints of similar phenomenon can be found in analyses of early studies of injury cases. In Chapter 1, I referred to Ross's study of insurance claims adjusters; Ross described the conflict between group goals and case goals in the following way (1980: 82).

> The first opportunity [for conflict of interest to arise between lawyer and client] is more likely to occur for the negligence specialist, who negotiates on a repeated basis with the same insurance companies. His goal of maximizing the return from any given case may conflict with the goal of maximizing returns from the total series of cases he represents. His negotiation opponent may, for example, plead for a lower settlement in case and offer in return more consideration in another, yielding the attorney a larger sum of fees in total. *Failure to oblige might additionally create more difficulty in obtaining settlements in the future* [emphasis added].

Carlin, in *Lawyers on Their Own* (1962: 78) noted that "upper-level personal injury practitioners" can obtain better settlements at least in part because "they handle a larger volume of cases and *are in a better position to establish a more permanent relationship with the [insurance] adjusters . . . "* [emphasis added]. In his study of lawyers in rural Missouri, Landon (1985) emphasized the importance the lawyers attribute to the need to maintain good working relationships with their colleagues in the bar, as emphasized by the comment made by one of his respondents whom I quoted in Chapter 1; "you can hire me to fight your case, but you can't hire me to hate the opposing attorney" (1985: 95).

One major difference between the criminal justice process and the civil justice process is that there may be an ongoing and important relationship between lawyer and client as well as among the lawyer and the other actors in the case. In Chapter 5, I presented evidence that prior representation was an important consideration for many lawyers in taking a case; this chapter discusses the existence of concerns about future relationships with other actors in the system. As I noted in the introduction to Part III, the survey questions that were asked about ongoing and future relationships have some major limitations; as a result, I will limit my discussion here to the simple presence of and variation in such relationships. In the analyses in Part IV of how the lawyers actually handle the cases in the sample, I will incorporate the variables discussed here as appropriate.

Before considering the presence of ongoing relationships with the other major actors in the civil justice process, it is important to note the likely role of future relationships with the lawyers' own clients. Unlike the criminal court workgroup, where future relationships between the defendant and the lawyer are likely to be of little importance (particularly when most defendants are represented by public defenders), the lawyer in civil litigation may be very concerned about "repeat business" from the current client. Hence, the potential influence of ongoing relationships with workgroup members (and/or the opposing party) will often be mitigated by the lawyer's ongoing (and desired future) relationship with the current client.[2] Still, the brokerage image suggests that these ongoing relationships can serve the interests of the client instead of conflicting with them (as is suggested by the analyses of the criminal justice system).[3]

The Opposing Counsel

Lawyers possess a monopoly on the right to represent litigants in a court of law. One result of this restriction is to narrow substantially the group that the lawyer will find representing the opposing side. As suggested by Landon, particularly where the group of potential counsel is limited in size, there may be substantial pressure to maintain good relationships, both because of the need to have a tolerable work setting and because the opposing lawyer may be a source of case referrals in the future (e.g., where a case presents a conflict of interest or deals with an issue with which the other lawyer is not familiar). The lawyers in the survey were asked: "Before you took on this case, did you know the lawyer(s) for [the opposing party/parties] on a personal basis, outside of business?" Those who responded "yes" were asked several follow-up questions, including:

- Have you (and this lawyer/any of these lawyers) ever referred clients to one another?
- Do you expect that you will ever refer clients to one another in the future?

The first question is not worded to best address the issues I have raised. The wording was intended to capture personal acquaintance as opposed to knowledge of the other lawyer only by reputation; unfortunately, the last phrase affected the way the question was interpreted by many respondents. Futhermore, there is no reason that past and future referrals would necessarily be restricted to lawyers who had a personal relationship prior to any given case. However, even with these limitations, the data yield some interesting information.

First, 23 percent of the lawyers report having a personal relationship with the opposing lawyer at the time they took the current case; of these, 25 percent reported that they had previously referred cases to, or received cases from, that lawyer. The work of Ross and of Carlin looked at the relationship between the lawyer and the insurance adjuster; one might expect that relationship to spill over to lawyers representing insurance companies (given that those companies tend to retain the same lawyer repeatedly). Comparing the likelihood of a prior relationship existing for tort cases to nontort cases indicates that lawyers in tort cases are no more likely to know the opposing lawyer personally than lawyers in other kinds of cases; likewise, there is no difference in the likelihood of lawyers with a personal relationship having previously referred cases to one another. Interestingly, however, only 28 percent of lawyers in tort cases indicated that they expected *future referrals*, compared to 38 percent for lawyers in contract cases and 45 percent for lawyers in other cases (cases that were neither tort or contract). The low level of referrals for lawyers in tort cases is consistent with the studies of the bar that have shown there to be a deep cleavage between "plaintiffs'" lawyers and "defendants'" lawyers (see Watson and Downing, 1964).

Landon's work on lawyers outside of urban areas suggests that there might be some significant variation by district (since two districts are heavily urban, two are a mixture of urban and rural, and one is largely rural). In fact, the probability of an existing personal relationship is monotonically related to the degree of urbanness of the district: Central California (the Los Angeles area) — 7 percent, Eastern Pennsylvania (Philadelphia plus roughly the eastern third of the state) — 13 percent, Eastern Wisconsin (Milwaukee plus roughly the eastern third of the state) — 18 percent, New Mexico — 30 percent, and South Carolina — 49 percent. The patterns do not differ appreciably when one looks separately at tort and contract cases by district. Past referrals (among those lawyers with a prior personal relationship) are higher in the less urban districts, and expected future referrals are also higher in those same districts. The pattern reported here of the highest expectation of future referrals in "other" cases, followed by contract and then tort cases, generally holds up within individual districts (where there are enough cases for meaningful analysis).

The Opposing Party

While the opposing party in civil litigation is not a part of the courtroom workgroup, as that notion is used in studies of criminal justice, Galanter's distinction between "one-shot players" and "repeat players" (1974) has some important implications for the set of relationships within which the lawyers work. Galanter made his distinction as part of the consideration of the relative advantage of different kinds of parties: the "haves" seem to be more successful in the litigation process than the "have nots." For this analysis, one can draw a further distinction between the "repeat" player and the "routine" player. Both groups are experienced in litigation, but the latter group is involved in litigation as a matter of routine; the obvious example is the liability insurer. The frequency of the litigation activity of the "routine" player places that litigant into the set of relationships with which the lawyer is regularly involved. The earlier quotations from Carlin and Ross suggest the significance of these relationships for the insurance adjuster.

To what degree can one find systematic evidence in my data concerning the existence of ongoing relationships (actual or potential) between lawyers and opposing litigants? The lawyers responded to the question[4] "Do you expect that you will ever oppose this party in the future?" This question was included because it was thought that a lawyer's current behavior might be influenced by the possibility of having to deal with the opponent in the future. The potential effect on the lawyer is not altogether clear. It is possible that a lawyer will be more combative when future cases are expected so that the opponent will know that the lawyer "means business"; it is also possible that a lawyer will look at the current case as part of a long-term (or even short-term) package where the concern is to maximize the overall return vis-à-vis the overall "worth" of the cases (particularly when the lawyer is being paid on a percentage basis). For the present, I am not trying to sort out the effect of possible future cases but to ascertain the potential for such effects.

Overall, 34 percent of the lawyers reported that they thought that they would be involved in future cases with the opposing party. This figure is 44 percent for tort cases and 27 percent for nontorts (there is no difference between contracts and other nontort cases). Given that most tort plaintiffs are individuals (the archetypical "one-shot" player) and most tort defendants are effectively insurance companies, one would expect that in tort cases there would be a low likelihood of a defendant's lawyer encountering the same plaintiff again in the future and a high likelihood that a plaintiff's lawyer would encounter the same (insurance company) defendant again. This expectation is confirmed by the data: 16 percent of the defendants' lawyers expect to have future cases with the opposing party compared to 51 percent of the plaintiffs' lawyers expecting such cases. Actually, the latter figure is a likely understatement because of the ambiguity of who the defendant is in states that maintain the fiction that the tortfeasor rather than the insurer is the defendant.

In Chapter 3 I pointed out that plaintiffs tend to be individuals, and defendants, particularly when insured individual tortfeasors are ignored, tend to be organizations; while this pattern is strongest for tort cases, it also applies to other kinds of nondomestic relations cases. Given the thrust of the repeat player argument, one would expect the pattern described here to hold for nontort (nondomestic relations) cases as well. It does, but the pattern is weaker (as one would expect), with 21 percent of the defendants' lawyers and 37 percent of the plaintiffs' lawyers expecting future cases with the opposing party.

The Judge[5]

As with the opposing lawyer and the opposing party, lawyers were asked about nonbusiness, personal relationships with the judge and about the expectation that they would appear before the judge in future cases. These questions were asked only if the judge had made some "important rulings or decisions" in the case. Very few lawyers reported having personal relationships with the judges (only 7 percent, and this figure did not vary by type of case). Only those few who had such relationships were asked about the possibility of future cases before the judge, and 90 percent expected such cases; given the relatively small size of the bench (even in a very large court such as the Los Angeles Superior Court), it is very likely that most lawyers regularly practicing in a particular court — recall most of the lawyers in this study handled a lot of litigation — would have to anticipate future appearances before a given judge, unless that judge was visiting from another jurisdiction, was on assignment from a different kind of court, or was about to leave the bench.

Still, one might question whether it really mattered in most cases; very few cases ever get to the trial stage, where a judge might have some influence. The importance of the judge in the criminal process is clearer because the judge must usually at least ratify and accept the agreements reached between prosecuting and defense attorneys that specify charges, pleas, and frequently sentences; no ratification of settlements is required in most civil cases. Given that one can safely assume that lawyers will usually have to anticipate future dealings with most of the judges they appear before, the question of whether such appearances are likely to matter is probably more important than any variation in the likelihood of such appearances. Consequently, in this section, I want to digress slightly to this latter question.

First, it is worth noting that, as has been documented in a wide variety of research (Aldisert, 1968; Will, Merhige, and Rubin, 1977; Naythons, 1973; Lynch, 1978; Ryan, Ashman, Sales, and Shane-DuBow, 1980; Wall and Schiller, 1982; Stevenson, Watson, and Weissman, 1977; Schiller and Wall, 1981; Title, 1979; Galanter, 1985b, 1986; Menkel-Meadow, 1985a; Kritzer, 1982;

Provine, 1986a; Brazil, 1985), many judges are quite active in the settlement process. Judges seek to facilitate settlement through various indirect (e.g., relentlessly pushing cases toward trial) and direct (seeking to mediate differences between the parties in order to achieve a compromise) methods. While a number of writers have raised questions about settlements that result from judicial intervention (Bedlin and Nejelski, 1984) or have taken issue with the desirability of settlements (Fiss, 1984; Alschuler, 1986; but see McThenia and Shaffer, 1985), I want to look at the reality of the distinction between adjudicated and negotiated outcomes (see Eisenberg, 1976; Mnookin and Kornhauser, 1979; Cooter and Marks, 1982).

Anyone knowledgeable about the courts recognizes that very few cases get the full adjudicatory treatment ending with a verdict (by either judge or jury) and a judgment. The figures that are commonly cited range from 5 to 10 percent of cases filed ever getting to trial (e.g., Miller, 1984: 4). In my data the court records indicated that only 8 percent of the 1649 sampled state and federal cases went to trial (and some fraction of those were settled before the trial was completed). A typical assumption is that cases that are not resolved by trial are not adjudicated, are not influenced by adjudication (see Alschuler, 1986), and are simply settled. However, this is not an accurate description of what goes on in ordinary civil litigation. There are several ways that a case can be resolved between trial and settlement. In fact, as I will show, adjudication is an *explicit* factor in the outcome of many cases that never get to trial and, while I have no way of empirically demonstrating it, actual adjudicatory decisions short of termination are often an *implicit* factor in the settlement process.

Based on the court record, one cannot tell definitively whether a case was settled; however, one can determine the formal mode of termination, and there are several modes other than trial that clearly involve significant action on the part of the judge or another actor carrying out an adjudicatory function. For purposes of analysis, I have defined three categories between trial and settlement that are indicative of an adjudicatory function being invoked, two of which almost certainly involve action by the judge. I have labeled these categories as *arbitrated* (limited to cases from the Pennsylvania state courts, which have a mandatory arbitration rule for certain categories of cases), *decided* (cases terminated by a summary judgment or something equivalent), and *dismissed for cause* (cases terminated by a ruling on a motion that is not simply technical in nature). Table 6-1 shows the complete set of termination codes that were used and how I grouped those codes into categories, plus the percentage of cases in each category; note that since each case could involve multiple parties, and the termination vis-à-vis each party could be different, there can be multiple termination types for a given case (and therefore the percentages do not total 100 percent). One sees in the table that only 7 percent of cases terminated through trial (down slightly from the 8 percent that went to trial). Of more interest is the fact that an additional 13 percent of cases terminated through decisions or dismissal for cause; thus, about 20 percent of the cases terminated through a decision of a judge.

TABLE 6-1. Modes of Termination[a]

Percent	Type	Description
7	Tried	
		Trial by court — decision for plaintiff
		Trial by court — decision for defendant
		Trial by jury — verdict for plaintiff
		Trial by jury — verdict for defendant
		Federal Rule 42: liability by jury, damages by judge
2	Arbitrated	
		Arbitration award for plaintiff
		Arbitration award for defendant
9	Decided	
		Order enforcing summons for documents
		Remanded to state court
		Remanded to administrative law judge
		Remanded to administrative agency
		Summary judgment for plaintiff
		Summary judgment for defendant
		Judgment non pros
		Stipulated dismissal (after judgment)
4	Dismissed for cause	
		Improper pleadings
		Failure to state a claim
		Lack of jurisdiction
		Lack of diversity jurisdiction
		Denial of pauper status
		Expiration of statute of limitations
6	Defaulted	
		Default judgment for plaintiff
8	Dismissed for technical reasons	
		Moot
		Removed/transferred to another jurisdiction
		Suspended for inactivity
		Other dismissal
63	"Settled"	
		Withdrawn
		Voluntary dismissal (before pretrial)
		Voluntary dismissal (after pretrial)
		Stipulated dismissal (before judgment)
		Dismissed, failure to prosecute
		Stipulated judgment
		Consent judgment
		Settled in arbitration
		Settled, discontinued, ended
		Settled, discontinued, ended in conference
		Divorce decree
5	Other	
		Disposition order
		Other
		Not ascertained

[a]Table is based on 1,649 cases. Percentages may not add to 100 because cases may involve multiple types of terminations if there is more than one plaintiff or defendant.

But, as suggested, this is not all there is to adjudication. Many cases may settle because of an adverse decision on the part of a judge. I have no way of knowing for sure the role of specific decisions, but I can look at the frequency of rulings on motions that might lead to a decision to settle. In the court records there is detailed information on the types of motions that were filed in each case. One set of motions can be thought of as indicative of a significant, substantive decision on the part of the judge that might be instrumental in leading to a settlement; specifically, I included all motions to dismiss where an explicit basis for dismissal was given (except for consensual dismissals, dismissals for failure to prosecute, and dismissals for insufficient service), all motions for summary judgment, motions for immediate judicial intervention (e.g., for restraining orders and injuctions), and motions that could materially affect a party's ability to present its case (e.g., motions to exclude evidence or witnesses, motions to proceed as a class action). Table 6-2 shows a list of these motions. After selecting the motions to be examined, I looked at the frequency of rulings on those motions in the 78 percent of cases that were not terminated by trial, arbitration, decision, or dismissal for cause. Approximately 11 percent of the subset of cases involved such motions; this represents an additional 9 percent of the cases in the overall sample.[6] Recognizing that I may now be overestimating the importance of some of the motions that I have counted, let me add this figure to the earlier 20 percent of cases; we now have evidence of judicial involvement in the termination of as many as 29 percent of the cases in the sample.[7]

These figures concerning adjudication clearly indicate that judges play a significant, explicit role in a substantial proportion of cases,[8] and I have not even considered the part that might be played by direct involvement of the

TABLE 6–2. Adjudicatory Motions

Motion to proceed as class action
Motion to exclude evidence
Motion to exclude witness
Motion to quash
Motion to dismiss or (in the alternative) for summary judgment
Motion to dismiss for failure to join party
Motion to dismiss for failure to state a claim
Motion to dismiss for improper pleadings
Motion to dismiss for improper venue
Motion to dismiss for lack of jurisdiction
Motion to dismiss for lack of diversity jurisdiction
Motion to review magistrate's findings
Motion for summary judgment
Motion for summary reversal
Motion to strike

Motion for preliminary injunction
Motion for temporary restraining order
Motion for injunction

judges in the settlement process.[9] Given the assumption that lawyers appear before a small group of judges repeatedly regarding their various cases, the need to be aware of the judges' orientations and the need to maintain at least neutral, if not positive, relationships with those judges should be clear.

Discussion: The Lawyer's Working Relationships

The purpose of this chapter was to consider the argument that the lawyer qua broker is deeply embedded in a web of relationships that influence services provided to the litigant–client. The available data allow for only a very sketchy analysis, but the findings are not inconsistent with the expectations associated with the world of the broker. A more definitive analysis of the role and importance of the lawyer's relational web in ordinary litigation will have to await better data on this question.

The evidence that the lawyer's relationships with other actors in the system are important is strongest for plaintiffs' lawyers in tort cases. A majority of these lawyers report an expectation of future dealings with the opposing party (almost certainly the insurance companies); given that an insurance company tends to employ the services of a relatively small group of lawyers in a specific community, it is likely that appropriate questions about the opposing lawyer would have shown that both plaintiff and defense lawyers in tort cases expected future dealings with the opposing lawyers. While the likelihood of future cases with the opposing party was lower for nontort cases, a substantial minority of lawyers in such cases (excluding domestic relations) did indicate an expectation that they would face their opponent again in the future. The absence of questions in the lawyer survey concerning how anticipated future contacts had consciously influenced the lawyers' actions in the case (such questions were asked of the litigants vis-à-vis their opponents) limits the analysis here; however, in Chapter 8, I will assess the influence of expected future contacts on certain aspects of the lawyers' actions.

The analysis leaves little question about the importance of relationships with judges for lawyers handling ordinary civil litigation. Judges occupy a very important role in the disposition of civil cases, much greater than suggested by the prevalence of trials as a way of resolving everyday litigation. The lawyers must know the decisional propensities of judges who rule on the motions that resolve or shape the litigation process. This knowledge reflects a combination of a formal, abstract understanding of the law and the more informal, insider knowledge of how individual judges view specific questions. These two types of knowledge are necessary for lawyers to carry out their role as the broker between their clients (and the clients' cases) and the civil justice system (both the law that is applied by that system and the appliers of that law, the judges and juries).

IV

LITIGATING ORDINARY CASES

In Chapters 5 and 6, I examined the relational context in which lawyers handle ordinary civil cases. In the chapters in this part, I turn to the work that lawyers perform and the results they achieve. Two major themes are addressed in Chapters 7 and 8: what is the nature and amount of work that lawyers carry out, and how is that work, both in quantity and content terms, affected by the lawyers' relationships. To look at the first of these, I distinguish between *formal* legal activities (the kinds of things that are taught in law school and that are closely linked with the professional image of lawyers) and *informal* legal activities (the kinds of things that are learned by doing lots of litigation and that have more of an "insider" nature). In looking at the influence of lawyers' relationships, I develop comprehensive statistical models that incorporate many other variables (e.g., case characteristics, and lawyer attitudes, training, and experience) that are of interest in understanding the litigation process.

In Chapter 9, I analyze the outcomes from litigation. I consider both the results lawyers obtain for their clients, and—for contingent fee lawyers—the results the lawyers obtain for themselves. As with the analysis of the content of litigation, I present comprehensive models to account for the outcomes. In addition to the factors suggested by the professional and broker images, I include a variety of factors that are frequently thought to influence outcomes in litigation.

7

*The Work of the Litigator
in Ordinary Cases*

In distinguishing between the professional and the broker, one of the major differences is in the nature of the expertise used in the day-to-day work of the litigating lawyer. The professional's special knowledge is based on formal training associated with a university education which, in turn, is closely related to the type of research associated with an academic discipline. The broker's special knowledge, while possibly technical, is not centered on a formal discipline; it is gained from experience in the work setting. Obviously, this distinction does not allow for easily defined boundaries. If one takes the practice of clinical medicine as the archetypical application of formal knowledge, it is clear that much of what is involved is based more on the experience of seeing large numbers of patients than on theoretically oriented materials learned in a formal classroom setting.[1] However, formal medical education normally includes substantial amounts of clinical experience within its bounds.

For most of the twentieth century, legal education in the United States has been dominated by the "case method," as developed by Christopher Langdell at Harvard in the latter half of the nineteenth century. The emphasis of the case method is twofold: first, to train would-be lawyers in a particular mode of analytic thinking (i.e., teaching them to "think like a lawyer") and, second, to familiarize the students with broad legal principles, particularly in the traditional common law areas of property, contracts, and torts. Until recently, American law schools have provided little or no experience paralleling the clinical aspects of medical education, and few law schools are sufficiently oriented toward the specifics of substantive law that graduates feel comfortable taking the bar licensing examinations without extensive additional preparation such as that provided by "bar review" courses offered on a proprietary basis.

To look at the work of lawyers in litigation it is useful to distinguish between the kinds of things that are at the heart of the law school curriculum, such as conducting legal research and preparing written briefs, and the kinds of things learned by working in the litigation process (negotiation, factual investigation, etc.).[2] One might be tempted to label these different activities "legal" and "nonlegal," but I prefer to refer to them as "formal legal skills" and "informal legal skills" to emphasize the distinction between the kinds of legal expertise I associate with the "lawyer as professional" and the "lawyer as broker." Any practicing lawyer must apply a combination of these kinds of formal and informal skills, but the central question for this chapter concerns the relative balance of skills and knowledge used by the lawyers handling routine litigation.

In the pages that follow, I will (1) examine the work that makes up the process of ordinary civil litigation, (2) look at variations in that work, and (3) assess what the patterns described say about the two alternative images of the professional and the broker. The analysis focuses on three indicators of the work of litigation. The first indicator is the types of "events" or activities that show up in the court record; the second is the amount of effort, in hours, that a lawyer spends handling an ordinary case in the civil justice system; and the third is the relative distribution of the lawyer's time on the various activities that comprise litigation. The third of these is most important for assessing the broker and professional images, but the other two indicators are necessary to place the specific activities in perspective.

The Activities in Court in Ordinary Litigation

In this section I am interested in the activities taking place under the auspices of the court, and its rules and procedures. For purpose of analysis I have used the notion of court "event" as the building block of the civil court case; I define a court event as an entry on the court's "docket" sheet. The docket book is the standard court record book in which each case is recorded, usually having been assigned a "docket number"; in most American courts each "event" is recorded in the docket book, starting with the initial filing and concluding with some form of termination, such as dismissal, judgment, or satisfaction. The events that comprise cases can be examined to provide a profile of the processing of those cases.

Law students employed by the research project examined and coded information from the court record for each case in the sample; they recorded information on 16 different general types of events (each of these general types had from 1 to over 100 different specific subtypes).[3] For purposes of the discussion that follows, I have collapsed the 16 event types into nine groups: pleadings, discovery (collapsed form discovery motions, depositions, and other types of discovery events), nondiscovery motions (collapsed from substantive pretrial motions, procedural pretrial motions, and posttrial motions), briefs, pretrial hearings, continuance requests, and judicial actions (typically consisting of rulings on motions). The other categories of events are included only in the overall summary category of "all events" because of small numbers of occurrences (trials, appeals, and court-annexed arbitration[4]) or because of their miscellaneous nature (affidavits and the catchall "other" category).

General Patterns in Court Events

Overall, the typical (median) case involved 11 court events; as Table 7–1*a* shows, 25 percent of the cases involved 5 events or fewer, and 4 percent involved 50 or more. Clearly, there is substantial variation among cases in the amount of court-oriented activity, although cases are more likely to involve a relatively small number of events than they are to involve many events. In terms of assessing ordinary litigation as a whole, these figures may be deceptive

TABLE 7–1. Level of Court Activity Overall and by Type of Court

(a) All Events

	Number of Events							
	1–2	3–5	6–10	11–15	16–20	21–30	31 and Up	*n*
Both courts	5%	20%	24%	18%	10%	22%	11%	1,648
Federal	4	13	19	18	12	15	19	809
State	6	27	28	18	9	8	5	839

(b) By Event Type

	Number of Events						
	0	1–2	3–5	6–10	11–20	21 and Up	*n*
Pleadings[a]	1	71	21	5	*	*	1,648
Federal	1	70	21	7	1	*	809
State	1	73	22	3	*	0	839
Motions	18	54	22	5	1	*	1,648
Federal	12	51	28	7	2	*	809
State	23	57	16	3	*	0	839
Discovery	53	15	13	11	6	2	1,648
Federal	49	15	12	13	7	4	809
State	58	14	14	9	4	1	839
Briefs	66	17	12	4	2	*	1,648
Federal	42	25	21	8	3	*	809
State	88	9	2	*	*	0	839
Continuances	73	21	4	1	*	0	1,648
Federal	54	34	8	3	*	0	809
State	92	8	*	0	0	0	839
Judicial actions	6	52	28	11	3	*	1,648
Federal	6	38	34	16	5	1	809
State	6	64	22	6	1	0	839
Pretrials	71	20	8	**	**	**	1,648
Federal	54	30	16	**	**	**	809
State	88	10	2	**	**	**	839

[a] The first row of each set is federal and state cases combined.

*Less than 1/2 of 1 percent.

**Collapsed with the 3–5 category (i.e., the 3–5 category is actually 3 or more).

because the sampling design for the study took approximately equal numbers of cases from the federal and state courts even though civil litigation in the federal courts comprises less than 5 percent of the total of ordinary litigation (even less if small claims were to be included). Thus, to get a better picture of what goes on in "most" cases, it is necessary to look at federal and state cases separately.

Table 7-1*a* also shows the numbers of events in state and federal courts. In the state courts in the study, 61 percent of the cases involve 10 court events or fewer, compared to only 36 percent of the federal cases in that range; on the other hand, 34 percent of the federal cases involve more than 20 events, while the comparable figure for state courts is only 13 percent. This reflects in part the generally higher stakes in federal cases as compared to state cases, although federal cases involve more events than do state cases even after taking into account differences in stakes.

This picture is sharpened by looking at specific types of events (pleadings, motions, discovery, briefs, continuance requests, judicial actions, and pretrials). As Table 7-1*b* shows, there is little difference between state and federal courts in the number of pleading events, although the few cases that do have substantial numbers of such events are more likely to be in the federal courts than in the state courts. There is slightly more of a gap between federal and state courts regarding motions; state cases are notably more likely to involve no motions (23 percent compared to 12 percent), and federal cases are more likely to involve three motions or more (35 percent compared to 20 percent). Still, a majority of both state and federal cases (57 percent and 51 percent) involve one or two motions. This general lack of major differences between state and federal courts holds up for discovery as well. Similar percentages of cases have no discovery at all (49 percent, 58 percent), or relatively small amounts of discovery; 27 percent of the federal and 28 percent of the state cases have one to five discovery events. Larger numbers of discovery events are more likely to be found in the federal courts (24 percent) than in the state courts (14 percent), but the gaps are not large and the percentage of cases involved are small; in fact, given the relative numbers of cases in the two kinds of courts, there are almost certainly many more large discovery cases in the state courts than in the federal courts.

Larger differences begin to appear for the other types of events. For example, only 12 percent of state cases involve any briefs at all, while 58 percent of federal cases involve at least one brief and 33 percent involve three briefs or more. Similarly, few state cases (8 percent) have any continuances, while 46 percent of federal cases have one continuance or more (Table 7-1*b*). In almost all cases, both state and federal, there is at least one judicial action but 64 percent of the state cases are in the one or two action category compared to only 38 percent of the federal cases; 22 percent of the federal cases involve six judicial actions or more compared to only 7 percent of the state cases. Last, pretrial conferences are relatively rare in state cases (12 percent have one or more) but fairly common in federal cases (46 percent have one or more, and 27 percent have two or more).

Before discussing the implications of these patterns, let me assess the degree to which they hold up once controls are introduced for two variables one might logically expect to influence the level and nature of court-oriented activity: stakes and area of law (there are substantial differences between state and federal court cases on both characteristics). Recall that I have measured stakes using the lawyers' evaluations of what would constitute an appropriate resolution, all things considered. For cases where multiple stakes estimates were obtained, I have used the average of the largest amount given by each respondent; Table 7–2 also shows the event patterns for cases where no stakes information was available.[6]

The figures in Table 7–2 show that the overall amount of court activity is related to *both* stakes and court. As one would expect, the number of docket entries increases as the amount at stake increases, and this partly accounts for differences between state and federal cases. Still, there is clearly more activity in the federal court than in the state court: for virtually every comparison of federal and state cases within a given range, federal cases tend to have more activity. While it is not shown in Table 7–2, this pattern clearly holds up for individual event types, both for types of events where there are large overall differences between the two courts (briefs, pretrial conferences, and continuances) and for events where the differences between the two courts is much more modest (e.g., motions and discovery); detailed breakdowns by event type, stakes, and court are shown in Appendix Table 7–A1.

If the difference between federal and state courts is not explained by stakes, is it explained by the differences in the mix of areas of law dealt with by the two courts? Recall that area of law is not a variable with mutually exclusive categories (a case can involve more than one area); Table 7–3 shows tabulations for each of eight areas of law, with cases involving more than one area included under each applicable category. The figures in the table show that area of law

TABLE 7–2. Level of Court Activity by Stakes: All Events

	Number of Events							
	1–2	3–5	6–10	11–15	16–20	21–30	31 and Up	n
No stakes[a]	6%	24%	24%	18%	10%	9%	8%	1,003
Federal	5	16	19	21	12	13	13	484
State	8	32	29	16	7	5	4	519
Under $10,000	2	15	28	23	12	10	10	332
Federal	2	8	25	21	14	11	20	118
State	2	19	30	24	11	9	5	214
$10,000–50,000	3	11	22	13	13	19	19	229
Federal	4	9	19	10	13	20	25	137
State	2	14	26	16	13	17	11	92
Over $50,000	2	10	11	8	7	19	28	84
Federal	1	6	10	9	9	21	44	70
State	7	29	14	7	0	7	36	14

[a] The first row of each set is federal and state cases combined.

Table 7-3. Level of Court Activity by Area of Law

	Number of Events							
	1–2	3–5	6–10	11–15	16–20	21–30	31 and Up	*n*
Torts								
Federal	4%	8%	20%	18%	12%	16%	21%	239
State	3	16	30	17	10	9	6	414
Contract/commercial								
Federal	6	15	18	15	10	12	25	280
State	12	28	26	20	7	6	2	233
Real property								
Federal	4	15	17	23	11	17	11	53
State	1	29	23	16	5	17	8	92
Business regulation								
Federal	3	21	19	13	7	14	22	131
Discrimination/civil rights								
Federal	2	8	15	14	15	23	22	105
Government action								
Federal	0	14	12	16	21	27	9	56
Government benefits								
Federal	0	9	19	41	23	5	4	79
Domestic relations								
State	9	28	34	16	7	3	3	116

Note. Percentages are computed across rows and may not add to 100 due to rounding.

does not account for the differences between federal and state courts in the number of court events. What is perhaps most striking about this table is the relative consistency within each court across areas of law; the only within-court category that stands out is government benefits.[7] Government benefits stands out among cases in federal court because of the relatively *small* numbers of events compared to other kinds of cases in that court. Thus, the differences in the level of activity in the two kinds of courts cannot be explained by differences in the types of issues brought to the courts, at least with regard to the ordinary cases that make up this sample.[8]

The preceding contrasts are intriguing; the civil justice process in the federal courts seems to be more judge centered[9] than the process in the state courts.[10] This is most clear in the frequency of judicial actions and pretrials, but it is also true regarding briefs, which are documents prepared primarily for the benefit of the judge rather than as work products that are helpful to the parties themselves. One might also argue that it is the judge centeredness of the process that leads to the higher number of continuances in federal cases, since it is the judges who typically create and/or enforce the deadlines that raise the need for continuances. It is this judge centeredness and not the level of stakes, which one would expect to account for higher numbers of motions and larger amounts of discovery, that seems to be the most important component of general levels of activity.

Discussion

The reason for examining court events is to set the context for my analysis of the lawyers' descriptions of what they devote their time to when handling civil litigation. There are several points to keep in mind as I turn to the specifics of the lawyers' activities. First, there are very important differences in what goes on in federal and state cases and, as I will show, this carries over into the specifics of the lawyers' activities. In thinking about ordinary litigation, it is necessary to keep in mind that state cases represent more than 95 percent of the action, and one must discount heavily the findings for federal courts when putting together the overall picture; I am not suggesting that federal cases are unimportant, only that they constitute a small and unique corner of the world.

Second, in considering the kinds of expertise that lawyers employ in handling civil litigation, the one type of event that stands out in its use of the range of formal skills typically taught in law school, the preparation of the written brief, is relatively infrequent, except in the federal courts; only 12 percent of state cases involved the preparation of even a single brief. This finding begins to suggest the relative importance of differing kinds of skills and expertise applied in civil litigation. At the same time, one must be cautious about jumping to a conclusion that formal legal skills are unimportant in ordinary litigation because the one virtually universal event in litigation, the pleadings in which the lawyers state and respond to the legal bases of the action, draws very directly on the formal legal knowledge of the lawyer; however, as I pointed out in Chapter 4, in much of what I have characterized as ordinary litigation, lawyers are able to routinize the pleading process by using preprinted "fill in the blank" forms to prepare complaints and answers.

How Much Time Do Lawyers Devote to Ordinary Cases?

How much time do lawyers actually devote to individual cases? While this does not relate to the specific kinds of skills that lawyers use in their litigation work, one of the major theoretical questions that has been raised about the impact of fee arrangements on the work of lawyers concerns the amount of lawyer time spent on cases. I will explore that specific question in some detail in Chapter 8;[11] here I provide a preliminary analysis of the level of lawyer effort required in ordinary litigation.[12] The overall amount of lawyer activity *is* relevant for understanding patterns and variations in content because that information establishes a point of perspective.[13]

Analysis

The level of lawyer activity in most civil cases is modest. Table 7-4*a* shows the overall distribution of time devoted to cases. In the median case, a lawyer spends 30 hours. In 25 percent of the cases, lawyers spend 12 hours or less; in another 25 percent of the cases, lawyers spend 62 hours or more. At the upper

TABLE 7-4. Amount of Time Lawyers Devote to Ordinary Cases

Category	0–8 Hours	9–20 Hours	21–40 Hours	41–80 Hours	81 Hours and Up	Median Hours	n
(a) All Cases							
	15%	26%	22%	17%	20%	30	1,288
(b) Court							
(chi square=158.6, *p* < .0001)							
Federal	10	18	22	23	28	45	772
State	22	36	22	12	8	19	566
(c) Stakes							
(chi square=260.0, *p* < .0001)							
Under $10,000	20	35	25	12	7	20	460
$10,000–50,000	6	15	22	30	27	50	253
Over $50,000	4	3	9	17	66	122.5	92
(d) Area of Law							
Torts	16	25	23	18	18	30	547
Federal	9	13	22	25	31	52	227
State	21	33	24	13	8	20	320
Contract/commercial	18	24	21	15	22	28	443
Federal	12	18	22	18	30	40	283
State	28	36	19	11	6	17	160
Domestic relations	23	54	8	5	10	13	39
Real property	16	30	22	9	23	25	100
Federal	11	24	8	11	47	60	38
State	19	34	31	8	8	18	62
Business regulation	12	22	19	18	29	40	159
Discrimination/civil rights	3	14	18	41	24	54	93
Government actions	9	12	19	34	25	56	32
Government benefits	0	18	29	32	21	42	38
(e) Complexity							
(chi square=386.1, *p* < .0001)							
1 simple	33	40	16	7	5	12	305
2	12	32	28	18	9	25	375
3	10	18	24	26	21	40	315
4	4	12	17	23	44	70	184
5 very complex	5	7	14	15	60	100	87
(f) Size of Law Firm							
(chi square=47.8, *p* < .0001)							
1–4 lawyers	18	29	21	15	16	25	603
5–19	14	26	23	17	20	30	470
20–49	8	16	18	26	31	50	125
50 or more	9	12	25	23	30	50	56
(g) Percent of Practice Devoted to Litigation							
(chi square=22.7, *p* < .05)							
25% or less	19	29	28	13	20	22	151
26–50%	18	29	25	14	15	25	262
51–75%	12	27	20	19	22	30	288
76% or more	15	22	22	20	20	30	570

(continued)

TABLE 7-4. *Continued*

Category	0–8 Hours	9–20 Hours	21–40 Hours	41–80 Hours	81 Hours and Up	Median Hours	n
(h) Lawyer's Income							
(chi square = 30.1, $p < .01$)							
Under $25,000	15	27	25	17	16	25	229
$25,000–50,000	18	28	20	15	19	25	492
$50,000–100,000	11	23	23	24	18	35	381
Over $100,000	16	19	17	21	27	40	89
(i) Years of Experience							
(chi square = 18.0, $p > .10$)							
5 or fewer	17	24	20	17	22	30	435
6–10	11	30	21	22	16	30	308
11–20	14	24	25	15	21	30	283
21 or more	18	24	21	18	19	27	248

The percentages in the first five columns across may not add to 100 due to rounding.

end, 10 percent of cases involve 125 hours or more, 5 percent involve 225 hours or more, and 1 percent take 620 hours or more. There are cases that take a lot of lawyer time, but most cases do not involve very substantial amounts of effort by a person formally trained in the law.

There are three kinds of variables that might be related to lawyer effort: the institution where the case is processed, the nature of the case, and the nature of the lawyer. The major institutional variable that I have is type of court (state and federal). The three case-related aspects I will look at are area of law, stakes, and complexity, and the lawyer characteristics considered will consist of size of firm, years of experience, percent of time devoted to litigation, and income. The one set of variables I am deferring to Chapter 8 is one concerning the lawyers' relationships with their clients and with opposing parties.

Table 7-4b shows the variation by court. There is a sharp difference in the amount of time spent on cases in the two types of courts: the median for federal cases is 45 hours compared to only 19 hours for state cases. This follows directly from the finding that federal cases involve more court events (discussed in the previous section), which was at least partly attributable to the fact that federal cases tend to have more at stake.[14] Should one accept a simple stakes explanation of differences in amount of lawyer effort devoted to state versus federal cases? Earlier, I showed that the amount of court activity, measured in court events, could not be explained simply by stakes, or by another easily measured difference in state and federal cases: area of law. In fact extensive analyses of these data (see Kritzer et al., 1984b) were unable to account for the federal-state difference even after introducing controls for many variables that might differentiate between the cases in the two courts; the best explanation for the federal-state difference is again the judge centeredness of litigation in federal court, plus a possible "pride" element whereby lawyers in federal cases view that court as more prestigious and strive to perform better there by devoting more time to case preparation.

Turning to case characteristics, one might be tempted to assume a simple stakes-to-effort relationship: if one thinks about litigation as a kind of investment, where the substance of the investment was resources (mostly lawyer effort) devoted to "winning" the case in hopes for a return on that investment, one would expect greater resources to be invested when more is at stake. Certainly, this is partly true; however, it neglects the important interactive component in the litigation process. That is, while litigation may be a form of investment, there are factors other than expected return influencing the amount invested, partly because the amount invested only marginally influences the level of the *potential* return; most important, the amount invested by one side will have a major influence on the amount invested by the other. Instead of thinking of stakes "pushing" the level of investment, it makes more sense to think of stakes as serving as the basis of a "cap"; that is, stakes do not so much determine how much will be spent on a case, but instead, determine the *potential* for spending on a case.

Regardless of how one thinks about the role of stakes in the determination of the amount of lawyer effort, Table 7–4c shows very clearly that there is a strong relationship between stakes and effort, with the median smaller case (under $10,000) involving 20 hours of effort, the median medium case ($10,000 to $50,000) involving 50 hours, and the median larger case (over $50,000) involving 122.5 hours. What this simple analysis does not show is that the relationship between stakes and effort is curvilinear; that is, effort rises most rapidly as stakes rise in the more modest cases, with a declining rate of increase as stakes get larger and larger. This makes sense for two reasons. First, there is an element of fixed, or semifixed, costs involved in litigation, and these costs occur even in the more modest cases. Second, common sense would lead one to expect that a $5,000 increase in stakes would change a litigant's willingness to invest in the case much more if the change was to increase stakes from $1,000 to $6,000 than it would if the increase was from $95,000 to $100,000.[15]

The two other characteristics (shown in Table 7–4d and Table 7–4e) also seem to produce notable variations in lawyer effort. Effort *seems* to vary substantially by area of law. Domestic relations cases take the least amount of lawyer time, while government action cases take the most (followed closely by discrimination/civil rights cases). The three traditional areas of torts, contract/commercial, and real property all take roughly the same amount of time. In fact, these apparent differences may be due to court rather than to area of law. Recall that only torts, contract/commercial, and real property have substantial numbers of cases in both courts; domestic relations falls almost exclusively in state courts, and other areas (business regulation, discrimination/civil rights, government action, and government benefits) are primarily in the federal courts. When the three areas in both courts are split out into federal and state cases, the pattern clearly shows that there is one level of effort for state cases (about 15 to 20 hours) and a substantially higher level of effort for federal cases (40 to 60 hours); there *is* some variation among the areas in the federal court, but the greater variations are between the two courts. The relationship between effort and complexity (the latter measured by the subjective judgment of the lawyer) was exactly as one would expect: as complexity increases, the amount of lawyer time increases; the relationship is clear and quite strong.

The remainder of Table 7–4 shows the relationships between the four lawyer characteristics and lawyer effort. Three of the four relationships are significant in a statistical sense; however, compared to the relationships between effort and case characteristics, they are quite weak and clearly of less substantive importance. Lawyer effort goes up moderately as the size of the law firm increases; this partly reflects the fact that as the amount at stake increases, the likelihood that the law firm will be large goes up, and also the fact that state court cases are less likely to involve large law firms than are federal court cases. Still, even after introducing controls for stakes and forum, the relationship between effort and firm size remains. There is a similar pattern for effort and lawyer's income from the practice of law: amount of effort goes up as income goes up, and this relationship is weakened but not fully accounted for by controlling for stakes or forum (although the controlled relationships are notably weaker than the controlled relationships for firm size). There is no relationship between years of experience and effort, and only the slightest of relationships between percent of practice devoted to litigation and effort.

Discussion

In this section I have briefly examined the amount of lawyer time that is devoted to ordinary cases. I found that the typical case involves a modest amount of lawyer effort. Keeping in mind that most cases are in the state courts, the analysis indicates that the typical civil case in the United States involves something less than 20 hours of lawyer time per side of the case. The corresponding figure in the federal courts is significantly higher, reflecting in part differences in the cases in the two types of courts and in part differences in the courts themselves. Variations in the amount of lawyer effort is also related strongly to case characteristics, but only slightly (if at all) to lawyer characteristics.

These findings show some of the tensions between the professional and broker roles. One of the central realities of ordinary litigation is that *most* cases take only modest amounts of lawyer effort. This pattern suggests that ordinary litigation is not highly complex, and it could be interpreted to mean that the services of formally trained, highly skilled professionals is not necessary to carry out such work. Perhaps most cases are so cut and dried that they can be easily reduced to a routine that draws in only a minimal way on a lawyer's formal training and knowledge; most (or at least many) cases really need only a broker's skill: the experience to assess efficiently what a case is worth, and the knowledge of how to go about quickly convincing the other side of the validity of that assessment.

There are, however, alternate arguments that emphasize the other perspective. Even if all of the preceding is correct, there is a fundamental core of formal, abstract knowledge that creates the framework in which a broker works. This knowledge could be learned by extensive experience, perhaps through an apprenticeship arrangement, but it is, in fact, what is conveyed in formal legal education. Moreover, while most cases may be routine, it takes someone with expertise beyond the routine to identify the nonroutine when it does occur. Both of these lines of argument support the proposition that there is more to handling ordinary litigation than insider knowledge, although it may be no more than the need for a kind of professional "triage."[16]

Finally, there is an alternate interpretation of the modest lawyer effort that supports the professional role: lawyer–professionals are able to handle cases efficiently with a relatively small amount of effort because of their extremely high level of formal knowledge and technical expertise. This last point implies that the balance of work in ordinary civil litigation is heavily weighted toward the formal legal skills learned in law school and not toward the informal legal skills learned by working extensively in the system. The next section discusses in more detail the content of the lawyer's work in ordinary civil litigation.

What Do Lawyers Do in Civil Cases?

As noted previously a key distinction that contrasts the images of the professional and the broker has to do with the nature of the activities that are performed and the kinds of knowledge and expertise required for that performance. The work of the professional is marked by the need for "formal" knowledge of the type usually associated with a formal academic program. The work of the broker is oriented to a different kind of expertise: the insider knowledge more associated with working in a setting day-in and day-out. The line between these is difficult to draw but, in the discussion that follows, I will try to distinguish between formal legal activities and informal legal activities.[17]

As a basis of division I will use the knowledge *traditionally* associated with the actual training provided by law schools. Thus, I label the following as formal legal activities: preparing pleadings and motions, conducting legal research, and courtroom (including appellate) advocacy. In contrast, I label talking to the client, factual investigation (including discovery), and negotiation as informal legal activities. There is a natural ambiguity in these categories because one can make a case that many activities belong totally or partly in the other category. For example, the preparation of pleadings in many simple cases may involve nothing more than filling in a preprinted form (or a pattern form on a word processor), and legal research involves knowing how to use computerized legal search services such as Westlaw and Lexis.[18] Or, on the other side, lawyer–client discussions may involve the lawyer educating the client on the legal standing of the client's position.[19] Despite the inherent ambiguities, I believe that my classification is fundamentally valid, *particularly regarding ordinary cases*; it may be more suspect for big-time litigation.

The data on which I draw come from the lawyers' estimates of the proportion of their time devoted to each of the following kinds of activities.

Conferring with your client.

Discovery.

Factual investigation other than discovery.

Discussions aimed at settlement.

Preparing and responding to pleadings and motions.

Legal research.

Immediate preparation for and participation in trial or hearings.

Appeal or enforcement activities.

All other activities.

While I could translate the proportions into number of hours on each activity, the variations would primarily reflect the total effort of the lawyer rather than the variations in the relative distribution of effort, which is of more concern given the discussion of typical levels of effort. Thus, in the discussion that follows, I will look at the percentages reported by the lawyers.[20]

Analysis

There is no indication that lawyers tend to concentrate their time on any one of the activity areas listed.[21] Table 7–5a shows the distribution of proportions of time in each of the nine activities.[22] The table shows both the percentages for all respondents (the top row for each activity) and the percentage of time for those respondents reporting that they spent at least some time on the activity (the second row, which is shown in italics); in addition, the table shows the mean proportion for each area, again both for all respondents and for those who spent at least some time on the particular activity. Overall, what is most striking about this table is the relative balance among the areas, except for trials, hearings, and appeals, where majorities of respondents had no activity. No one area stands out as dominant, and the mean proportions generally fall between .10 and .20; the notable exception is that subset of cases where there is at least some discovery, where the proportion of time on discovery rises to .23. This indicates that the work involved in handling a case is quite varied and that the ordinary litigator must be able to handle all of the activities, both formal legal activities and informal legal activities.

Despite the need to deal with both kinds of activities, the work in ordinary litigation seems to be weighted substantially toward the informal legal activities. Table 7-6 shows the distribution of the proportions of time on the combined set of formal legal activities (defined as legal research, pleadings and motions, trials and hearings, and appeals) and on the set of informal legal activities (defined as conferring with clients, discovery, factual investigation other than discovery, and settlement discussions). The ratio of informal to formal activity seems to be approximately 3 to 2, with the mean proportion on informal legal activity being .60 compared to .40 for formal legal activities.

TABLE 7-5. Percentage of Time Devoted to Specific Activities[a]

Activity	None	.01–.05	.06–.10	.11–.20	.21–.30	.31–.50	.51–1.00	Mean
				Proportion of Time				
Conferring with	2%	19%	26%	31%	13%	7%	2%	.16
client		*19*[b]	*26*	*32*	*13*	*7*	*2*	*.16*
Discovery	37	7	9	20	12	12	3	.15
		11	*15*	*32*	*19*	*19*	*5*	*.23*
Factual investiga-	18	17	25	23	11	5	*	.12
tion other than		*28*	*24*	*24*	*12*	*10*	*2*	*.15*
discovery								
Settlement discus-	17	23	20	20	10	8	2	.14
sions		*28*	*24*	*24*	*12*	*10*	*2*	*.16*
Pleadings and mo-	9	14	24	30	14	6	3	.16
tions		*15*	*26*	*33*	*15*	*7*	*3*	*.18*
Legal research	28	18	20	19	8	5	2	.11
		25	*28*	*27*	*11*	*7*	*2*	*.16*
Hearings and Trial	52	9	12	13	7	6	1	.09
		19	*25*	*26*	*14*	*13*	*3*	*.18*
Appeals	93	3	2	2	1	*	*	.01
		36	*21*	*28*	*8*	*5*	*2*	*.13*
Other	64	10	9	9	4	3	1	.06
		27	*25*	*25*	*11*	*8*	*4*	*.17*

[a] The table is based on 1,307 cases; the figures in the body of the table add to 100 across (excluding the mean column) and represent the percentage of cases falling into the particular category of proportion of time on the respective activity.

[b] The italicized figures are for the subset of cases that involved at least some time devoted to the particular activity.

*Less than 1 percent.

In the previous sections of this chapter, I argued that because of the design of my sample it is necessary to look separately at federal and state cases to understand the activities of ordinary litigation; specifically, state cases provide a better image of the bulk of ordinary litigation. In comparing the summary categories of formal legal activities and informal legal activities, lawyers in both courts report spending the dominant proportion of their time on informal

TABLE 7-6. Percentage of Time Devoted to Formal and Informal Legal Activities[a]

Activity	.00–.10	.11–.25	.26–.50	.51–.75	.76–.89	.90–1.00	Mean
			Proportion of Time				
Formal legal	10%	22%	39%	21%	6%	2%	.40
Informal legal	2	8	26	39	17	10	.60

[a] The table is based on 1,307 cases; the figures in the body of the table add to 100 across (excluding the mean column) and represent the percentage of cases falling into the particular category of proportion of time on the type of activity.

legal activities; the mean proportion is .58 for lawyers in federal cases and .63 for those in state cases (the complementary proportions for formal legal activities are .42 and .37 for federal and state courts, respectively).[23] While the difference in the mean proportion for lawyers in federal cases is significant in a statistical sense ($t = 3.96$) from the mean proportion for lawyers in state cases, the gap is no where near as striking as is the more than 100 percent differential in the median *amount* of time lawyers in the two courts spend on their cases. Still, given that most cases are to be found in the state courts, these data indicate that almost twice as much time is spent on informal legal activities as on formal legal activities.

Let us look briefly at the details behind the two summary categories of formal and informal legal activities. Table 7–7 shows summary statistics for seven of the activities.[24] The table shows, separately for lawyers in state and federal cases, the percentage of lawyers reporting that no time was spent on a given activity, the percentage reporting having spent more than 20 percent of their time on the activity, the mean proportion on the activity, and the mean proportion on the activity omitting those lawyers reporting having spent no time on the activity. Recall that when I discussed court events in the first section in this chapter, I pointed out that federal cases were more likely to include briefs (which are one of the major results of legal research) and more likely to involve formal discovery than were state cases. This is consistent with the percentage of lawyers in cases in the two courts reporting having spent no time on discovery (42 percent state, 34 percent federal) or on legal research (43 percent state, 17 percent federal), and the fact that the mean proportions for both discovery and legal research differ significantly between federal and state cases. It is interesting, however, that all of the gap in the means for discovery and about 50 percent of the gap for legal research reflects the difference in the likelihood that any time will be spent on the activity. For cases where the lawyer spends time on discovery, there is no difference in the proportion of time spent on it for state and federal cases; that is, discovery is just as time consuming (taking 24 percent of the lawyers's time) in state and federal cases, but it is more likely to occur in federal cases. The persistence of the gap, albeit reduced in size, for legal research is consistent with the high likelihood that in federal cases the research will be reflected in a formal product that will be reviewed by a judge (i.e., a written brief) instead of done only to clarify the legal issues in the case for the lawyer's own benefit.

As for the other activities, the only one for which there seems to be a substantial difference in the likelihood that *any* time will be devoted to it is factual investigation other than discovery. Lawyers in state cases are simply much less likely to spend time on factual investigation regardless of whether or not it is formalized discovery; 12 percent of lawyers in state cases report no time on investigation compared to only 7 percent in federal cases. Likewise, the average proportion of time spent on both kinds of investigation in state cases is .26 (.30 for that subset of lawyers who spent some time on investigation) compared to .30 in federal cases (.32 for that subset spending time on investigation). Notice, however, that lawyers in state cases spend, on average, a greater

TABLE 7-7. Type of Activity by Court[a]

Activity	Percent No Time on Activity			Percent > .20 of Time on Activity			Mean Proportion All Respondents			Mean Proportion Respondents with Some Time		
	Both[b]	Federal	State	Both	Federal	State	Both	Federal	State	Both	Federal	State
Conferring with client	2	2	2	27	21	35	.18	.15	.20	.18	.16	.20
Discovery	37	34	42	31	33	28	.15	.16	.14	.24	.24	.24
Factual investigation other than discovery	18	15	22	19	22	16	.13	.14	.12	.16	.17	.15
Settlement discussions	17	19	14	25	20	31	.15	.13	.17	.17	.16	.20
Pleadings and motions	9	9	10	28	24	28	.17	.18	.17	.19	.19	.19
Legal research	28	17	43	18	23	11	.12	.15	.08	.17	.18	.14
Hearings and trial	52	53	51	17	15	19	.09	.09	.10	.20	.19	.21

[a] The ns for the first three columns are 1,308 for both courts combined, 736 for the federal cases, and 572 for the state cases. Approximate ns for the last column can be obtained by subtracting the percentage of cases shown in the first column from the appropriate n.

[b] The figures for both courts combined differ from those in Table 7–5 because the proportions were renormalized to add to 1.0 after eliminating the "other" activity category.

proportion of time conferring with their clients, .20 compared to .15 for federal cases (t=6.36); this difference is almost equal to the difference in combined
proportion for discovery and other investigation.[25] One interpretation of this
pattern is that in the lower-stakes cases in the state courts, lawyers are more
likely to limit their investigations to what can be gleaned from discussions with
their clients (and from what might be said by the other side in settlement
discussions).[26]

This interpretation can be evaluated by examining the relationship among
stakes, court, and the way the lawyers spend their time in their work on litigation. Table 7–8 extends the previous table by adding stakes as a control variable. For the first three activities shown in the table, conferring with the client,
discovery, and factual investigation other than discovery, the figures in the
table show that stakes do account for some of the difference between state and
federal cases in the amount of time spent on discovery and other investigative
activities. However, stakes do not account for the differences in the amount of
time spent conferring with clients—in state court cases about 20 percent of the
lawyer's time is spent conferring with the client regardless of the level of stakes.
There is still a significant gap between state and federal cases in the proportion
of time spent on investigative activities (discovery and other factual investigation combined) in big cases (.40 for federal cases versus .30 for state cases,
t=2.42); this may in part reflect that the big cases in federal courts are bigger
(median stakes of $150,000) than state cases (median stakes of $75,000).[27] One
of the major issues in debates over reform of civil litigation, particularly in the
federal courts, has to do with the costs of discovery; it is interesting, however,
that within the range of cases in this sample, there is only a modest increase in
the proportion of time devoted to discovery as stakes rise (going from .17 for
small cases under $10,000 to .21 for "big" cases over $50,000).

As for the relationships between stakes and the other kinds of activities
(also shown in Table 7–8), there are no *strong* relationships between stakes and
the content of activities. Given that all cases have to involve some pleadings,
one might expect the proportion devoted to pleadings to go down as the stakes
go up; this is true for federal cases (dropping from .18 to .11) but not for state
cases. One might also expect that the pressures for a quick, cheap settlement
would decline with the increase in stakes, but there is no clear pattern at all
between stakes and proportion of time devoted to settlement discussions. Going in the other direction, one might expect the proportion of time spent on
legal research to increase with stakes; however, while the likelihood that at least
some time will be spent on legal research does go up with increases in stakes for
both federal and state cases, there is no increase in the proportion of time for
federal cases, and only a slight rise for state cases.

If stakes do not systematically explain variations in the way lawyers choose
to use their time, what about area of law? Recall that some kinds of cases are
found in both courts (torts, contracts, and real property), while others tend to
be found either in the federal court (business regulation, civil rights/discrimina-
tion, government benefits, and government action) or the state court (domestic
relations). Given that there are substantial differences in what lawyers do in

TABLE 7-8. Type of Activity by Stakes and Court[a]

Activity	Stakes	Percent No Time on Activity		Percent >.20 of Time on Activity		Mean Proportion All Respondents		Mean Proportion Respondents with Some Time	
		Federal	State	Federal	State	Federal	State	Federal	State
Conferring with client	Low	1	2	30	30	.17	.20	.17	.20
	Medium	0	1	18	31	.15	.18	.15	.18
	High	1	0	14	35	.13	.19	.13	.19
Discovery	Low	29	40	35	29	.17	.15	.23	.24
	Medium	25	27	34	36	.18	.18	.24	.24
	High	21	29	46	29	.21	.14	.27	.20
Factual investigation other than discovery	Low	15	22	18	15	.13	.12	.15	.15
	Medium	9	14	22	17	.15	.13	.16	.15
	High	5	6	38	18	.19	.14	.20	.15
Settlement discussions	Low	10	6	20	37	.14	.20	.16	.21
	Medium	9	10	26	28	.16	.16	.17	.17
	High	6	6	11	24	.11	.17	.12	.19

Pleadings and motions	Low	8	12	31	30	.18	.16	.19	.19	
	Medium	7	6	21	20	.15	.15	.16	.16	
	High	6	0	8	12	.11	.15	.12	.14	
Legal research	Low	17	48	20	11	.14	.07	.16	.14	
	Medium	14	34	17	8	.12	.08	.15	.11	
	High	10	24	17	6	.14	.10	.16	.13	
Hearings and trial	Low	56	58	13	18	.08	.10	.19	.23	
	Medium	52	44	16	20	.09	.12	.18	.21	
	High	38	47	15	24	.10	.10	.16	.19	

[a]The ns for the first three pairs of columns are:

Stakes	Federal	State
Low	158	265
Medium	190	113
High	84	17

Approximate ns for the last column can be obtained by subtracting the percentage of cases shown in the first column from the appropriate n.

97

cases in the two courts, I have split the three common areas by court (Table 7–9), and I have included only cases from one court for the other five areas (Table 7–11).[28]

Table 7–9 is similar in form to Table 7–8, with area of law replacing stakes as the additional control variable. Recall that federal cases tend to have a greater proportion of effort devoted to work of a formal legal nature than do state cases; this primarily reflects increased effort on legal research in federal cases. Also, federal cases involve more emphasis on investigation, through the discovery process and through other means; lawyers in state cases seem to rely more on what they can learn from their own clients. With the exception of investigation outside of discovery (where the proportion is pretty constant both across the two courts and across the three areas), these patterns of difference across the courts hold up within each of the three areas of law commonly found in both courts. Lawyers in state cases spend more of their time conferring with their clients (the proportion is around .20) than do lawyers in federal cases (who spend .13 to .15 of their time on a case talking to their clients). Lawyers in federal cases spend more of their time on discovery than do lawyers in state cases in each of the three areas, although it is also true that lawyers in tort cases spend more of their time on discovery than do lawyers in contract/commercial cases who, in turn, spend more of their time on discovery than lawyers in real property cases (although lawyers in federal real property cases spend more time on discovery than do lawyers in state contract/commercial cases). The importance of legal research in federal cases stands up within areas of law, although federal tort cases involve substantially less emphasis on legal research than do other kinds of cases in the federal courts. Except for real property cases, settlement discussions receive a greater proportion of time in state cases than in federal cases, as was true in the overall contrast of state and federal cases.

While these differences in what lawyers do in similar state and federal cases are interesting and important, they are generally small in comparison to the differences by area of law. Concentrating first on the summary category of formal legal activities shown in Table 7–10, in the state cases, the proportion of time spent on formal legal activities goes from a low of .32 in tort cases up to .44 in real property cases, with contract/commercial and domestic relations falling in between at .39. The variations in the proportion of time devoted to formal legal activities derive from different sources, depending on area of law. For the area involving the largest proportion of formal legal activity, real property, slightly higher proportions are devoted to all of the separate activities forming this group (pleading and motions, legal research, and hearings and trial). In contrast, for domestic relations (see Table 7–11), the dominant formal legal activity is hearings and trial, with pleadings and motions actually taking a smaller proportion of time than is the case for torts; keep in mind that the domestic relations cases for which interviews were conducted all involved an active dispute over property division, child custody, and/or child support, so many of these hearings are probably not simply the *pro forma* hearings typically associated with a simple, uncontested divorce. As for contract/commercial

TABLE 7-9. Type of Activity by Selected Area of Law and Court[a]

Activity	Area of Law	Percent No Time on Activity		Percent >.20 of Time on Activity		Mean Proportion All Respondents		Mean Proportion Respondents with Some Time	
		Federal	State	Federal	State	Federal	State	Federal	State
Conferring with client	Torts	2	3	21	31	.14	.19	.15	.19
	Contract/commercial	3	3	20	34	.15	.20	.15	.20
	Real property	5	2	16	38	.13	.20	.14	.20
Discovery	Torts	12	26	50	40	.24	.20	.27	.27
	Contract/commercial	41	54	30	20	.15	.10	.25	.22
	Real property	37	61	24	9	.13	.07	.20	.17
Factual investigation other than discovery	Torts	11	19	26	17	.16	.13	.18	.16
	Contract/commercial	16	25	22	20	.13	.13	.16	.17
	Real property	21	19	24	20	.13	.13	.17	.16
Settlement discussions	Torts	14	12	13	30	.11	.17	.13	.19
	Contract/commercial	18	13	25	35	.15	.19	.18	.21
	Real property	16	19	29	34	.16	.16	.19	.20

(continued)

TABLE 7-9. *Continued*

Activity	Area of Law	Percent No Time on Activity		Percent >.20 of Time on Activity		Mean Proportion All Respondents		Mean Proportion Respondents with Some Time	
		Federal	State	Federal	State	Federal	State	Federal	State
Pleadings and motions	Torts	8	10	19	26	.14	.16	.15	.18
	Contract/commercial	8	9	32	33	.19	.18	.21	.20
	Real property	11	6	45	31	.21	.19	.24	.20
Legal research	Torts	19	50	14	8	.11	.06	.14	.13
	Contract/commercial	19	37	25	13	.15	.09	.19	.15
	Real property	18	28	21	11	.15	.09	.19	.12
Hearings and trial	Torts	45	58	16	16	.10	.09	.19	.21
	Contract/commercial	62	56	11	18	.06	.09	.17	.21
	Real property	63	34	8	25	.07	.14	.20	.21

[a]The ns for the first three pairs of columns are:

	Federal	State
Torts	239	325
Contracts/commercial	158	158
Real property	38	64

Approximate ns for the last pair of columns can be obtained by subtracting the percentage of cases shown in the first column from the appropriate n.

TABLE 7-10. Time on Formal Legal Activities by Area of Law and Court*

Area of Law	Mean Proportion of Time on Formal Legal Activities	
	Federal Cases	State Cases
Torts	.35	.32
n	237	325
Contract/commercial	.42	.39
n	288	158
Real property	.45	.44
n	38	64
Domestic relations	*	.39
n	2	39
Business regulation	.44	*
n	148	12
Civil rights/discrimination	.49	*
n	90	1
Government action	.55	*
n	28	5
Government benefits	.64	*
n	37	1

*Too few cases for analysis.

cases, more time is spent on pleadings and motions and on legal research. The area in which torts stand out as high is discovery; it is generally this informal legal activity that is the trade-off for the formal legal activities in the other areas of law because, for the other three informal legal activities (conferring with the client, factual investigations other than discovery, and settlement discussions), the proportions are pretty constant across areas of law for cases in state courts.

The differences for federal cases are much more striking. Looking at the summary category of formal legal activities, the proportion goes from a low of .35 for torts to a high of .64 for government benefits. Again, the sources of the variation differ, depending on the area of law:

Torts. Very high on discovery (.24, with the next highest being civil rights/ discrimination at .16) and very low on legal research for federal cases (.11, with contract/commercial and real property tied as the next lowest at .15) although still higher than any of the areas in state court (Table 7-9).

Contract/commercial. This category is lowest in the proportion of time spent on hearings and trial, but otherwise tends to the middle of the range of proportions for the other activities (Table 7-9).

Real property. This is generally another middle-range category on most activities, but it is the second highest (after government benefits) on pleadings and motions (Table 7-9).

TABLE 7-11. Type of Activity for Areas of Law in One Type of Court Only[a]

Activity	Area of Law	Court	Percent No Time on Activity	Percent > .20 of Time on Activity	Mean Proportion All Respondents	Mean Proportion Respondents with Some Time
Conferring with client	Domestic relations	State	0	62	.30	.30
	Business regulation	Federal	1	24	.16	.17
	Civil rights/discrimination	Federal	0	14	.14	.14
	Government action	Federal	0	11	.13	.13
	Government benefits	Federal	8	16	.15	.16
Discovery	Domestic relations	State	69	5	.03	.12
	Business regulation	Federal	41	26	.13	.22
	Civil rights/discrimination	Federal	31	32	.16	.23
	Government action	Federal	50	25	.11	.23
	Government benefits	Federal	73	3	.02	.08
Factual investigation other than discovery	Domestic relations	State	38	3	.07	.11
	Business regulation	Federal	20	20	.12	.15
	Civil rights/discrimination	Federal	12	18	.14	.16
	Government action	Federal	14	14	.13	.15
	Government benefits	Federal	11	22	.16	.18
Settlement discussions	Domestic relations	State	18	38	.20	.24
	Business regulation	Federal	17	24	.15	.18
	Civil rights/discrimination	Federal	19	10	.08	.10
	Government action	Federal	36	11	.08	.13
	Government benefits	Federal	70	3	.03	.11

Pleadings and motions	Domestic relations	State	8	.13	.14
	Business regulation	Federal	11	.19	.22
	Civil rights/discrimination	Federal	4	.18	.19
	Government action	Federal	7	.19	.20
	Government benefits	Federal	11	.24	.27
Legal research	Domestic relations	State	49	.06	.12
	Business regulation	Federal	18	.16	.20
	Civil rights/discrimination	Federal	7	.17	.18
	Government action	Federal	0	.24	.24
	Government benefits	Federal	5	.23	.24
Hearings and trial	Domestic relations	State	18	.19	.23
	Business regulation	Federal	59	.07	.18
	Civil rights/discrimination	Federal	39	.13	.22
	Government action	Federal	32	.12	.18
	Government benefits	Federal	32	.15	.22

*The ns for the first three columns are:

	Domestic Relations	Business Regulation	Civil Rights Discrimination	Government Action	Government Benefits
Federal	39	148	90	28	37

[a] The ns for the last column can be obtained by subtracting the percentage of cases shown in the first column from the appropriate n.

Business regulation. Except for its low proportion on hearings and trial, this category also tends to fall in the middle of the range of proportions on most activities (Table 7–11).

Civil rights/discrimination. On the high side for hearings and trial and the low side for settlement discussions (Table 7–11).

Government actions. On the low side for settlement discussions and the highest (at .24) for legal research (Table 7–11).

Government benefits. The lowest by far on discovery (.02), the lowest on settlement discussions (.03), almost as high on legal research as government action (at .23), and highest on pleadings and motions (at .24) and hearings and trials (at .15) (Table 7–11).

There is not a lot of variation among the various kinds of cases in the proportions spent on conferring with the client (.13 to .16) or on factual investigation other than discovery (also .13 to .16).

Clearly, different kinds of cases in federal court require different kinds of skill. Cases involving the government as an adversary draw most heavily on the formal legal skills of the lawyer, while the typical tort case in the federal courts relies much more heavily on the informal skills the lawyer gains from experience dealing with those kinds of cases. In some ways this should not be surprising, since torts are the most ordinary of the ordinary everyday cases in the federal courts, while the cases against government agencies form the smallest proportions of the sample of cases in the study (but remember that lawyers working as direct employees of government agencies were not included in the survey through which the data under discussion were obtained, so the proportion of lawyers handling cases involving government parties is lower in the sample than in actual fact[29]).

Discussion

The analyses in this chapter show that the stakes, the forum, and the substance of the case at issue all have important effects on the work of the lawyer in ordinary litigation. The contrast between the state courts and the federal courts stands out most strongly in creating distinctions in the work of the lawyer. In the section on court events, I described the federal court as having a more judge-centered process, and this feature shows up again in the greater amount of time spent by lawyers in federal cases (even after controlling for stakes and area of law) and in the larger proportion of time spent on legal research, which is an activity likely to be aimed at the judge. As one would expect, stakes have an important influence on the amount of time a lawyer is able to spend on a case, although I suggested that the mechanism of influence is in terms of placing a limit on what the lawyer will do rather than fueling the work process. Stakes seem to have a minimal influence on the content of the lawyers' work.

The content is most strongly influenced by the substance of the case, particularly in the range of cases found in the federal court.

In assessing the meaning of these findings for the professional and the broker images, one must keep in mind the small slice of the pie represented by federal cases. The most dominant portion of civil litigation is contract and tort cases in the state courts.[30] The typical state tort case takes only 20 hours of lawyer time on each side of the case, and 68 percent of that time is made up of informal legal activities. Fifty percent of the formal legal activity in the typical tort case consists of drawing up and answering the pleadings, most of which are probably based on form pleadings either in a preprinted or electronic format; almost no time is spent in the typical state tort case on legal research. The next most common case is the state contract case; this actually involves less time on the part of the lawyer (the median is 17 hours), although the proportion of time devoted to formal legal activities is slightly higher at .39.[31] In contested domestic relations cases, the typical case involves the same proportion of formal legal activity but only 13 hours of time.

Thus, the kinds of cases that make up the bulk of the work of the state courts do not draw heavily on the formal, highly technical skills for legal research and courtroom advocacy that are the core of the curriculum of most American law schools. The question that I cannot answer from the data before me is the degree to which the work of lawyers in those cases draws extensively on specific knowledge of the law of a kind that could not easily be conveyed through a less extensive and encompassing kind of training than that provided by the 3-year curriculum leading to a J.D. or L.L.B. in an American law school. I seriously question whether that training is needed to handle most of these ordinary state cases.[32]

The work of the lawyer litigating cases in federal courts is more varied, but it is still strongly oriented toward torts and contract cases.[33] Cases outside of torts and contracts clearly call more heavily on the formal legal training of the lawyers involved, at least in part because they deal with less settled areas of law, questions only recently subject to legal consideration (e.g., business regulation, discrimination, etc.) or issues in a state of relatively constant flux and change (e.g., regulations dealing with government benefits). Probably of equal or greater importance, however, is the more central role of the judge in federal cases. One can think of a lawyer's preparation of a case as being directed in part to the other side, in part to the judge, and in part to a potential jury. The analyses in this chapter suggest that in federal cases a more substantial portion of the preparation is directed toward the judge than is true in state cases, and that the preparation must be the most concerned with the formal legal aspects of the case.

APPENDIX 7A

Level of Court Activity by Stakes
for Individual Event Types

TABLE 7A-1. Level of Court Activity by Stakes for Individual Event Types

	Number of Events						
	0	1–2	3–5	6–10	11–20	21 and Up	*n*
Briefs							
No stakes[a]	68	16	11	4	1	*	1,003
Federal	44	25	22	7	2	*	484
State	91	8	2	*	0	0	519
Under $10,000	73	13	8	4	2	*	332
Federal	48	19	19	8	4	1	118
State	86	9	1	*	0	0	214
$10,000–50,000	57	21	16	4	2	*	229
Federal	41	27	22	7	3	1	137
State	80	12	7	0	1	0	92
Over $50,000	36	27	15	14	7	0	84
Federal	27	30	17	17	9	0	70
State	79	14	7	0	0	0	14
Continuances							
No stakes	76	19	3	1	*	0	1,003
Federal	57	33	7	2	*	0	484
State	94	6	0	0	0	0	519
Under $10,000	22	17	14	9	0	0	332
Federal	56	35	8	2	0	0	118
State	91	9	*	0	0	0	214
$10,000–50,000	62	29	6	2	*	0	229
Federal	50	36	9	4	1	0	137
State	80	18	1	0	0	0	92
Over $50,000	48	35	13	5	0	0	84
Federal	41	37	16	6	0	0	70
State	79	21	0	0	0	0	14
Motions							
No stakes	21	54	20	5	1	0	1,003
Federal	13	53	27	7	1	0	484
State	28	55	14	3	0	0	519
Under $10,000	14	57	23	5	1	0	332
Federal	6	54	27	10	3	0	118
State	18	58	20	3	*	0	214
$10,000–50,000	11	56	24	6	2	0	229
Federal	15	52	26	7	1	0	137
State	7	63	22	5	3	0	92
Over $50,000	11	40	35	7	7	0	84
Federal	7	41	40	4	7	0	70
State	29	26	7	21	7	0	14

	Number of Events						
	0	1–2	3–5	6–10	11–20	21 and Up	*n*
Discovery							
No stakes	65	12	10	8	4	1	1,003
Federal	62	13	8	10	5	2	484
State	67	11	12	7	3	*	519
Under $10,000	41	22	18	13	5	2	332
Federal	35	21	19	15	7	3	118
State	44	22	17	12	4	1	214
$10,000–50,000	34	17	17	17	11	3	229
Federal	31	19	15	17	14	4	137
State	39	13	20	18	8	2	92
Over $50,000	25	11	14	14	17	19	84
Federal	21	10	16	17	16	20	70
State	43	14	7	0	21	14	14
Pretrials							
No stakes	79	16	5	**	**	**	1,003
Federal	64	25	11	**	**	**	484
State	92	8	*	**	**	**	519
Under $10,000	68	23	9	**	**	**	332
Federal	40	41	19	**	**	**	118
State	84	13	3	**	**	**	214
$10,000–50,000	54	31	15	**	**	**	229
Federal	42	39	19	**	**	**	137
State	73	20	7	**	**	**	92
Over $50,000	43	27	30	**	**	**	84
Federal	33	31	36	**	**	**	70
State	93	7	0	**	**	**	14

[a] The first row of each set is federal and state cases combined.

*Less than 1/2 of 1 percent.

**Collapsed with 3–5 category.

8

The Impact of Relationships
on the Lawyer's Work
in Ordinary Civil Litigation

In Chapters 5 to 7 I discussed aspects of lawyering in civil litigation that reflect some of the tensions between the lawyer as professional and the lawyer as broker: (1) the role of the web of relationships within which lawyers carry on their work in litigation, and (2) the specific nature of that work. In this chapter, I will combine these to consider the impact of the lawyers' relationships on the work that they do in litigation. In the first part of the chapter, I will consider the impact of relationships on the amount of effort that lawyers devote to their cases; in the second part, I will examine the impact on the content of the work.

The Amount of Lawyer Effort[1]

There are several aspects of the lawyers' web of relationships that might be considered as factors in accounting for the amount of effort devoted to a case: fee arrangement, degree of control exercised by the client, expectation of future representation of the client, expectation of future cases against the opposing lawyer, and expectation of future cases against the opposing party. I have direct information available for three of these, indirect information for one (future representation[2]), and no usable information for one (future cases against the opposing lawyer).[3]

The American legal system offers a range of options for paying for legal services: hourly fees, contingent fees, flat fees, prepaid legal insurance, and direct representation (i.e., representation by in-house lawyers). Most litigation, other than simple divorce cases (and perhaps simple collections cases), is handled on either an hourly fee or a contingent fee basis. As many authors have pointed out (Franklin et al., 1961; MacKinnon, 1964; Schwartz and Mitchell, 1970; Rosenthal, 1974; Johnson, 1980–1981; Danzon, 1983; See, 1984), these two fee arrangements create different kinds of incentive situations for the lawyers.[4] The hourly fee arrangement makes it advantageous, at least in the short run, for the lawyer to devote more time to the case; at the extreme, it is, to paraphrase Rhode (1985: 635), to the lawyer's advantage "to leave no stone unturned, given that he or she is charging by the stone." This, of course, presumes (1) that the lawyer has no better use of time (i.e., there is no other activity that yields equal or better rewards), and (2) that the client is able and willing to pay whatever fee the lawyer ultimately bills.

The American contingent fee system of lawyer compensation, whereby the lawyer receives payment only if money is recovered from the opposing party, has been the target of a variety of criticisms. The traditional attack (see Mac-Kinnon, 1964; Benson Commission, 1979: 176–177) is that by joining the interests of lawyer and client, the lawyer is less able to exercise the kind of dispassionate, "professional" judgment that should be provided to the client.[5] Recent analyses have relied on the specific nature of virtually all American contingent fees: they are simply "percentage" fees whereby the lawyer retains a percentage of whatever is recovered; the "contingency" element arises from the fact that any percentage times zero yields nothing. The latter discussions have taken issue with the idea that the contingent fee lawyer becomes the client's "partner" in the case and have pointed out that it may be in the lawyer's interest to accept a settlement much less favorable to the client than might be obtainable (see in particular Rosenthal, 1974; and Johnson, 1980–1981). The logic of this latter position follows from the recognition that the goal of economically rational lawyers should be to maximize the hourly return from their efforts, and very quick, even small, settlements will frequently yield larger fees per hour of effort than will larger settlements achieved after substantial expenditures of time on the part of the lawyers. While this critique of contingent fees has merit, it presumes (1) that the lawyers have alternative ways of using their time that will yield *higher* hourly returns (this is the opposite of the assumption that was inherent in the expectation that hourly fee lawyers would spend too much time on cases), (2) that the lawyers' efforts on individual cases are not related (e.g., a lawyer's reputation derived from one case will not affect either the flow of business or the ability to achieve "good" outcomes in future cases), and (3) that the lawyers are not influenced by noneconomic considerations (e.g., the norms of what constitutes adequate representation).

Thus, there are two contrasting hypotheses about how fee arrangement[6] will influence the amount of effort a lawyer will devote to a case: an hourly fee lawyer is expected to devote "too much" and a contingent fee lawyer is expected to devote "too little." Defining "too much" or "too little" borders on a hopeless task, but it is possible to combine the two hypotheses to yield the expectation that the hourly fee lawyer would devote more time to a case than a contingent fee lawyer, everything else being the same. In the discussion that follows, I will refer to this as the *magnitude effect*.

But there is another way in which fee arrangement might influence lawyer effort, and this complicates any simple comparison of the amount of time spent by hourly and contingent fee lawyers. As I will show, it is the case that fee arrangement *structures* the process that determines the amount of time a lawyer will devote to a given case: the things that influence an hourly fee lawyer differ, either in presence or magnitude, from the things influencing a contingent fee lawyer; that is, some things influencing the contingent fee lawyer do not influence the hourly fee lawyer and vice versa, and the degree of influence of some factors varies depending on the fee arrangement.

The differences in the factors influencing effort allocation by hourly and contingent fee lawyers constitutes the *structuring effect* of fee arrangement. If fee arrangement did not have a structuring effect, testing for the magnitude effect would be straightforward: simply control for the differences in cases handled by hourly and contingent fee lawyers and determine if hourly fee lawyers devote more effort than contingent fee lawyers. As it is, the magnitude effect can be considered only in a limited fashion and only within the context of the structuring effect.[7]

Fee arrangement between lawyer and client is only one aspect of the web of relationships within which the litigator works. One of the other relational web variables, client control of the lawyer, provides a good example of how the structuring effect of fee arrangement might work. The literature on client control suggests that client control should work in opposite ways for the hourly and contingent fee lawyer. Given that the problem of the hourly fee lawyer is an incentive to "overwork" a case, the function of client control should be to place limits on the amount of effort the lawyer expends (see Wessel, 1976). In contrast, for the contingent fee lawyer, the client will (in the modest case) want the lawyer to devote more effort to the case than is necessarily in the lawyer's financial best interest; in this situation, client control should be exercised to insure that the case receives adequate attention (see Rosenthal, 1974).

As for the other two relational web variables, one might expect a lawyer who anticipates future representation of a client to behave differently than a lawyer who sees a client as only a one-time player. The nature of the effect of potential future representation would probably be similar to that associated with the client control variable: the hourly fee lawyer will seek to handle the case in as economical a fashion as possible (by avoiding unnecessary and costly activities), while the contingent fee lawyer will strive to obtain a result that the client will recognize as good even if that means expending more effort than the lawyer would normally devote to the case. Given the lack of a good direct question about future representation,[8] I will rely on past representation as an indicator of the expectation of future representation; that is, if the lawyer took the case at least partly because of past representation of the client, I will assume that the lawyer is more concerned about future representation than would be true if past representation had no role in the decision to accept the case.

The expectation of future cases against the current opposing party is likely to be of particular concern to the contingent fee lawyer, since it is really that party who is paying the lawyer's fee. The most reasonable expectation is that potential future cases would lead a lawyer (regardless of fee arrangement) to devote more effort to a case in order to insure that the party will take the lawyer seriously in future cases. At the same time, the expectation of future cases is likely to be indicative of past cases (particularly for contingent fee, tort lawyers), and it may well be true in such situations that the lawyer already has a well-established reputation, making it possible to spend less actual time on the average case involving that opposing party.

To summarize, the lawyer's web of relationships can have important influences on the amount of time that the lawyer devotes to a case; those influences may be reflected in the magnitude of the lawyer's effort or, in regard to fee arrangement, the relationship may structure the effort allocation decisions of the lawyer. To examine these complex questions empirically, it is necessary to examine lawyer effort within the context of an overall explanatory model.

Explaining Lawyer Effort

Many individual factors might influence the amount of time that a lawyer will devote to a case. For statistical reasons, it is important that all variables that might have a major influence on the lawyer be included in the kind of analysis needed to describe the structuring and magnitude effects of fee arrangement as well as the effects of the other relational web variables.[9] To insure this completeness, I constructed a regression model using 31 distinct variables. Table 8-1 summarizes each of the individual items; Appendix 8.A describes each one in detail and explains the rationale for each variable's inclusion.

The factors, in addition to the relational web variables, can be grouped into five categories.

Party interaction. Litigation is fundamentally a process of interaction, with the activities of one side determined in substantial part by the activities of the other.

Case characteristics. The amount of effort that a lawyer will devote to a case is affected by the size of the case,[10] its complexity, and its duration.[11]

Participant characteristics. Lawyer effort may be influenced by characteristics of the client (specifically, the type of client as indicated in the court record), the lawyer's own experience and expertise, and the lawyer's attitudes.

Participant goals. Both the client's goals (getting a maximal monetary result, a fair monetary result, or some other goal) and the lawyer's goals (as indicated by the factors influencing the lawyer's decision to take the case) might influence how much time a lawyer devotes to a case.

Case processing factors. How the case is processed (i.e., which court— federal or state—handles the case, whether there is a trial and/or settlement discussions, and the use—versus nonuse or absence—by the lawyer of standard operating procedures) is likely to affect the amount of effort going into a case.

The individual variables (all 31 of them) were combined into an additive equation to predict the amount of effort a lawyer would devote to a case. The method used for the analysis was multiple regression, in which the effect of each variable is expressed as the amount of change in the dependent variable (i.e., hours worked) that can be expected if an explanatory variable changes by

TABLE 8-1. Summary Descriptions of the Variables in the Lawyer Effort Model

Cluster	Variable	Type	Description	Means (Standard Deviations)	
				Hourly	Contingent
Party interaction — measures of pretrial activities by the other side					
	1. Pleadings	Count[a]	Number of pleading documents filed by other side	1.50 (1.30)	1.43 (1.91)
	2. Motions	Count	Number of motions initiated by other side	0.84 (1.20)	0.82 (1.26)
	3. Discovery	Count	Number of discovery events (dispositions, motions, etc.) initiated by the other side	2.13 (3.12)	2.28 (3.34)
	4. Briefs	Count	Number of briefs filed by the other side	0.71 (1.34)	0.63 (1.36)
Case Characteristics[b]					
	5. Stakes[b]	Lawyer's estimate	The lawyer's estimate in dollars of what the client should have been willing to accept or do to settle the case	$19,985 ($37,025)	$23,529 ($39,733)
	6. Complexity	Lawyer's estimate	Lawyer's subjective estimate of the complexity of the case (five-point scale)	2.39 (1.11)	2.52 (1.17)
	7. Duration	Count	Number of days from filing to termination	422 (283)	417 (289)
Participant Characteristics					
	8. Client type	Dummy	1 for individuals, 0 for organizations (as indicated by the court record)	0.28 (0.45)	0.84 (0.36)
	9. Specialization	Factor score	Indicator of degree to which the case fell within an area that the lawyer considered to be a specialty	0.08 (0.91)	0.07 (0.84)
	10. Law school performance	Factor score	Indicator of lawyer's performance based on rank in class and participation on law review	0.05 (0.69)	−0.00 (0.67)
	11. Years of practice	Count	Number of years lawyer has been practicing law	11.41 (8.92)	10.22 (9.04)

12. Litigation proportion	Lawyer's estimate	Proportion of time devoted to litigation	68.45 (27.35)	66.52 (24.10)
13. Personal capacity	Factor score	Measure based on items taken from Robinson and Shaver's (1969: 102–105) scale.	0.03 (0.67)	−0.04 (0.64)
14. Commitment to craft	Lawyer's estimate	Lawyer's commitment to the legal craft (three-point scale)	2.51 (0.69)	2.49 (0.68)
Participant Goals				
Client goals				
15. Get most/pay least	Dichotomy	Client sought to get the most or pay the least (coded 1); client did not have this goal (coded 0)	0.44 (0.50)	0.32 (0.47)
16. Get fair/pay fair	Dichotomy	Client sought to get a fair amount or pay a fair amount (coded 1); client did not have this goal (coded 0)	0.32 (0.47)	0.48 (0.50)
Lawyer goals – as measured by reasons lawyer took the case				
17. Challenge	Factor score	Lawyer took case because it presented a challenge	−0.08 (0.86)	0.07 (0.88)
18. Public service	Factor score	Lawyer took case because it provided an opportunity to serve the public or because of sympathy for the client	−0.15 (0.71)	0.06 (0.67)
19. Professional visibility	Factor score	The case would increase the lawyer's community standing or improve lawyer's position in the firm	0.03 (0.72)	0.05 (0.68)
20. Making money	Factor score	The case was taken because of the amount money that could be earned	−0.08 (0.57)	0.26 (0.66)
Processing characteristics				
21. Type of court	Dichotomy	Federal court (1); state court (0)	0.56 (0.50)	0.47 (0.50)
22. Settlement discussions	Dichotomy	Did occur (1); did not occur (0)	0.90 (0.30)	0.90 (0.30)
23. Trial	Dichotomy	Case did go to trial (1); case did not go to trial (0)	0.11 (0.32)	0.12 (0.32)
24. Pretrial events SOP	Factor score	Use of SOPs for pretrial activities such as pleadings, motions, and discovery	0.01 (0.99)	−.06 (1.01)
25. Estimating case value SOP	Factor score	Use of SOPs for estimating the value of the case	−0.03 (0.97)	−0.05 (1.02)

(continued)

TABLE 8–1. *Continued*

Cluster	Variable	Type	Description	Means (Standard Deviations)	
				Hourly	Contingent
Processing Characteristics (*continued*)					
	26. Plan for motions	Dichotomy	Lawyer used a plan for motions (1); no plan used (0)	0.20 (0.40)	0.12 (0.33)
	27. Plan for settlement	Dichotomy	Lawyer used a plan for obtaining a settlement (1); no plan was used (0)	0.70 (0.46)	0.68 (0.47)
	28. Plan for discovery	Dichotomy	Lawyer used a plan in conducting discovery (1); no plan used (0)	0.60 (0.50)	0.64 (0.48)
The lawyer's relationships					
	29. Service to regular client	Dichotomy	The lawyer took the case to provide service to a regular client	0.62 (0.49)	0.15 (0.36)
	30. Client control and participation	Factor score	Client sought to exercise control over the lawyer's activity and to participate actively in decision making regarding the case	0.20 (0.72)	-0.24 (0.71)
	31. Expectation of future cases against opposing party	Dichotomy	The lawyer expects to have cases against the current opposing party in the future	0.17 (0.38)	0.44 (0.50)
Dependent variable					
	Hours worked	Lawyer's report	The number of hours of effort by lawyers in the respondent's firm	51.65 (66.37)	52.76 (61.41)
	n			374	273

[a]"Count" indicates that the variable was a simple count of some type of event or some other discrete entity (e.g., days—for duration).

[b]In the actual analysis, stakes was adjusted for nonlinearity; the particular adjustment used was to take the square root of stakes.

one unit, assuming that all other variables remain unchanged; these effects are represented as the "coefficients" of the equation (with one coefficient for each predictor variable). Since the measurement units of the predictor variables are important for interpreting the magnitudes of the corresponding regression coefficients, they are shown in the summary in Table 8-1. A separate regression equation was computed for hourly and for contingent fee lawyers, yielding one estimate of the coefficient associated with each of the 31 predictor variables for the hourly fee lawyer and another coefficient estimate for each variable for the contingent fee lawyer.[12] The structuring effect of fee arrangement is found in the differences in the two sets of coefficients.[13]

Results and Discussion

THE STRUCTURING EFFECT

Selected coefficients from the regression analysis are shown in Table 8-2; appendix Table 8-B1 shows the complete set of regression results, including all of the separate coefficients for the hourly fee lawyers and contingent fee lawyers. The structuring effect, as represented in the differences between coefficients for contingent and hourly fee lawyers, can be seen clearly in the table.[14] For example, while the variables in both the party interaction and case characteristics groups are important in explaining the level of effort for both sets of lawyers, the nature of the impacts of the individual variables in these groups differ in important ways, depending on the fee arrangement. The variable that has the biggest impact for hourly fee lawyers, filing of briefs by the opposing party (which typically necessitates preparing a brief in response), also has the largest impact for contingent fee lawyers, but that impact is less than half as large— about 4 hours (4.029) compared to 8½ hours (8.543); given that preparing a brief is a very individual matter, it is not surprising that contingent fee lawyers, who must consider whether there are more productive ways of spending their time, will devote less time to it than will hourly fee lawyers, who can look to their clients for compensation for the effort that goes into brief writing. In the case characteristics group, *all* the variables are significant for both groups, but the impacts of both stakes (.303 and .227 for contingent and hourly fee lawyers, respectively) and complexity (6.065 and 3.885) are larger for contingent fee lawyers.

Further evidence of the structuring effect can be seen in the other variable groups. The participant goal variables are much more important for hourly fee lawyers, both in terms of the number of statistically significant coefficients and the magnitude of the effects of the individual variables. For example, both of the indicators of client goals are significant for hourly fee lawyers, indicating that more time is likely to be spent on a case if the client has goals other than getting the best and/or a fair monetary outcome (effort goes down by 18.381 hours if the goal is get most/pay least and by 20.307 if it is get fair/pay fair); in contrast, only one—get most/pay least—is significant for contingent fee lawyers, and that coefficient is about half the size (−9.234) of the corresponding coefficient for hourly fee lawyers. None of the lawyer goal variables show an

TABLE 8-2. Selected Regression Results for Hourly and Contingent Fee Lawyers

	Contingent		All Hourly	
	b	Standard Error	b	Standard Error
I. Party interaction				
3. Discovery	2.910***	0.874	2.885***	0.817
4. Briefs	4.029*	2.195	8.543***	1.879
II. Case characteristics				
5. Stakes	.303***	0.047	.227***	0.050
6. Complexity	6.065***	1.784	3.885**	1.459
7. Duration	.012*	.005	.013*	0.006
III. Participant characteristics				
8. Individual/organization	−9.292*	4.321	−2.035	3.846
14. Commitment to craft	.096	2.177	6.810**	2.346
IV. Participant goals				
Client goals				
15. Get most/pay least	−9.234*	4.335	−18.381***	3.712
16. Get fair/pay fair	0.887	3.588	−20.307***	4.249
Lawyer goals				
18. Public service	3.089	2.516	−10.957***	2.303
19. Professional visibility	0.686	2.610	6.249***	2.037
V. Processing characteristics				
21. State/federal	0.252	4.248	14.067***	3.401
26. Plan for motions	−11.055	6.665	11.186**	4.033
27. Plan for settlement	−3.400	3.375	−7.267*	3.669
28. Plan for discovery	−1.235	3.477	16.114***	3.320
VI. The lawyer's relationships				
29. Took case because of prior representation	−13.047**	5.104	3.275	3.401
30. Client control and participation	1.635	2.407	−4.897*	2.211
R^2	0.48[a]		0.47[a]	
n	273		374	

[a]Obtained from the regression equation prior to the heteroscedasticity correction.

  *$p < .05$.

  **$p < .01$.

  ***$p < .001$.

influence on the level of effort for contingent fee lawyers, while two (of six) influence the hourly fee lawyer—public service (which *decreases* effort, −10.957) and professional visibility (6.249).

Likewise, none of the processing characteristic variables are significant for contingent fee lawyers, while some (half in this case) are significant for hourly fee lawyers;[15] it is particularly interesting to note that a contingent fee lawyer will spend no more time on a federal case than on a state case once controls have been introduced for other kinds of factors, while a very substantial time gap between federal and state cases—over 14 hours (14.067)—remains for the hourly fee lawyer.[16] Only one participant characteristic affects each group of lawyers, and it is different for each group—type of client for contingent fee lawyers (effort goes down by 9.292 for an individual client as compared to an organizational client[17]) and commitment to craft (6.810) for hourly fee lawyers. Similarly, different relationship variables (to be discussed in more detail in a separate section) affect each of the two lawyer groups.

While it does not relate to evidence concerning the structuring effect of fee arrangement, it is interesting to note that none of the indicators of technical expertise—experience, specialization, litigation proportion, law school performance—appear in Table 8-2. *None* of these variables have any significant effect on the amount of effort expended by either group of lawyers.[18] This may indicate one of two things. First, it may be that the actual variation in these characteristics is so small among these lawyers that there is no room for the variables to account for differences in the level of effort. Alternatively, ordinary litigation may be so routine that the work involved does not draw on these characteristics in any appreciable fashion. The indicators of variation for the individual variables shown in Table 8-1 seem to suggest that the first explanation has less validity than the second, even though the complex construction of indicators such as specialization and law school performance obscures the variation in the constituent variables.

In summary, fee arrangement has a substantial impact on the process by which lawyers allocate time to cases. Contingent fee lawyers seem to be highly sensitive to the potential productivity of their time, and they are less affected by craft-oriented factors. This effect can be seen most clearly in two variables: commitment to craft and response to opposing party's briefs. The contingent fee lawyer does spend time in response to the opposing side's briefs, but that response involves half as much time per brief as the response of hourly fee lawyers. While the hourly fee lawyer is strongly influenced by commitment to craft, the contingent fee lawyer does not seem to be so influenced. On the other hand, the level of effort of contingent fee lawyers goes up at a faster rate as the level of stakes increases than it does for the hourly fee lawyer. The contingent fee lawyer seems sensitive to the potential return to be achieved from a case, which is closely related to the stakes. The hourly fee lawyer's return from a case is not as tied up with the stakes, and other types of considerations (the client's goals, the nature of the forum, etc.) have a greater influence.[19] This broad comparison suggests that the contingent fee lawyer's behavior in terms of the amount of resources put into the case is controlled primarily by the exigencies of the case; those factors also influence the hourly fee lawyer's behavior but are modified in important ways by other considerations. Given that the contingent fee lawyer's return on the investment in a case is directly determined by the case's characteristics and the processing of the case that leads to an eventual outcome, it is not surprising that other factors have relatively little impact.

THE MAGNITUDE HYPOTHESIS

Turning now to the question of whether a contingent fee lawyer will spend less time on a case than will an hourly fee lawyer, all other factors being held constant, the basic answer has to be "Maybe, but it depends." It depends on the nature of the case, the nature of client goals, and all the other variables that I described as influencing the amount of effort a lawyer devotes to handling a case.

The best way to illustrate this is by looking at lawyer behavior under different conditions and seeing whether or not there are significant differences in lawyer effort in these situations. This can be done by using the full regression equations (see Table 8–B1) to estimate the number of hours each type of lawyer would spend in a hypothetical case, where the hypothetical case is defined in terms of a set of values for the variables that influence lawyer effort; an example of one such hypothetical case might be the "average case," where all variables in the predictive equation for lawyer effort take on their mean value. Once a hypothetical case is defined in this way, the number of hours that the *hourly fee* lawyer would spend on that case is estimated by multiplying each of the values that have been assigned to the 31 predictor variables in the equation by the corresponding regression coefficient;the sum[20] of these products yields an estimate of the amount of effort one would expect an hourly fee lawyer to devote to the hypothetical case. The estimate for the *contingent fee* lawyer is obtained in exactly the same way, only substituting the relevant coefficients for the contingent fee lawyer.

For purposes of discussion, I defined three different hypothetical cases.

The "average" case for the contingent fee lawyer (i.e., using the means shown for contingent fee lawyers in Table 8–1).

The "average" case for the hourly fee lawyer (i.e., using the means shown for hourly fee lawyers in Table 8–1).

The "average" case for the two groups of lawyers combined (i.e., using the means for the predictor variables without distinguishing between hourly and contingent fee lawyers[21]).

Table 8–3 shows the "predicted" number of hours for each fee arrangement for each of the three hypothetical cases.[22] What is striking about the table is the general lack of differences. Only for the hypothetical case based on the aver-

TABLE 8–3. Predicted Number of Hours for the "Typical" Case

	Hourly Fee Lawyer	Contingent Fee Lawyer
"Average" hourly fee case	50.6	42.1
"Average" contingent fee case	47.9	50.7
Overall "average" case	49.5	45.7

ages for the hourly fee lawyers is there a substantial difference in the hypothesized direction. When the hypothetical case based on the averages for the contingent fee lawyer is used, the direction of differences reverses, although it is less substantial.[23]

What happens if I take one of these hypothetical cases and systematically vary the level of stakes? Figure 8-1 uses the hypothetical case based on the overall averages as the baseline; the solid line represents the estimated time investment of hourly fee lawyers and the broken line that of contingent fee lawyers. This figure indicates that contingent fee lawyers tend to put in less effort for small cases than do hourly fee lawyers, but they put in more time for big cases. This result makes sense for the economically rational contingent fee lawyer. That lawyer's potential return is closely related to the potential recovery (i.e., stakes) and, if a greater effort with a big case will significantly increase the recovery, the lawyer who is to be paid a percentage of that recovery will want to put in that extra time.

There are, however, problems with this interpretation of the pattern shown in the figure. One is that the apparent differences shown may not be statistically significant. The lines shown in Figure 8-1 are estimates of the average expected time investment for a given level of stakes; since these averages are estimates, they are subject to the normal error associated with any kind of estimate derived from a sample.[24] In order to have some confidence about whether the apparent differences reflect real differences, I performed a series of statistical tests to determine if the means for hourly and contingent fee lawyers differ significantly; separate tests were done setting stakes at $1,000, $2,000, $3,000 and increasing in this way up to $100,000. Only when the stakes were set at $6,000 or less was the difference in effort between hourly and contingent fee lawyers statistically significant; none of the differences where stakes were set to a value of more than $6,000 were significant, or even close to being significant.

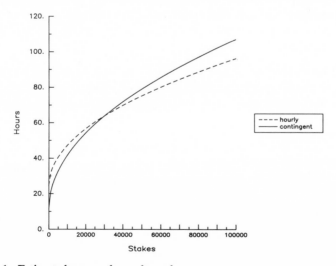

FIGURE 8-1. Estimated average hours by stakes.

This indicates that fee arrangement may actually make a difference in level of effort only in relatively modest cases. At the last point of statistical significance, $6,000, the gap is about 7 hours.[25]

There are two conclusions to be drawn from this limited analysis of the magnitude hypothesis concerning the impact of fee arrangement on lawyer effort. First, while the effect seems to be limited in scope regarding the *kinds* of cases to which it applies, it is not limited with regard to the *number* of cases because most cases, which are in the state courts, involve stakes that fall within the range where an hourly fee lawyer is likely to spend more time than a contingent fee lawyer. The second, closely related conclusion, is that the "effort gap," while measurable, is not large in absolute terms, primarily because small amounts of time tend to be spent on the cases where the differential exists.

While in relative terms the gap is sizable, in absolute terms the difference, 25 hours versus 32 hours for a $6,000 case, is not large. The obvious follow-up question is whether or not this difference in effort makes any difference in outcome. This is a difficult question to answer given that hourly fee lawyers tend to represent defendants while contingent fee lawyers represent plaintiffs and that the notion of success is very different for plaintiffs as compared to defendants. Nonetheless, it is an important question, and I will consider it, along with the complications involved, in Chapter 9.

IMPACT OF THE OTHER RELATIONAL WEB VARIABLES
Clearly, fee arrangement has powerful influences on how lawyers handle the ordinary cases that are brought to them. Interestingly, with one exception, none of the other relational web variables have strong influences on the level of effort that lawyers devote to the cases. Table 8-4 shows the regression coefficients for prior representation (as an indicator of future representation), client control and participation, and expectation of future cases against the current opposing party. As the table shows, none of the hypotheses concerning these variables are strongly supported by the statistical analysis.

TABLE 8-4. Impact of Relational Web on Lawyer Effort

	Contingent		All Hourly	
	b	Standard Error	*b*	Standard Error
Took case because of prior representation	−13.047**	5.104	3.275	3.401
Client control and participation	1.635	2.407	−4.897*	2.211
Expects future cases against opposing party	−.736	3.324	1.235	4.456
n	273		374	

*p<.05.
**p<.01.
***p<.001.

One of the relational variables, expectation of *future cases* against the current opposing party, does not systematically predict the amount of lawyer effort, regardless of the fee arrangement. The other two variables do show some relationship with lawyer effort, one for the hourly fee lawyer only and one for the contingent fee lawyer only. As hypothesized, the effort of the hourly fee lawyer is inversely related to the degree of *client control* (effort goes down as client control goes up); there is no support for the hypothesis that the reverse is true for the contingent fee lawyer. In some ways this is not surprising, considering that the contingent fee lawyer's direct stake in the outcome should lead the lawyer to resist efforts at control by the client.

The role of *prior representation* in the decision of the lawyer to take the case (which I have suggested can be thought of as an indicator of the likely influence of a concern about future representation) is strongly negative for the contingent fee lawyer and nonsignificant for the hourly fee lawyer. The hypothesis concerning this variable for the contingent fee lawyer was that it should increase, not decrease, lawyer effort. In fact, the regression coefficient (-13.047) indicates that if a contingent fee lawyer takes a case in whole or in part because of prior representation, the lawyer will, on average, decrease the amount of effort devoted to the case by 13 hours.[26] One interpretation of this apparent reversal is that in some situations a lawyer may agree to take a contingent fee case for an existing client even if it is a case that the lawyer would normally decline;[27] if this is true,[28] and if the reason the lawyer would not have normally taken the case is a recognition that the case is not likely to return a reasonable fee, then it makes sense that the lawyer would try to minimize the amount of time devoted to the case.[29]

As for the lack of influence of past representation on the level of effort by hourly fee lawyers, the available information does not allow for anything more than speculation. It may be that the potential conflict between the desire to impress the client by doing a particularly good job on a case and the need to impress the client by keeping the cost of representation as reasonable as possible cancels any systematic effect of prior representation on lawyer effort. Given that the cases are relatively small and that most hourly fee clients are organizations, the lawyer may perceive little room to maneuver in making a decision to put in more time.

Relationships and the Content of the Lawyer's Work
In Ordinary Litigation

The impact of the lawyer's web of relationships, particularly the fee-paying aspects of the lawyer–client relationship, on the amount of effort lawyers devote to ordinary cases is clear from the preceding analysis. That leads to the second question about the connection between the lawyer's work and the lawyer's relationships: Do those relationships affect the content of the lawyer's work in handling a civil case in any systematic fashion? The analysis in Chapter 7 showed that work content was very strongly influenced by case characteristics, particularly area of law; there was also some link between the work content and the forum, with there being a slightly higher formal legal component for cases in federal court than in state court (even after controlling for area of law).

Because of the existence of these influences, they must be taken into account in considering connections between the lawyer's relationships and work content. As with the amount of lawyer effort, multiple regression is the natural statistical tool for carrying out this analysis. The following set of variables were regressed against the indicators of the content of the lawyer's work.

Area of law.[30]

Court.

Logarithm of stakes.[31]

Complexity.

Fee arrangement.[32]

Client control and participation.

Expectation of future cases against the opposing party.

Past representation of client as a factor in accepting the case.

The regression model used here is less well developed theoretically than that used in the previous section; nonetheless, it is unlikely that there are any omitted variables whose inclusion would significantly alter the results with regard to the relational web variables of primary interest here.[33]

Results

What is most striking about the results of these regression analyses is the general lack of connection between the relational web variables and work content. The few relationships that do appear are small in comparison to those between content and case characteristics (particularly area of law).[34]

Fee arrangement. Nonhourly fee lawyers tended to spend a slightly higher proportion (a .02 to .05 increase, depending on the specific arrangement) of their time conferring with their clients, but this shift was not drawn clearly from any of the other specific task areas.

Client control and participation. There was a small positive relationship between this variable and proportion of time on discovery, and a slight negative relationship between this indicator and proportion of time on factual investigation other than discovery. If anything, this is the reverse of what one would probably hypothesize given complaints about the high cost of discovery, and the need to exercise control over lawyers to insure that they do not overdo it when it comes to engaging in discovery activities (one might expect this kind of control to be implicit, showing up as a connection between prior representation and the proportion of time on discovery, but no such connection appears). In contrast to this reversed relationship with discovery, the proportion of time on trial and hearings goes down with increases in client control and participation; while this makes sense in that it might reflect a greater client involvement in efforts to settle the case without the expense of hearings and trial, there is no commensurate increase in the proportion of the lawyer's time devoted to settlement discussions.

Prior representation. The only relationship with any of the indicators of work content for this variable is with the proportion of time spent on pleadings and motions; this proportion is higher if the lawyer took the current case because of prior representation.

Expectation of future cases with the current opposing party. This has minor relationships with proportion of effort on discovery (a negative coefficient of about −.02) and with proportion of time on the summary category of formal legal activities (a positive coefficient of .03).

Thus, overall the results of this analysis indicate that the web of relationships within which lawyers carry out their work in ordinary litigation does not greatly influence the content of that work, *at least as measured by the indicators just used*.

While relationships do not seem to control the allocation of time to the kinds of categories that make up what I have described as comprising formal legal and informal legal activities, there is another level at which the lawyer's web of relationships might influence the content of litigation work. Specifically, relationships might affect the details of the content of the various general types of activities.

- The kind of discussions that take place with the client.
- What actually goes on in settlement negotiations with the opposing party.
- The way that factual investigation, both through discovery and otherwise, is carried out.

Unfortunately, I have virtually no specific information on work content at this degree of specificity; however, that which I do have suggests strongly the ways in which relationships can influence specific content.

Fee Arrangement and Negotiation[35]

The subject of negotiation, and the skills that can lead to satisfactory results through negotiation, has been a popular one in recent years, resulting in important writing dealing with negotiation in general (e.g., Fisher and Ury, 1981; Raiffa, 1983; see also the relatively new *Negotiation Journal*) and with negotiation in a specifically legal context (e.g., Williams, 1983; Menkel-Meadow, 1984). However, when one starts to consider the applicability of much of this writing to ordinary litigation, one is struck by the failure to take into account the fact that some lawyers work on litigation on an hourly fee basis while others work on a contingent fee basis. The point of this section is that the contingency arrangement has very important implications for the substance of the negotiation in which lawyers in civil cases engage. Specifically, given that contingent fee lawyers receive a share of the ultimate recovery, they have an incentive to see to it that recovery is, in fact, shareable.

The importance of this point is clearest when one considers the argument that lawyers should move away from "adversary" (also called "zero sum" or "distributive") bargaining toward a "problem-solving" (also called "positive sum" or "integrative") mode of negotiation. While there are strong normative reasons for accepting the value of this position, it presents some real difficulties when applied to the contingent fee lawyer. Let me illustrate this by drawing on an example used by Menkel-Meadow (1984: 772).

> Ms. Brown buys a car from Mr. Snead, a used car salesman. After a short time the car ceases to function, despite repeated attempts by Ms. Brown to have the car repaired. Ms. Brown, therefore, sues Mr. Snead for rescission of the sales contract, claiming misrepresentation in the sale of the car, or, in the alternative, breach of warranty, with consequential damages, including lost income from the loss of a job due to repeated latenesses and absences as a result of the malfunctioning car. Mr. Snead counterclaims for the balance due on the car [plus attorneys fees as permitted under the sales contract], claiming that the warranty period has ended and the dealership was given insufficient time in which to cure any possible defects.

As Menkel-Meadow points out, while the lawsuit is over money, the parties both really want something more than simple dollars and cents (even though the concerns can be monetized relatively easily). Ms. Brown wants a reliable form of transportation (and her job); Mr. Snead wants both to retain his profit on this sale and for Ms. Brown (and her friends) to buy cars from him in the future.

One can easily imagine an outcome where both parties go away fairly happy, and that differs from what can be obtained through the typical damages-oriented lawsuit.

> Mr. Snead provides Ms. Brown with another car from his (large) inventory, and gives her an extended warranty on that car to compensate her for her difficulties; he can then proceed to repair the car originally sold to Ms. Brown and sell it to another customer (at least one would hope he would repair it before putting it back on his lot).

However, if Ms. Brown hires a lawyer on a contingency fee basis, this kind of creative solution is no longer viable. Even if the lawyer considers the preceding scenario, or other ways of resolving the case without a direct exchange of money, the lawyer has to make a living from the practice of law;[36] Ms. Brown does not have the funds to pay the lawyer on an hourly basis, and there is no way that the lawyer can take one third of a car. A contingent fee lawyer who sought nonmonetary resolutions for clients, even if those resolutions were better from the clients' perspective, would soon go out of business unless there were some alternate payment method available for such settlements.[37]

What happens in actual cases? Are contingent fee lawyers more oriented to money in what they seek in negotiation than are hourly fee lawyers or lawyers paid on some other basis (flat fees, legal aid, salaried employees, etc.)? The survey of lawyers included information on up to three offers or demands. Using only the data on what the respondent offered or demanded (i.e., ignoring the offers or demands of the opposing party), I classified the content of negotiation as monetary (when the demand was for a specific or nonspecific sum of money), nonmonetary (when the demand or offer was for something that was not explicitly monetary), and mixed (when there was a combination of monetary and nonmonetary demands or offers). This latter category includes situations where an individual demand or offer contained both monetary and nonmonetary elements and situations where the demands or offers changed in nature from one exchange to another.

Table 8–5a shows a tabulation of the content of the negotiation from the respondent's side and the way in which the respondent was to be paid. The table shows clearly the overriding importance of money in the demands of the contingent fee lawyer: only 3 percent of the contingent fee lawyers reported making demands that contained no monetary element compared to 19 percent for the hourly fee lawyers' demands and offers; 77 percent of the contingent fee lawyers' demands were entirely monetary compared to 51 percent for the hourly fee lawyer. There is an element of self-fulfilling prophecy here, since it is no doubt true that contingent fee lawyers will normally turn down cases that are not amenable to a monetary recovery; such cases will have to be handled by a lawyer being paid on some other basis. Still, when one looks at Table 8–5b, which shows only the cases in which the lawyer–respondent was able to express stakes in clearly monetary terms, the basic relationship is still present, although somewhat muted because the negotiations of the lawyers paid on other than a contingency basis are more monetary in orientation.

TABLE 8–5. Negotiation Content by Fee Arrangement

(a) All Respondents

	Monetary	Nonmonetary	Mixed	*n*
Hourly	51%	19%	29%	547
Contingent	77%	3%	20%	349
Other	44%	28%	28%	109

Chi square=90.55; $p<.001$.

(b) Only Respondents Who Monetized Stakes

	Monetary	Nonmonetary	Mixed	*n*
Hourly	63%	5%	32%	370
Contingent	78%	1%	21%	300
Other	62%	8%	30%	60

Chi square=27.04; $p<.001$.

Discussion

In this chapter I have considered the connection between the web of relationships in which a lawyer handles civil cases and the actual work those cases
involve. The analysis reveals very clear and strong influences of the "business"
connections (i.e., the nature of the fee arrangement) tying lawyer and client
together on the amount of effort that lawyers put into their work in ordinary
civil litigation. In particular, the kinds of factors influencing lawyers' effort
allocation decisions depend on how the lawyer is being paid, and even the
actual amount of effort seems to be affected by the fee arrangement (although
this is a function of how the other factors combine in the allocation process).
There is also some evidence, albeit much weaker, that the content of the lawyers' efforts depends in some ways on the business relationship, particularly as
that relationship creates a specific self-interest for the lawyer.

   There is only weak evidence linking the other aspects of the lawyers' relationships to the quantity and content of the work carried out in handling civil
cases, but the specific presence and absence of relationships is interesting, given
the tension between the lawyer as professional and the lawyer as broker. For
example, client control does seem to work in the expected direction for hourly
fee lawyers, but it has no apparent effect for contingent fee lawyers. The client
control arguments derive from a prescriptive literature about how litigants
should interact with their lawyers, and it is not surprising that the more sophisticated clients (generally repeat player organizations) of hourly fee lawyers are
more responsive to those prescriptions than are the usually naive individual
clients of the contingent fee lawyer. Furthermore, while hourly fee lawyers
often depend on repeat work from their organizational clients, contingent fee
lawyers have no such direct dependence on one-shot individual clients. One
implication is that the hourly fee lawyers may see it as in their long-term
interest to defer to the clients' control, even if that reduces the fees that might
be obtained for particular cases; on the other hand, contingent fee lawyers
need not be as sensitive to such demands by clients who are "here today and
gone tomorrow," particularly if the demands run strongly counter to the lawyers' interests.

   The professionalism image of lawyers and their work does not lead one to
expect there to be any of the kinds of linkages discussed in this chapter, and the
extant discussions of the impact of relationships on lawyers' work is often cast
as raising serious "professional" and ethical problems. This is most clear in the
literature on contingency fees (e.g., Clermont and Currivan, 1978; Rosenthal,
1974).[38] On the other hand, the broker image suggests that relationships are
important in understanding the work lawyers do. While one expects a broker to
behave "professionally" (in the sense of adhering to some basic norms of
honesty and openness with clients), one also expects brokers to rely on and be
influenced by their relationships. Brokers are recognized as being in a "business" that is governed heavily by the fee-paying (or commission-paying) relationship. One would immediately expect that the way brokers are to be paid

would influence how they carry out the tasks they had been hired to perform. Moreover, one would certainly expect that brokers would draw on and be influenced by the standing relationships they have with the other players in whatever system one was dealing with.

The impacts of the fee-paying aspects of the lawyer–client relationship that have been described in the preceding pages is difficult to reconcile with the professionalism image of the lawyer. It is, on the other hand, to be expected in the context of the broker image that considerations influencing how much time hourly and contingent fee lawyers devote to cases are different; in fact, it is probably somewhat surprising that this same kind of differential pattern did not carry over to the categories of work content discussed before (although that lack of impact may be more apparent than real given the very general nature of the categories that were used[39]).

APPENDIX 8A

Description of Variables

Thirty-one predictor variables were used in the regression on hours worked. This appendix provides more details on how those variables were operationalized.

(1) Opposing Party's Pleadings, (2) Motions, (3) Discovery, and (4) Briefs

The party interaction variables presume that one important determinant of lawyer effort is the need to respond to actions initiated by the other side. To this end, the model includes counts of the number of (1) pleadings, (2) motions, (3) discovery events, and (4) briefs filed by the opposing party.[40] These variables were the simple counts of the number of docket entries in each category initiated by the opposing party. Discovery motions were counted in the discovery category rather than in the motions category.

(5) Stakes

Stakes were measured as the amount that the lawyer felt that the client should take or pay to settle the case; if several estimates were given, the largest value was used in the regression analysis. Probes were used to try to get nonmonetary components expressed in terms of money and, where this was not successful, the respondent was omitted from the analysis. Where the response included a periodic payment, that payment was converted to a single sum by figuring the present value of those payments streams using the average prime interest in 1978 (9.06 percent) as a discount factor and establishing duration based on case type. Case types were determined by visual inspection of the court record coding form. Duration was then figured as shown in Table 8A–1.

(6) Complexity

This was the lawyer's subjective estimate of the complexity of the case as measured by the response to the question: "On a scale of 1 to 5, if 1 is simple and 5 is very complex, how would you rate this case as to its complexity of fact and law?"

TABLE 8A-1. Durations Used for Recurring Payments

Type of Case	Assumed Duration
Divorce, with child support	9 years (median of 0–18)
Divorce, without child support	2 years
Social Security, retirement, or black lung benefits	Life expectancy (according to sex) at age 65
Disability payments	Life expectancy (according to sex) at actual age, or if age unknown, at 43 (median of 21–65)
Mortgage payments	10 years (median of 0–20)
Consumer credit	2 years
Unemployment benefits	1 year
Tenant debt	2 years

(7) Duration

The variable is the time, in days, from filing to termination. The filing date was taken from the court record and the termination date was taken from either the court record or the survey, whichever date was earlier (lawyers often neglect to inform the court of a termination).

(8) Type of Client

This dichotomous variable was obtained from the court record and was coded 1 for individuals (73 percent) and 0 for organizations, including governmental organizations (27 percent). It is subject to some error in the case of individual defendants because outside of Wisconsin courts, none of the courts in the study explicitly named the defendant's insurer as a defendant of record. The literature suggests that organizations should be willing to invest more in litigation than individuals (see Galanter, 1974).

(9) Specialization, (10) Law School Performance,
(11) Years of Practice, (12) Litigation Proportion,
(13) Personal Capacity, and (14) Commitment to Craft

The lawyer characteristics included in the model are (9) specialization (i.e., does the case fall within the lawyer's self-defined area of specialization?), (10) law school performance as reported by the lawyer, (11) the number of years of law practice (as reported by the lawyer), (12) the proportion of time devoted to litigation (the lawyer's estimate of the proportion of time spent practicing law that was devoted to court cases), (13) personal efficacy as measured by a standard scale, and (14) commitment to craft as indicated by the likelihood, as reported by the lawyer, that extra time would be spent making marginal improvements on legal documents. Obviously, the last of these would tend to be associated with increased lawyer effort; notions of efficiency would lend one to expect that the other five lawyer characteristics would be inversely related to effort (i.e., a better, more experienced, more confident lawyer would be able to process cases more efficiently using less effort).

Three of these variables are scales created from a factor analysis of a set of nine items obtained from the lawyer survey.

PERCAP1. How likely are you to feel sure of yourself even when people disagree with you — very likely, somewhat likely, not too likely?

PERCAP2. How often do you have trouble making up your mind about important decisions — very often, somewhat often, occasionally, or hardly ever?

PERCAP3. How sure do you feel that your life will work out the way you want it to — very sure, somewhat sure, not too sure, or not sure at all?

LAWEXP. Whether or not the respondent reported serving on the law review while a law student (0 no, 1 yes, 2 officer of the review).

RANK. The respondent's rank in law school class as reported by the respondent.

LNND. The natural logarithm of the number of disputes in the field of law of the case that the lawyer had handled previously.

PERFIELD. The percentage of the respondent's practice in the field of law the case is in.

SELFRANK. The lawyer's self-ranking of substantive expertise in the area of law the case is in.

ACTS. A scale based on which of the following activities the lawyer had done with regard to the area of law in which the case fell: (1) taken a course, (2) taught a course or workshop or given a lecture, (3) written or edited book(s) and/or article(s), (4) served on bar association committees concerned with the area of law; and (5) served on government commissions concerned with the area of law. If the lawyer had done none of these, the item was scored 0, if the lawyer had done activity 1, 4, or 5, it was scored 1; if the lawyer had done activity 2 or 3, the item was scored 2.

The results of the factor analysis are shown in Table 8A–2.

(15) Get Most/Pay Least and (16) Get Fair/Pay Fair

The lawyers were asked to describe their clients' goals apart from a more specific statement of stakes (and thus these goals might be seen as modifying the stakes in some sense). Some of the lawyers described their clients as wanting to (15) get the most (or pay the least) they could; some described their client's desires in terms of (16) getting or paying what was fair; those who mentioned neither goal were presumed to have con-

TABLE 8A–2. Factor Analysis of Lawyer Characteristics Variables

	Specialization	Law School Performance	Personal Capacity
PERCAP1	−.10	−.04	.47
PERCAP2	−.02	.04	.50
PERCAP3	−.01	.04	.41
LAWEXP	.02	.57	.08
RANK	.04	.56	−.04
LNND	.71	−.06	−.07
PERFIELD	.78	−.01	.01
SELFRANK	.71	.07	−.14
ACTS	.37	.08	−.03

cerns over and above the monetary stakes. For analysis, both variables were treated as dichotomies, even though they are not necessarily exclusive (2 percent mentioned both "most/least" and "fair"). The first dichotomy was coded 1 if the maximize/minimize goal was mentioned, and 0 otherwise; the second was coded 1 if "fair" was mentioned and 0 otherwise.

(17) Challenge, (18) Public Service, (19) Professional Visibility, and (20) Make Money

The lawyer's own goals were measured in terms of the reasons for taking the case (other than simply to service an existing client). Four specific indicators were used in the regression analysis.

(17) Challenge. Did the case present a professional challenge? Was it intellectually interesting?

(18) Public service. Did it provide an opportunity for service to the public? Was it taken out of sympathy for the client?

(19) Professional visibility. Would the case increase the attorney's community standing, improve the attorney's position in the firm, and/or create publicity for the lawyer or the firm?

(20) Making money. Was the case taken primarily for the amount of money the lawyer would earn?

The indicators were derived from a factor analysis of 10 items that measured the importance of specific considerations in the lawyer's decision to take the cases. The lawyer was asked to rate each of the following items on a three-point scale (very important, important, not important).

- Community standing.
- Forming a new relationship with a promising new client.
- The intellectual interest of the case.
- Sympathy for the client's predicament.
- The challenge involved.
- The amount of money to be made on the case.
- Standing in the firm/office.
- Public service.
- Opportunity for experience in a new field of law.
- Obtaining publicity for the firm/office.

A factor score was created for each of the dimensions reflected in the factor loading shown in Table 8A-3. The scores were constructed so that a high value indicated that the dimension was important in the lawyer's decision.

(21) Court, (22) Settlement, and (23) Trial

Processing characteristics included a variety of variables relating to decisions made about how to handle the case. The analysis in Chapter 7 showed that the choice of (21) court (coded 1 for cases from the federal court and 0 for cases from the state court) has a substantial influence on the amount of lawyer effort. The decision whether to engage in (22) settlement discussions (coded 1 if the lawyer reported that settlement discussions with the opposing party had taken place and 0 otherwise) and whether to take the case

TABLE 8A-3. Factor Analysis of Lawyer Goals

	Challenge	Public Service	Professional Visibility	Making Money
Community standing	.20	.07	.61	−.03
Forming a new relationship	.02	−.15	.23	−.18
Intellectual interest	.79	.16	.15	−.03
Sympathy for client	.31	.59	−.08	−.03
Challenge involved	.73	.27	.19	.04
Amount of money expected	.07	−.12	.13	.62
Standing in firm/office	.11	−.02	.47	.10
Public service	.16	.65	.16	−.09
Experience in new field	.42	.09	.21	.11
Publicity for firm/office	.07	.07	.33	.07

to (23) trial (coded 1 if the court record indicated that a trial had occurred whether or not the trial had been completed and 0 otherwise) also may have an impact on lawyer effort.

(24) Pretrial Events SOP and (25) Estimating Case Value SOP

One thing that lawyers might do to manage a case that might influence their level of effort level would be to use standard operating procedures (SOPs) for things such as (24) estimating case value or for (25) pretrial activity (pleadings, motions, and/or discovery); using such SOPs could make it possible for a lawyer to get those parts of the work done in less time. To measure the impact of SOPs on lawyer effort, two factor scores based on a principal-components analysis were constructed. Lawyers were asked whether they had, and used, SOPs for estimating the value of a case or whether they used preprinted forms for pleadings, motions, and/or discovery. An indicator was created for each of the activities, coded in the following way.

  −1 Has a standard procedure or preprinted form and used it.

   0 Did not have a standard procedure or use preprinted forms.

  +1 Had a standard procedure or preprinted form but had to deviate from it in this case.

Lawyers were not asked about deviations from SOPs for individual activities; thus a lawyer who reported SOPs for two activities and then indicated having to deviate from SOPs was coded as 1 on both activities for which SOPs were reported. The coding of individual items reflected the presumption that if one took a no SOP situation as a baseline, having and using SOPs would reduce the amount of time spent while having and not using SOPs would actually increase the amount of time spent. The conversion to factor scores was necessitated by the high level of multicollinearity among the individual items; the results of the principal components analysis are shown in Table 8A-4.

(26) Plans for Motions, (27) Settlement, and (28) Discovery

Another thing that lawyers might do that might speed their work (and thus reduce their level of effort) would be to develop and use explicit plans for (26) motions, (27) settle-

TABLE 8A–4. Principal Components Analysis of
Standard Operating Procedures (SOPs)

SOPs for	Pretrial Events SOP	Estimating Case Value SOP
Estimating case value	.31	.95
Pleadings	.88	.29
Motions	.89	.24
Discovery	.85	.36

ment negotiations, and/or (28) discovery. Lawyers were asked whether they had and used a plan for each of these three activities. The indicators were coded 1 if the lawyers had used a plan for the respective activity; otherwise, the indicator was coded 0.

(29) Prior Representation as a Consideration in Taking the Current Case

The item was coded 1 if the lawyer took the current case because of prior representation of the client.

(30) Client Control and Participation

This is a single factor score based on the following variables from the lawyer interviews (the number in parentheses following each item is the factor loading for the variable).

Client involvement in determining case strategy (.70).

Presence of an understanding about the client's role in decision making about the case (.28).

Actual role client played in decision making about the case (.61).

Nature of reports to the client by the lawyer (.36).

Client participation in the decision to file (.22).

The scale is scored so that high values indicate a high level of client participation and control.

(31) Future Cases Against Current Opposing Party

This variable was coded 1 if the lawyer responded affirmatively to the question "Do you expect that you will ever oppose this party in the future?"; otherwise, it was coded 0.

APPENDIX 8B

Regression Results for Hourly and Contingent Fee Lawyers

TABLE 8B-1. Regression Results for Hourly and Contingent Fee Lawyers

	Contingent		Hourly	
	b	Standard Error	*b*	Standard Error
I. Party interaction				
1. Pleadings	−1.998	1.446	−3.254	1.743
2. Motions	0.030	1.742	−.968	1.740
3. Discovery	2.910***	0.874	2.885***	0.817
4. Briefs	4.029*	2.195	8.543***	1.879
II. Case characteristics				
5. Stakes	.303***	0.047	.227***	0.050
6. Complexity	6.065***	1.784	3.885**	1.459
7. Duration	.012*	.005	.013*	0.006
III. Participant characteristics				
8. Individual/organization	−9.292*	4.321	−2.035	3.846
9. Specialization	2.493	2.136	1.762	1.826
10. Law school performance	2.696	2.771	3.526	2.121
11. Years of practice	−.043	0.181	−.008	0.179
12. Litigation proportion	−.036	0.068	.031	0.062
13. Personal capacity	1.152	2.351	− 1.215	2.388
14. Commitment to craft	.096	2.177	6.810**	2.346
IV. Participant goals				
Client goals				
15. Get most/pay least	−9.234*	4.335	−18.381***	3.712
16. Get fair/pay fair	0.887	3.588	−20.307***	4.249
Lawyer goals				
17. Challenge	2.485	2.075	1.017	1.884
18. Public service	3.089	2.516	−10.957***	2.303
19. Professional visibility	0.686	2.610	6.249***	2.037
20. Make money	3.157	2.466	1.893	2.661
V. Processing characteristics				
21. State/federal	0.252	4.248	14.067***	3.401
22. Trial	0.209	6.604	4.624	5.704
23. Settlement discussions	11.087	6.085	3.366	5.930
24. Pretrial events SOP	0.816	1.765	2.571	1.518
25. Estimating case value SOP	0.930	1.551	1.377	1.587
26. Plan for motions	−11.055	6.665	11.186**	4.033
27. Plan for settlement	−3.400	3.375	−7.267*	3.669
28. Plan for discovery	−1.235	3.477	16.114***	3.320

(continued)

TABLE 8B–1. *Continued*

	Contingent		Hourly	
	b	Standard Error	b	Standard Error
VI. Lawyer's relationships				
29. Took case because of prior representation	−13.047**	5.104	3.275	3.401
30. Client control and participation	1.635	2.407	−4.897*	2.211
31. Expects future cases against opposing party	−.736	3.324	1.235	4.456
Constant	−3.566		−20.496	
R^2	0.48[a]		0.47[a]	
n	273		374	

[a]Obtained from the regression equation prior to the heteroscedasticity correction.

  *$p < .05$.

 **$p < .01$.

***$p < .001$.

9

Winning and Losing in Litigation: Does the Lawyer Deliver?

In one of the first systematic efforts to understand the outcomes of litigation, Galanter (1974) examined the question of "Why the Haves Come Out Ahead." Galanter was responding to an analysis that defined the "winner" in a given case as simply the party that "prevailed" at judgment time.[1] Unfortunately, as I will detail in this chapter, that simple definition misses much of what results from litigation. Since most litigation does not terminate through a judgment in favor of one side or the other, outcomes achieved through settlement, as well as outcomes that *might have been* achieved by settlement, must be taken into account to arrive at an understanding of who ultimately wins and loses from litigation. Once results achieved through settlement are included in the picture, the idea of what constitutes a "favorable" outcome takes on different meanings for each of the *three* litigation players with a clear stake in that outcome.

There are two points in this last statement. First, not only do the litigants themselves (i.e., the plaintiff and the defendant) have a direct interest in the outcome of the case, but there is often a contingent fee lawyer who has a direct financial concern in the result as well. Second, there are many cases in which both sides of a dispute might view an outcome as favorable; it is also possible for both parties to be very dissatisfied with the outcome and to think of themselves as losers. In this sense, it may not be correct to think of litigation as a zero sum game, whereby whatever one side gets, the other side by definition must give up. This reflects ambiguity in what is at stake in a case in the civil justice system: if defendants think that they have more to lose than plaintiffs think they have to win, then it is very easy for both sides to see themselves as "winners," particularly if the defendant concedes liability.[2]

This discussion provides a brief summary of the issues I will confront in more detail now. In the next section, I present a preliminary discussion regarding case *outcomes*, which refers to what ultimately changes hands without regard to the perceived stakes. I will use several different measures of *relative outcomes* (outcomes relative to some base) to consider first the contingent fee lawyer followed by the defendant and the plaintiff. This ordering reflects the complexity of defining good outcomes (i.e., of identifying an appropriate base of comparison) for each of the players: it is most straightforward for the lawyer and most ambiguous for the plaintiff.

Outcomes

It should not be surprising that the outcome in the typical, everyday court case is modest; given the modest nature of the stakes, it would be difficult for the outcomes to differ markedly. The first three columns of Table 9-1 provide a basic description of the outcomes in the cases in the sample, both for all cases and for federal and state cases separately. Note that the cases represented in the table are only those for which the outcome was monetary in nature; interviewers did not attempt to have the respondents monetize the nonmonetary aspects of settlements and judgments, and thus cases where the outcomes were wholly or partially nonmonetary were not used in the analysis.

The median outcome (recovery for plaintiffs or payment for defendants) was only $3,500 in state court cases and $6,500 in federal court cases. Both figures are lower than the typical stakes figures reported in Chapter 3, where the medians were $4,500 and $15,000 for the state and federal courts, respectively. The figures for the federal courts are particularly interesting for two reasons. First, the typical recovery falls below the jurisdictional minimum ($10,000 in the 1970s) for diversity of citizenship cases, which comprise 57 percent of the cases in this sample; if one looks only at the outcomes for diversity cases, the median rises to $13,072, but 43 percent of these cases still fall under the $10,000 boundary.[3] Second, the aggregate stakes to outcome ratio is much lower for federal courts (6500/15000=.43) than for state courts (3500/4500=.78). This difference might reflect a variety of factors, although the most obvious is that those with modest expectations do better than those

TABLE 9-1. Adjusted and Unadjusted Case Outcomes by Court

Amount	Unadjusted Outcomes Percent of Cases			Adjusted Outcomes Percent of Cases		
	All	State	Federal	All	State	Federal
Less than $0[a]	—	—	—	6	5	7
$0–2,500	38	41	35	26	64	19
$2,501–5,000	17	23	10	18	23	12
$5,001–10,000	13	16	12	17	19	16
$10,001–25,000	18	15	21	17	14	21
$25,001–50,000	6	5	8	8	4	11
$50,001 and up	8	1	13	8	1	14
Median	$4,289	$3,500	$6,500	$5,069	$3,081	$8,946
n	767	372	395	676	333	343

[a] These are plaintiffs only (who paid out more in legal fees than they recovered).

who think there is a "large" amount at stake. In fact, this is the case: the aggregate outcome to stakes ratios for cases involving $10,000 or less are .75 and .83 for federal and state cases, respectively, compared to .68 and .62 for cases involving more than $10,000.

The initial figures in Table 9–1 are misleading in one regard: they represent the gross recovery. That is, the figures in the table ignore the costs of litigation. It might be more helpful to look at the outcomes adjusted for the major transaction cost: fees and expenses[4] paid to the lawyer. For plaintiffs the adjusted outcome would be the net amount recovered after paying the costs associated with the litigation; I will use as an estimate of this figure the gross recovery *minus* the amount paid to the lawyer. For defendants, the adjusted outcome would be the total outlay including both the amount paid to the plaintiff and the costs associated with getting to the point where that payment is made; my estimate of this figure will be the gross recovery *plus* the lawyer's fee.[5]

The last three columns of Table 9–1 present the adjusted outcome figures. These figures do not differ sharply from the unadjusted outcomes: they are still modest and are substantially below the original stakes figures (at least in the aggregate). Perhaps the most interesting additional item of information in the table is the top row, which shows the percentage of plaintiffs who suffered a net loss (i.e., paid more in lawyer fees than they were able to recover). When the "profit/loss" information is broken down by fee arrangement, one finds that 22 percent of the plaintiffs with lawyers retained on an hourly fee basis suffered a net loss (i.e., paid more in fees than they recovered); interestingly, this was also true of 7 percent of the plaintiffs who retained their lawyer on a contingency basis. Thus it is clear that litigation can be a losing proposition, even when the supposedly "safe" mechanism of contingency fees is used.[6]

I could proceed to delineate patterns of outcomes by the same types of variables as I looked at in Chapter 3 as part of the discussion of stakes. This would add little to the understanding of outcomes because those variations would, by necessity, closely parallel the variations for stakes. One can get a sense of this by simply looking at the relationship between stakes and outcomes. The simple correlations between stakes and unadjusted outcome is .91 (.89 for adjusted outcome); not surprisingly, if we know the general level of stakes, we can pretty accurately predict the level of the outcome.[7]

Success from the Lawyer's Point of View

One of the implications of the magnitude effect (i.e., that a contingent fee lawyer may put in less work in modest cases than an hourly fee lawyer would in the same situation) discussed in Chapter 8 is that there may be conflicts of interest between contingent fee lawyers and their clients, particularly in the relatively modest cases that constitute the core of ordinary litigation.[8] Because of this, it is not possible to evaluate the outcome of a case from the lawyer's viewpoint by simply looking at the result from the perspective of the client.[9]

From the lawyer's viewpoint, it may be advantageous to settle for a relatively small proportion of the potential recovery if that settlement can be achieved quickly and with relatively little time investment; the best outcome (most successful) from the client's perspective may require much more of the lawyer's time while increasing the fee in an amount that is not proportional to that time increment. For example, in a $5,000 case with a 33 percent contingent fee, it might be possible for the lawyer to obtain a settlement of $1,200 with 2 hours of work; this would yield a fee of $400, or $200 per hour. With an investment of 10 hours, the lawyer might be able to achieve a settlement of $2,400; this would mean a fee of $800, or $80 per hour. Going to trial to get the full $5,000 might take another 20 hours (for a total of 30 hours of lawyer time); this would mean a fee of $1,667, which works out to only $56 per hour. From the lawyer's viewpoint, the most successful outcome would be the first (presuming that other work is available that will yield at least $80 per hour), even though that is not the best for the client. While this example is simplistic—it ignores the nonmonetary aspects of success for the lawyer (implications for professional reputation, professional obligations to the client, etc.)—it illustrates how success for the contingent fee lawyer can be examined apart from success for the litigant.

The preceding discussion also suggests a useful indicator of success from the perspective of the contingent fee lawyer: effective hourly rate (fee[10] received divided by hours spent on the case). Because the commodity that lawyers are selling is time (and the expertise that time represents) and because that commodity is limited in quantity for the individual lawyer,[11] the more that lawyers can get for their time, the more successful they are in dollar terms. Moreover, lawyers who are motivated solely by economic rationality would seek to devote their time to activities that paid at the highest rate. Thus, effective hourly rate is an excellent indicator of success for lawyers who are paid a percentage of recovery.

Results

Table 9–2 summarizes information about success for contingent fee lawyers. The overall median effective hourly rate for contingent fee lawyers is $42; this is somewhat lower than the median hourly rate for hourly fee lawyers, which is $50 but, as I will show, that apparent gap disappears for the most traditional areas of torts and contracts.[12] Thus, in an overall sense, contingent fee lawyers do not do better than they would do charging on an hourly fee basis, at least in ordinary litigation. As one would expect, there is substantial variation in the level of success achieved: 19 percent of the lawyers receive no payment for their services, 25 percent receive $7 per hour or less, 25 percent receive $94 or more, and 10 percent receive $198 or more per hour. Much of the criticism of contingent fees (Burger, 1984; Grady, 1976) is directed at fees that are perceived as being excessive in relationship to the amount of time devoted to the case. Exactly what constitutes an "excessive" fee, once translated into hourly terms, has never been dealt with explicitly.[13] The figures in Table 9–2 suggest that,

TABLE 9-2. Effective Hourly Rates for Contingent Fee Lawyers

Group	Median	First Quartile	Second Quartile	Ninetieth Percentile	No Fee	*n*
All cases	$42	$7[a]	$94	$198	19%	349
By stakes						
<$10,000	$36	$12	$70	$155	14%	129
$10,000–50,000	$57	$10	$105	$220	18%	120
>$50,000	$58	$19	$160	$270	18%	33
By court						
Federal	$40	$0	$92	$182	26%	167
State	$43	$16	$95	$200	13%	182
By area of law						
Torts						
All	$49	$14	$101	$209	17%	232
Federal	$56	$0	$104	$250	26%	90
State	$44	$19	$100	$200	12%	142
Contracts						
All	$47	$19	$117	$205	17%	71
Federal	$56	$37	$138	$205	14%	35
State	$45	$4	$94	$205	19%	36
Neither torts nor contracts						
All	$6	$0	$45	$71	38%	50
Federal	$5	$0	$41	$75	42%	40
State	$25	–[b]	–	–	20%	10

[a] The first quartile for all cases is less than that for all categories broken down by stakes because of missing data concerning stakes.

[b] Insufficient number of cases to compute a meaningful statistic.

while there may be fees that are excessive, they constitute a very small proportion of the fees obtained; furthermore, those very high effective hourly rates are offset by the large proportion of cases that earn very low effective hourly rates.

This general conclusion is reinforced when effective hourly rate is broken down by the magnitude of the stakes. For small cases, under $10,000 at stake, the median hourly rate is $36; for moderate cases, in the $10,000 to $50,000 range, the median rises markedly to $57; however, at $58, the median for big cases (over $50,000) is more or less the same as that for moderate cases.[14] At the same time, as indicated by the figures associated with the third quartiles (i.e., the top quarter in each group), those at the upper end of the big cases do substantially better ($160 per hour) than those at the upper end of the moderate ($105 per hour) or small cases ($70 per hour). While $160 per hour is a lot better than $58 per hour, it is not, by the standard of rates frequently charged to clients by corporate lawyers, excessive. There is a relatively small fringe group of cases (at most 5 percent of the cases) where the effective hourly rates approach and exceed $300 per hour;[15] in such situations one might argue that the fees received by contingent fee lawyers are excessive (although senior partners in major law firms often charge at rates in the $300 per hour range[16]). However, these rates are achieved in both moderate and large cases; they most likely reflect "lucky" outcomes achieved quickly with relatively little time and effort.[17] While an argument might be made that it is unfair or unjust that lawyers receive outlandish fees of this type, such fees are sufficiently rare that creating a system for reviewing fees would probably introduce a burden that could far outweigh the inequities that arise under the existing system.[18] One could imagine a modification to contingent fee contracts that required lawyers to provide an accounting of their time to their clients and placing a "cap" on the effective hourly rate that they receive, but such a modification would affect a small proportion of cases unless the cap was set at a low figure.[19]

Two other somewhat related contrasts are shown in Table 9-2. The first is between effective hourly rates for state and federal cases. In terms of the typical rates, there is no real difference between state and federal courts; the medians are $43 and $40, respectively. The most interesting contrast seems to be at the bottom end of the success scale. Lawyers handling cases on a contingent fee basis in the federal courts are twice as likely to be "total losers" (i.e., they receive no payment for their efforts) than are contingent fee lawyers in the state courts; 26 percent of the lawyers in federal court "lose" compared to only 13 percent in the state courts.

As shown at the bottom of Table 9-2, this reflects a combination of factors. First, contingency fees are particularly risky outside of the traditional areas of tort and contract, and a much higher proportion of nontraditional cases are to be found in the federal courts than in the state courts. Second, tort cases are riskier in federal court than in state court.[20] I do not have an empirically based explanation for this difference, but it may reflect more rigorous use of summary judgment procedures in the federal courts;[21] however, while there is some evidence to support that explanation (see Kritzer, 1986: 164), there is a similar difference in the use of such procedures in contract cases even though there is no similar gap in the likelihood of receiving a fee in the two courts. In fact, if anything, contingent fee lawyers in state contract cases are more likely to be paid nothing than if such cases are brought in federal courts; this may simply reflect the difficulty of collecting judgments and/or settlements in small contract cases (as compared to small tort cases, where there is an insurance company that routinely pays once a resolution is reached).

Other than those that I have just described, there are no appreciable differences between contract and tort cases. However, the greater risk involved in cases outside contract and tort carries over even for cases where some recovery is achieved. Looking only at federal cases (because there are too few state cases outside contracts and torts for meaningful analysis), the median effective hourly rate for nontort/noncontract cases where some recovery is achieved is only $39; this can be contrasted to $77 for tort cases and $60 for contract cases.

Given these connections between key case characteristics and success from the contingent fee lawyer's perspective, let me now turn to an examination of the impact on effective hourly rates of factors such as professional skills, what the lawyer actually does in the case, and the lawyer's relationships. To do this, I will again use multiple regression. The regression equation includes the variables just discussed (court, stakes, area of law) plus the other variables needed to answer the questions of interest[22]:

Case characteristics.
 Log of stakes.
 Subjective complexity.
 Area of law (neither tort nor contract versus tort and/or contract).

Processing characteristics.
 Court.
 Log of amount of court activity (as measured by the total number of docket entries).
 Percent of time spent on each of the following activities:
  Conferring with the client.
  Discovery.
  Factual investigation other than discovery.
  Settlement discussions.
  Pleading and motions.
  Legal research.
 Log of duration.
 Trial/no trial.
 Log of hours of lawyer effort.
 Number of exchanges of demands and offers, with more than three recorded as three.
 Log of ratio of first demand to stakes, with cases without any reported demands coded as 0.

Lawyers characteristics.
 Size of law firm.
 Commitment to craft.
 Years in practice.
 Percentage of time on litigation.
 Specialization/expertise.

Relationships.
 Expectation of future cases against opposing party.
 Prior representation of client.

As this list indicates, several variables were transformed by taking the natural logarithm before being entered into the regression equation; all of the variables that were transformed in this way are relatively open ended in the upper range of values. Preliminary analyses indicated that for all of them, the logarithm transformation provided the best description of the relationship with effective hourly rate (as compared to either no transformation or the square root transformation). The maximum value of three for the number of exchanges of demands and offers was necessary because the survey included questions about no more than that number of exchanges; in fact, this introduces little distortion, because 85 percent of the respondents reported less than three exchanges.

Including stakes as a variable necessitated omitting cases for which no stakes estimate was obtained but, given the strength of the relationship, omitting stakes would have led to a severely misspecified model.

The significant results from the regression analysis are reported in Table 9–3 (the complete set of results can be found in appendix Table 9–A1); the table shows results for three subsets of cases:

All cases.

Extreme cases (effective hourly rates exceeding $250) excluded.

Extreme cases and losers (where the lawyer received no fee at all) excluded.

For the first two sets of cases, the regression equation achieves a moderate level of explanation, with virtually identical coefficients of determination (.32 and .33); for the last subset (without big winners and complete losers), the coefficient of determination rises to .55. Regarding the effects of specific variables, the relatively small number of coefficients shown in Table 9–3 indicates that most of the variables do not have a statistically significant impact on effective hourly rate. Neither the indicators that might be linked to professionalism (formal legal activities, experience and expertise, etc.) nor those linked to the alternate broker image (e.g., the informal legal activities and the relationship variables) have significant links to effective hourly rate; the two possible excep-

TABLE 9–3. Significant Influences on Lawyer Success

	Regression Coefficients		
Variable	All Cases	Excluding Outliers	Excluding Losers and Outliers
Log of stakes	70.69***	26.40***	44.83***
	(9.63)[a]	(3.41)	(3.60)
Nontort/noncontract	−44.71	−35.79***	−18.35
	(32.52)	(11.12)	(11.34)
Log of hours worked	−72.71***	−26.70***	−51.30***
	(11.02)	(4.08)	(4.40)
Strategic bargaining[b]	27.85	8.67	11.36*
	(15.65)	(5.29)	(5.76)
Specialization	22.25	9.66*	12.86
	(12.45)	(4.42)	(3.83)
Commitment to craft	−33.44*	−3.05	−2.95
	(13.47)	(4.76)	(4.29)
Coefficient of determination (R^2)	.32	.33	.55
Adjusted coefficient of determination	.26	.26	.50
n	274	255	209

[a]Figures in parentheses are standard errors of the regression coefficients.

[b]Log of the ratio of first demand to highest stakes evaluation.

*$p < .05$.

**$p < .01$.

***$p < .001$.

tions shown in Table 9-3, both on the professionalism side, are specialization and commitment to craft, and they cut in opposite directions, with specialization tending to increase success and commitment to craft to decrease it.[23]

The results of the regression analysis indicate that the effective hourly rates that contingent fee lawyers are able to obtain are primarily the result of case (e.g., stakes, area of law) and processing (e.g., hours worked, negotiation) factors and have relatively little to do directly with the other kinds of variables in the model. It is worth noting that, as suggested by the literature on contingent fees, success goes down sharply as the amount of time worked goes up.[24] *Keep in mind the kinds of cases in this sample; this may not be true for the kinds of big cases that attract media attention.* From the lawyer's perspective, the better outcomes are achieved when stakes are high and the case involves a tort or contract dispute.[25]

Success from the Defendant's Perspective

The simplest way of viewing outcomes from the defendant's position would be to treat only the outcomes in which nothing is paid to the plaintiff as indicating success. However, this presumes that the dispute is over whether *anything* should be paid by the defendant to the plaintiff. In fact, in many disputes there is little or no difference of opinion over whether something is owed to the plaintiff; instead, the question to be resolved is *how much* should be paid. From the defendant's perspective, if there was nothing to be gained by incurring the costs of litigation, it would make sense simply to pay the plaintiff what was requested; the likelihood of avoiding some or all of that payment makes it rational to force the plaintiff to invoke the litigation process.[26]

From a defendant's viewpoint, it can be cost effective to end up paying a substantial amount to the plaintiff and also to pay a substantial amount to one's own lawyer if the result is that the savings in what is paid to the plaintiff exceeds the amount paid to the lawyer. As an example, assume a case in which the plaintiff expects to recover $10,000 but, in the end, the defendant pays only $3,000, with the defendant's lawyer receiving a fee of $2,000. In this situation, the defendant has a net savings of $5,000, even with a total outlay of $5,000. Thus, the purpose of the defendant's litigation investment is to reduce or eliminate an expenditure the defendant would otherwise have to incur; when presented with a claim, a defendant sees the expenditure on lawyer's fees as a way to avoid paying some or all of the amount claimed. If the lawyer's work reduces the payment by an amount greater than the buyer's fee, the defendant's investment in litigation has been successful.

This leaves the problem of measuring the amount of the claim in order to measure the result of the lawyer's work. Various indicators could be used in this regard. One might use the amount that the defendants thought they might have to pay based on what the plaintiffs initially demanded ("exposure"); this is likely to overestimate the potential benefit because plaintiffs will often ask for more than they expect to get for tactical reasons. Alternatively, one could use the plaintiffs' (highest) estimate of what was at stake; while the defendants will not usually be aware of this figure, it is a more accurate indicator of the potential loss to the defendants than is a possibly exaggerated demand. A third possible measure, which is likely to be on the low side, is the amount that the defendants felt would be an appropriate payment; this figure is likely to underestimate the defendants' success because it is usually lower than what the plaintiffs are seeking.[27] In the analysis presented here, I will rely on the second indicator (the plaintiffs' estimate of stakes); I have information from 139 pairs of opposing plaintiff's lawyers and defendant's lawyers.[28]

That leaves the problem of defining a specific measure of success to use in the analysis of defendant's success. From the preceding discussion, the most obvious measure would be:

$$ds = \frac{\text{Plaintiff's Stakes} - (\text{Recovery} + \text{Fees})}{\text{Plaintiff's Stakes}}$$

For this measure, any positive value indicates success, in that the combination of what was paid to the plaintiff and what was paid to the defendant's lawyer was less than what the plaintiff was seeking. This formula can be algebraically manipulated to yield an alternate formula for defendant's success.[29]

$$DS = \frac{\text{Plaintiff's Stakes}}{\text{Recovery} + \text{Fees}}$$

This second measure is always positive, with values greater than 1.0 indicating success (i.e., less was paid out in fees and recovery than the plaintiff had sought) and values less than 1.0 indicating failure (the defendant would have been better off simply paying the plaintiff the plaintiff's estimate of stakes — if the defendant had known what that figure was). In the analysis that follows, I will use the second formula because it closely parallels the measure of success that I will use in looking at plaintiffs in the next section.[30] Let us now turn to the results of the analysis of success from the defendant's perspective.

Results

Table 9–4 shows some summary information for defendant's success. *For 65 percent of the defendants, their lawyer saved more in reduced payments to plaintiffs than the lawyer was paid in fees.* Thus, for most defendants, litigation was successful.[31] This does not necessarily mean that 65 percent of the defendants won while that proportion of plaintiffs lost; instead, relative to what they might have lost, defendants' positions are improved by the work of the lawyer.

The various breakdowns in Table 9–4 shows a remarkable general lack of variation in level and likelihood of success for different groups of cases: defendants do just as well in state and federal courts and in big and small cases. It seems that there might be some variation by area of law (again using the

TABLE 9–4. Defendant Success

Group of Cases	Median	First Quartile	Third Quartile	Percent Successful[a]	n
All cases	1.38	.88	2.44	65	139
Size of recovery					
<$10,000	1.52	.89	2.80	66	90
$10,000–50,000	1.22	.84	1.67	65	40
>$50,000	1.47	.99	2.03	63	9
Court					
Federal	1.27	.84	2.58	63	75
State	1.44	.96	2.27	69	64
Area of law					
Torts	1.52	.99	2.81	70	79
Contract	1.12	.78	1.74	62	48
Not torts or contract	1.27	.77	2.40	58	19

[a] This is the percentage of cases with success ratios greater than 1.0.

categories of torts, contracts, and other, since there are not enough cases in each of the other individual areas for meaningful analysis): tort defendants seem to do slightly better than defendants in other kinds of cases, with a 70 percent success rate and a median success ratio of 1.52, compared to success rates of 62 percent and 58 percent, and success ratios of 1.12 and 1.27 for contract and "other" cases, respectively. However, as I will show next, these apparent differences disappear once controls for other variables are introduced.

These controls were introduced by replicating the regression analysis discussed in the last section using the measure of defendant's success as the dependent variable. There were two changes to the predictor variables. First, because of the pattern of variation by area of law (see Table 9–4), that variable was introduced as three dummy variables: torts, contracts, and both torts and contracts, while the "other" cases served as the base of comparison. Second, the ratio of demand to stakes was replaced by the log of the ratio of opposing party's stakes estimate to initial offer;[32] thus, if strategic bargaining (i.e., making a low initial offer) is related to success, this ratio should have a positive regression coefficient in this analysis.[33]

The regression (detailed results can be found in Table 9–A2[34]) achieves a moderate level of explanatory power with an adjusted R^2 of .36.[35] However, there are only two individual coefficients that are statistically significant: (1) the indicator of strategic bargaining (the log of the ratio of opponents stakes estimate to first offer)—the lower the first offer relative to opponents stakes evaluation, the better the outcome from the defendant's perspective, and (2) the indicator of specialization—the greater the level of specialization, the better the outcome. The apparent effect of area of law that appeared in Table 9–4 disappears.

At first look this suggests that expertise does make a difference, but further examination indicates that the expertise factor probably contributes little if anything to the explanation of defendant success. Given the strength of the relationship between the strategic bargaining indicator and defendant's success and the fact that specialization was the only other variable that contributed significantly to the prediction of defendant success,[36] I carried out a regression analysis with just two predictor variables: strategic bargaining and specialization. In this analysis only the strategic bargaining indicator achieves statistical significance. In fact, repeating the regression using the bargaining variable alone results in an R^2 (both adjusted and unadjusted) of .38;[37] a statistical test of the improvement in the coefficients achieved by including the other variables confirms that they contribute nothing to the explanation of success from the defendant's viewpoint.[38]

What this means is that the success of defendants is not systematically improved by the lawyers concentrating their effort on certain activities, it is not improved by going to trial or by settling short of trial, and it is not improved by using a lawyer with more experience or expertise. The only apparent factor that seems to make a systematic difference is a tough negotiating stance.[39] Despite the failure to account for much of the variation in defendant's success, it is clear that defendants usually come out ahead from the litigation process in that they save more than they pay out in expenses to their legal counsel. Note that this does not take into account the internal costs that are incurred, that is, the value of the time of the people who are directly affiliated with the defendant (such as the defendant personally if it is an individual or the employees of the defendant if it is an organization); however, much, if not most, of these costs would be incurred regardless of whether or not the dispute was taken to court.[40] Even though most defendants come out ahead, a sizable proportion (35 percent) do not, and there is a substantial amount of variation in the degree to which defendants profit or lose by litigation.

As for the professional and the broker images, the results of this analysis are more consistent with the latter; negotiating skills are more clearly linked to insider knowledge than to formal legal knowledge. None of the indicators of specialization (which include both experience and expertise in the legal area of the case) and none of the indicators of concentration on formal legal activities have any apparent relationship to defendant success. This is not to say that the legal ability of the lawyer makes no difference at all; it may be the situation that in most cases the opposing lawyers are fairly evenly matched with regard to professionalism factors, so the effect of variations in skills related to professionalism is difficult to detect.[41]

Success from the Plaintiff's Perspective

The question of winning and losing in litigation is most complex when viewed from the plaintiff's perspective. First, do we mean winning as a result of litigation, or do we simply meaning winning, period? This is an important distinction. It is possible that a specific outcome achieved as a result of litigation is no better than that which could have been achieved in *that* case without ever involving the court or lawyers. Consider the following hypothetical case.[42]

> You signed a contract with a local contractor to renovate an old fireplace in your home. The agreed price was $1,700 ($500 in advance), including labor and materials, and was to be completed within four weeks. Because it was a relatively small job, the contractor had workers come when there was slack elsewhere. After dismantling the old fireplace, the workers did not reappear for several weeks. Eventually you started calling the contractor and complaining about the delays. When a couple of workers finally did show up at your house, they didn't have the materials (e.g., the damper, the fire box, etc.) needed to do the job. After you angrily called the contractor and discovered that the materials had never been ordered, you went to the local supplier and for $750 purchased the materials yourself. When you got back to the house, you discovered that the workers had gone elsewhere. A week later, after several more calls, two other workers showed up at your house, and over the next 2 days finished the job to your satisfaction.
>
> Ten days later, a bill arrived in the mail for the $1,200 balance due. When you phoned the contractor and pointed out that you had in fact paid for the materials and spent a good bit of your own time going to get them (and hassling with the contractor generally), they offered to reduce the bill by $450, which was the *wholesale* cost of the materials (what the contractor would have paid for them from the distributor), leaving a balance of $750. You demanded that the bill be reduced by $850 (leaving a balance of $350), the $750 you paid for the materials plus $100 to compensate for the time you spent on the matter. After that offer was refused, you informed them that you would not pay anything on the bill until they agreed to your figure and, in response, they threatened to take you to court, claiming the $750 plus attorney's fees and interest (as provided for under the terms of the contract).
>
> When the case came up in small claims court a year later, the contractor claimed $750 plus interest of 1.5 percent per month and $300 in attorney's fees (a total of $1,196.71). You appeared with your receipt from the materials supplier, and a list of the telephone calls you made to the contractor. After hearing both sides, the judge ruled that you should pay the contractor $400 (i.e., $50 more than the amount you had offered without interest or attorney's fees).

If one were to look at this case in the court record, it would seem to be a partial victory for the plaintiff: they had sued for almost $1,200 and had gotten $400. However, an alternative interpretation would be that the dispute was not over the $1,200 but over the difference between $750 and $350; seen in this way, one could say that the plaintiff essentially lost and the defendant enjoyed a near total victory. From this perspective, the plaintiff's success must be considered in light of what could have been obtained without turning to formal legal processes; that is, success should be evaluated in terms of what is really at stake, not what is nominally at stake.

It is important that the example used in the preceding discussion is drawn from a contract dispute, because there is a general belief that people should pay their debts, and this belief leads most people most of the time to pay what they owe without really taking into account the possibility that they will probably be taken to court if they fail to meet such obligations. If the dispute over payment had arisen not because of the problems dealing with the contractor, but because a member of your family had badly sprained an ankle after tripping over a tool left lying in the middle of the room by one of the workers, you might feel that you could properly claim that you should pay nothing to the contractor as a way of obtaining compensation for the injury, even if the actual out-of-pocket medical costs were only $150.

In a pure contract dispute, you might decide to go ahead and offer to pay the contractor $350 *because you (or your lawyer) estimated that if the case went to court there was a good chance that you would be ordered to pay something on the order of that amount.* That is, in many (perhaps most) cases it is likely that what can be achieved in the absence of litigation depends greatly on what would result from litigation. The alternatives to litigation, whether they be bilateral settlement without the intervention of any third party or the use of some third party other than the court (e.g., arbitration, mediation) are able to achieve results in substantial part because of the *shadow* of the court (cf. Mnookin and Kornhauser, 1979); in the absence of that shadow, it would be difficult in cases where the social–cultural norms did not create a strong inclination toward providing redress for claimants to obtain any satisfaction for their grievance. If one thinks about the area of medical malpractice, the strength of this argument is immediately clear: without litigation, there would be little or no compensation for medical errors.[43]

Moreover, outside of the contracts area, where amounts of claims can be determined with relative precision, it is the litigation process itself that places valuations on claims, albeit with a tremendous amount of imprecision. Without litigation and in the absence of some other kind of valuation procedure (such as amounts set through statute, as has been the practice in some areas), there would be no way of assessing the appropriate level of damages in cases involving things such as personal injury or discrimination.[44] The levels of compensation achieved through the most common alternative to litigation, settlement, tend to represent "going rates" (sometimes called "shadow verdicts"; see Danzon, 1982) that can only be established through litigation (see Daniels, 1986; Galanter, 1981: 6; Ross, 1980: 5–6, 115).

There is an interesting but separate question of what might have been achieved if a specific claimant had decided *not* to turn to the courts, but this is fundamentally different from the question of what would have been obtained *in the absence of litigation* (i.e., if litigation had not been available). Any analysis of the individual choice question would be complicated by the fact that in the process of turning to the courts (e.g., by going to a lawyer), a potential litigant's perception of what might be at stake could be substantially changed (Felstiner, Abel, and Sarat, 1980–1981; see also Ross, 1980: 192–198);[45] the stakes estimates for disputes that do go to court and for those that do not go may be fundamentally different because of this "transformation" process. A further complication may be related to the selection process, either by the claimant or the lawyer; it may well be only those cases in which there are substantial questions about liability (see Priest and Klein, 1984) or discrepancies between the parties in the evaluation of damages (Wittman, 1985) that result in court processes being invoked, or it may be only bigger cases in which there is more room for ambiguity about what is at stake. In the absence of any kind of truly random assignment process, it would be extremely difficult to compare litigation and its alternatives accurately.

The conclusion of this discussion is that the best base of comparison to assess the success of plaintiffs is what they were seeking, even if they might have been able to obtain some portion of that without invoking the court process *in their individual case.* With this said, there are still at least two ways that one might go about assessing winning and losing from the plaintiff's perspective. First, one might take an approach resembling a cost-benefit analysis by comparing fees paid to amount recovered. The difficulty with this approach is that for most plaintiffs the ratio of fees to recovery is fixed by the percentage (contingent) fee agreement; thus the cost-benefit approach is applicable only to the relatively small group (around 20 percent of the sample) of plaintiffs who paid their lawyers on some basis other than a contingent fee.[46]

The second approach of assessing plaintiff success is to compare the outcome, net of transaction costs, against the amount at stake. This leads to a definition of plaintiff's success that is a ratio that is very similar to that used in the previous section for defendant's success.

$$PS = \frac{\text{Recovery} - \text{Attorney's Fees and Expenses}}{\text{Plaintiff's Highest Stakes Estimate}}$$

The higher this ratio, the better the plaintiff has done in relation to expectations; negative ratios indicate litigants who incurred more in expenses than they recovered. Since the stakes question elicited the amount of money the case *should* settle for, not what the client should get after paying the attorney, success ratios above 1.0 would be exceptional. In a contingent fee case where the lawyer's fee equaled one third of the recovery, and the recovery was exactly the same as the stakes estimate, the ratio would be .67, or two-thirds.

Results

Table 9–5 shows separate success statistics for plaintiffs who used hourly and contingent fee lawyers. As the table shows, the patterns for those who used hourly fee lawyers and for those who were represented by contingent fee lawyers differ in several important respects. First, the contingent fee arrangement, whereby the lawyer always gets a percentage of the recovery, limits the level of success that can be achieved. Thus, for cases over $10,000, plaintiffs' hourly fee lawyers can achieve success ratios of .8 and .9, while the best that contingent fee lawyers achieve in typical (i.e., median) cases is ratios in the .5 to .6 range. Perhaps the most striking difference is the tendency of success to go down sharply with contingent fee lawyers as stakes increase above $50,000, while success goes sharply up for hourly fee lawyers as stakes increase. Another interesting difference is that hourly fee lawyers seem to do better in federal court than in state court, while contingent fee lawyers do better in state court than in federal court, although this primarily reflects the gap in stakes between federal and state cases.

TABLE 9–5. Plaintiffs' Success

Group of Cases	Median		First Quartile		Third Quartile		n	
	Hourly	Contingent	Hourly	Contingent	Hourly	Contingent	Hourly	Contingent
All cases	.60	.49	.19	.23	.95	.67	57	256
By size of recovery								
<$10,000	.38	.44	.00	.11	.56	.64	32	155
$10,000–50,000	.78	.57	.71	.28	.95	.68	13	79
>$50,000	.93	.52	.68	.37	1.00	.74	12	22
By court								
Federal	.71	.39	.06	.11	.94	.66	30	117
State	.54	.56	.31	.33	.95	.67	27	139
By area of law								
Torts	—[a]	.49	—	.27	—	.66	6	200
Contracts	.71	.63	.27	.23	.94	.70	42	45
Other	.42	.17	.00	-.01	.95	.60	10	19
By area of law and stakes								
Torts								
<$10,000	—	.56	—	.35	—	.69	—	93
$10,000–50,000	—	.60	—	.25	—	.66	—	76
>$50,000	—	.30	—	.16	—	.54	—	31
Contracts								
<$10,000	.44	.58	.00	.03	.78	.67	15	18
$10,000 and up	.76	.65	.48	.23	.94	.74	27	27
By area of law and courts								
Torts								
Federal	—	.38	—	.14	—	.66	—	84
State	—	.56	—	.35	—	.66	—	116
Contracts								
Federal	.74	.63	.40	.23	.94	.67	25	26
State	.48	.59	.27	.10	.84	.74	17	19

[a]Too few cases for analysis.

Some of these differences between hourly and contingent fee lawyers arise from the kinds of cases accepted under the two fee arrangements. Almost all of the tort cases (200 out of 207) were handled on a contingent fee basis; only six tort plaintiffs retained their lawyer on an hourly basis.[47] The 87 cases involving contract issues are evenly divided between contingent (45 cases) and hourly (42 cases) fee arrangements.[48] The nontort/noncontract cases are split between the two fee arrangements, with about twice as many employing lawyers on a contingent fee basis.[49] One set of rows in Table 9-5 shows plaintiff success by fee arrangement and area of law. In contract cases, where comparisons can be made most easily, hourly fee lawyers seem to do better for their clients than do contingent fee lawyers. When controls are introduced for stakes, one finds that hourly fee lawyers do better for their clients as stakes go up, with a median success ratio of .44 for cases under $10,000 and .76 for cases involving $10,000 or more; this is not surprising, since the proportion of the recovery consumed by legal fees is bound to be higher in small cases than large cases when those fees are computed on an hourly basis. With contingent fee lawyers in contract cases there is little appreciable difference, depending on stakes; the median success ratios are .58 for cases under $10,000 and .65 for cases involving $10,000 or more. Because of the percentage nature of the fee calculation, there must be some constraint on the upper bounds of plaintiff success (unless the fee percentage is computed on a sharply declining scale as the recovery increases). Interestingly, the level of success for a contingent fee lawyer handling a contract case falls between the level of success achieved by an hourly fee lawyer in smaller cases (under $10,000) and larger cases ($10,000 or more). Clearly, a plaintiff with a small contract claim is likely to do better hiring a lawyer on a contingency basis while, with a large claim, a better result can be achieved with a lawyer working on an hourly fee basis.

Focusing now on contingent fee lawyers only, overall they seem to do somewhat better in contract cases than in tort cases (median success ratios of .63 and .49, respectively). However, any comparison of success across areas of law needs to be drawn cautiously because of the greater ambiguity of the stakes in tort cases than in contract cases; that is, contract cases generally involve explicit and clearly identifiable sums of money, while civil litigation over tort issues frequently involves claims for more ambiguous things, such as "pain and suffering."[50] In tort cases, while it is not possible to compare the outcomes achieved by type of fee arrangement, there are some striking differences in results, depending on stakes. The best results seem to be achieved in the smaller cases (median ratio, .56), with slightly poorer results in cases involving $10,000 to $50,000 (median ratio, .50), and sharply worse results in larger cases involving more than $50,000 (median ratio, .30). An initial interpretation of these results might be that defendants are more likely to contest big cases and, consequently, there is a greater chance of a plaintiff getting nothing as the stakes go up. While there may be some validity to such an argument, it does not explain the results for this set of lawyers, since the proportion of losers was, in fact, smallest for the cases involving more than $50,000; the pattern holds up (with some slight diminution in the gap between small and medium cases) when the losers are left out of the analysis.

Another explanation that might be advanced to account for the poorer results achieved in larger cases has to do with the increasing margin for error in the evaluation of stakes as the amount at issue goes up. That is, it may be that the poorer performance in big cases represents errors in estimating the denominator of the success measure (stakes) rather than low values in the numerator (net recovery). This explanation is questionable because the estimates of stakes were provided by the lawyers themselves *after* the case was over; given this I would be more concerned that the lawyers have, in fact, adjusted their retrospective estimate of stakes to be more in line with the final result. Thus, it is more likely that these findings concerning outcomes overestimate the degree of success than that they underestimate it.[51]

Let us now turn to the results of regression analyses based on the set of variables used previously to examine effective hourly rates and defendant success. Several different theoretically relevant models were estimated.

1. A basic model that included the variables discussed previously, with the addition of dummy variables for fee arrangement (contingent fee versus hourly fee arrangement) and area of law (nontort/noncontract versus either tort or contract).[52]
2. A model that added a parameter to check for the effect of stakes conditional on fee arrangement. (Do stakes affect success differently for hourly and contingent fee lawyers?)
3. A model that added a parameter to check for the effect of lawyer effort conditional by fee arrangement. (Does lawyer effort affect plaintiff success differently for hourly and contingent fee lawyers?)

Selected results for these analyses are shown in Table 9-6 (complete results are shown in appendix Table 9-A3.)[53]

The first column, from the initial model, shows that only four variables significantly predict plaintiff's success: fee arrangement (the success ratio goes down .18 for contingent fee lawyers), the number of court events (success goes down as the number of events goes up), proportion of time devoted to legal research (for each percentage point more such research, the plaintiff's success ratio goes down by .0042), and strategic bargaining (the higher the first demand in relationship to stakes, the greater the ultimate success). The legal research item probably indicates that the plaintiff achieves less success in cases where questions of law are more at issue (requiring that more legal research be conducted), and the inverse relationship with the number of court events may mean that plaintiff success goes down as the contentiousness of the case goes up (i.e., the more the defendant resists the plaintiff's claim, the less success the plaintiff achieves). The other two significant predictors are generally consistent with the findings reported in this section (i.e., the lower level of success for contingent fee lawyers) and elsewhere in this chapter (the strong relationship between success and strategic bargaining).

A few paragraphs ago I discussed the apparently contrasting relationships between stakes and success, depending on fee arrangement. The second regres-

TABLE 9-6. Significant Influences on Plaintiff Success[a]

Variables	Regression Coefficients		
	Model 1	Model 2	Model 3
Log of number of events	−.07*	−.07	−.07
	(.03)[b]	(.04)	(.04)
Contingent fee	−.18**	0.61*	0.64*
	(.06)	(.31)	(.31)
Proportion of time devoted to legal research	−.43*	−.38	−.39
	(.21)	(.21)	(.21)
Strategic bargaining[c]	0.17***	0.16***	0.16***
	(.04)	(.04)	(.04)
Conditional effect of stakes for hourly fee lawyers	−	0.08**	0.10**
		(.03)	(.04)
Conditional effect of effort (hours) for hourly fee lawyers	−	−	−.05
			(.05)
Coefficient of determination (R^2)	.18	.20	.20
Adjusted coefficient of determination	.11	.13	.13

[a]Sample size for all three models is 313.

[b]Figures in parentheses are standard errors of the regression coefficients.

[c]Log of the ratio of first demand to highest stakes evaluation.

*$p<.05$.   **$p<.01$.   ***$p<.001$.

sion model provides a further test of this finding. The significant coefficient for conditional effect of stakes for hourly fee lawyers provides further evidence in behalf of the existence of differing effects. To interpret the meaning of the term, it must be combined with the coefficient for fee arrangement. The change in sign in fee arrangement term (from negative to positive) does not mean that contingent fee lawyers are now more successful than hourly fee lawyers; it simply reflects the fact that the two terms must be interpreted together.[54] For cases involving less than $1,768, contingent fee lawyers would be expected to achieve a higher success ratio for their clients than would hourly fee lawyers; above this figure the situation reverses, with hourly fee lawyers achieving a higher degree of success. This discussion presumes that all other variables remain constant as stakes increase which, in the real world, is quite unlikely. Extra caution is needed in interpreting these results because about 80 percent of the contingent fee cases involve tort issues while virtually none of the hourly fee cases involve this area of law.

In Chapter 8 I reported that the fee relationship did seem to be related to the amount of effort that lawyers expended on cases; at that time, I posed the question of whether or not this additional effort led to better results. I have now shown that there is a tendency for hourly fee lawyers to achieve better results than that achieved by contingent fee lawyers. Is this perhaps the result of hourly fee lawyers putting in more time? The analysis discussed so far provides no indication that the amount of effort is related to success. Furthermore, the third regression model, which adds a term for the conditional effect of effort for hourly fee lawyers, still provides no evidence of a relationship between effort and success; if anything, given the negative sign of this new coefficient, any additional effort by hourly fee lawyers seems to reduce success. In fact, given that the effort analysis in Chapter 8 indicated that the effort gap was in the hourly fee lawyer's favor for small cases and in the contingent fee lawyer's favor for large cases and that the success analysis indicated that hourly fee lawyers provide better results in larger cases (where the contingent fee lawyer might be putting in more time than the hourly fee lawyer), it should not be surprising that I can find no indication that the extra effort by hourly fee lawyers makes any systematic difference in outcomes achieved.

From this analysis, there is little evidence to support an argument that indicators of legal professionalism can account for the success (or lack thereof) achieved for plaintiff clients. The broker image provides a better basis of explanation. Plaintiff success can be partially explained by the bargaining strategy employed by the lawyer and by the lack of legal issues necessitating substantial concentration on the part of the lawyer on legal research; that is, it is just in those kinds of cases, where the lawyers have to draw on formal legal knowledge and skills, that the degree of success achieved goes down. More important, success seems to be related to the fee-paying relationship linking the lawyer and the client; again, this must be considered with some caution because of the strong correspondence between legal issues and fee arrangement (i.e., virtually all tort plaintiffs retain lawyers on a contingency basis).

It is not hard to see why there might be a decreasing level of success as stakes go up. First, contingent fee lawyers are probably more willing to undertake cases involving substantial uncertainty as to outcome as the amount they might earn increases; in small cases, they will want to be very sure of the likely outcome before agreeing to invest their own time. Second, the amount of effort that contingent fee lawyers put into cases rises quickly as stakes increase (see Chapter 8); as those sunk costs increase, the lawyer may well be anxious to achieve some return, even if that involves accepting a recovery that is far below the case's potential.[55] In any event, it is clear that the business relationship between the lawyer and the client has important influences on what the lawyer might be ultimately expected to achieve on the client's behalf; if nothing else, the contingency arrangement effectively puts a cap on the level of success in most cases because the lawyer will receive a more or less fixed percentage of the final recovery.[56]

How do things look from the plaintiff's perspective? That is, do the results obtained in litigation systematically affect the litigants' evaluations of the process and their experience? To look briefly at this question, I examined the responses of the litigants themselves from the surveys of individual and organizational disputants. As I said previously, these data must be used with great caution because of the low response rates; in order to maximize the number of respondents available for analysis, I have included the individuals and organizations who, while not part of the original sample of court cases, reported that their case had involved a lawsuit. While these data can at best be suggestive, they can give some indication of whether or not client satisfaction is at all related to degree of success achieved.

Questions about stakes, outcome, and lawyers' fees similar to those used in the lawyer survey were asked of the litigants. In addition, litigants were asked:

> Based on only your experience in this case, was having the case filed in court very ineffective, ineffective, just effective, or very effective in getting the problem resolved?

> Was it very useful in getting the problem resolved, just useful, not too useful, or not useful at all?

> Considering what you had to gain or lose in the case, was going to court very cheap, cheap, expensive, or very expensive?

> Overall, was your experience with the court very good, good, bad, or very bad?

For purposes of analysis all of the questions were coded so that high numbers indicated a positive evaluation and low numbers indicated a negative evaluation; consequently, if good outcomes from the litigant's viewpoint led to a positive evaluation of the experience of going to court, then there should be a positive correlation between success and the evaluation indices. The number of respondents for whom there was available both an indicator of success (which meant that information was available for monetized stakes, monetized outcome, and legal fees) and the evaluation indicators was approximately 115 (with some variation, depending on the specific evaluation question); only about 30 percent of the respondents were spokespersons for organizational disputants.

Taking both the individual and organizational plaintiffs together, there is *no* indication that there is a relationship between success and evaluation of the court experience. Two of the four correlations were in fact negative, including the largest coefficient (in absolute terms), −.14 between success and the good/bad question; none of the coefficients was statistically significant. When I looked separately at individuals and organizations, I found exactly the same pattern for individuals, but I found that *all* of the correlations for organizational plaintiffs were *negative*, and three of them were in the range of −.21 to −.28 (the exception was the good/bad question, which had a correlation of only −.07); still, because of the small sample size none of the correlations were statistically significant (applying a two-tailed test, although two would be significant if I had hypothesized a negative relationship between success and evaluation). The clear message of these findings is that, at least for plaintiffs, the success (measured in the terms that I defined before) that their lawyers achieve on their behalf has little or no influence on the litigants' evaluation of their experience with the court process.[57]

Discussion

Given the frequently expressed concern about the costs, delays, and uncertainties of litigation, one might reasonably want to ask, "Does anyone come out ahead?" As I noted at the beginning of this chapter, Galanter (1974) suggested one answer to that question some years ago when he discussed "why the 'haves' come out ahead." A recent analysis of decisions by state supreme courts over the last 100 years or so also came to the conclusion that the "haves" seem to be more likely to prevail than the "have nots," although the gap between the two groups was more modest than one might have presumed (Wheeler et al., 1987).

In the end, the analysis presented here cannot really answer the question of which side wins and which side loses in litigation. In fact, the point of much of the discussion is that in many, if not most, cases the perspectives of the various players are so different that for any one case all players may be losers, all may be winners, or there may be any of several combinations of winning and losing (e.g., the defendant and the plaintiff's contingent fee lawyer may do very well in the case, or the defendant and plaintiff may come out ahead while the plaintiff's lawyer achieves a very low effective hourly return for the time spent). As I have discussed, assessing success in terms of winning and losing is problematic because it really has to be considered in light of some baseline. That baseline is easiest to define theoretically for the contingent fee lawyer: the opportunity cost of the time devoted to the case (i.e., what the lawyer could have made doing something other than work on the specific case in question). The clarity of a baseline decreases as one turns to the defendant and becomes still murkier for the plaintiff; for this last actor, the problem of assessing results is severely complicated by the difficulty of separating the results of a single case from the workings of the system as a whole. Perhaps the apparent lack of relationship between success and satisfaction on the part of plaintiffs reflects an acknowledgment of this underlying complexity.

Despite the inability to come to any firm conclusion about who, on aggregate, comes out ahead in the litigation process,[58] the preceding analysis once again suggests the value of looking beyond the standard image of professionalism and formal professional skills in trying to understand litigation. By and large, the indicators of professionalism, in terms of the kinds of skills and activities most specifically linked to the "legal profession," explain little of the results achieved through the litigation process. The one variable that seems to have an impact for the litigants on the two sides of the case is strategic bargaining (demanding high for plaintiffs and offering low for defendants);[59] interestingly, this has no impact on the result from the perspective of the contingent fee lawyer.[60] Negotiation skills in the arena of litigation epitomize the kind of informal, insider knowledge that I have associated with the broker (in contrast to the professional's reliance on formal knowledge). The results from this analysis suggest that plaintiffs are disadvantaged in cases where their lawyers need to draw strongly on formal legal training to carry out substantial amounts of legal research; however, this probably is more reflective of case characteristics than of the lawyers' active decisions to devote time to legal research (a formal legal activity) as opposed to negotiation or fact gathering (informal legal activities).

One should not conclude that professional training is unimportant or that lawyers engaged in litigation do not need to have the formal legal skills associated with the professional. It is true that in explaining why some cases are successful (in monetary terms) and some are not, the kinds of characteristics linked to formalized professionalism are of little help. Instead, it is the skills associated with the experience of the insider, the broker, that seem to best account for results.

Moreover, the analysis suggests, but does not prove, that the fee-paying relationship between lawyers and their plaintiff clients has very important implications for the results achieved for the clients. Drawing firm conclusions here is difficult because of the almost total dominance of the contingent fee in the personal injury area. Nonetheless, the evidence suggests that clients are better served by the hourly fee lawyer in moderate to big cases and by the contingent fee lawyer in small cases. The latter reflects the fixed costs involved in the litigation process. The former reflects two considerations. First, the fixed proportion taken by the contingent fee lawyer limits the success that can be achieved. Second, contingent fee lawyers seem willing, particularly in tort cases, to obtain sharply decreasing proportions of the amount at issue as the stakes begin to get large; whether this reflects greater uncertainty in larger cases (lawyers may be more willing to roll the dice when the payoff may be large) or that in those cases lawyers can achieve a reasonably good effective hourly rate with a lower level of success (from the plaintiff's perspective) cannot be determined from the data I have available. Regardless of what explains these apparent differences, they are not particularly surprising within the context of the broker image, but they are extremely difficult to square with our expectations of the professional.

Finally, one might ask, given the evidence that strategic bargaining makes a significant difference in the outcome from the clients' viewpoint, Why don't lawyers (particularly contingent fee lawyers) rely more heavily on that style of bargaining? In my companion study of bargaining in civil litigation (Kritzer, forthcoming), I show that most lawyers in ordinary litigation do not engage in strategic bargaining; instead, lawyers tend to make initial demands or offers that are fairly close to their evaluation of what the case is worth. If there is a distinction to be drawn among lawyers, it is between plaintiffs' and defendants' lawyers, with the latter more likely to engage in strategic bargaining. One explanation of the low likelihood of plaintiffs' lawyers engaging in strategic bargaining in ordinary litigation is that it is not in their own interest: effective hourly rate is best improved by getting quick settlements, and engaging in strategic bargaining has no systematic influence on the hourly rate achieved! Thus, it is fast turnover that is important to the financial success of the contingent fee lawyer–broker handling ordinary, everyday cases. Satisfaction and pride may come from a strong commitment to craft but, in specific cases, that does not necessarily pay. At the same time, just as I argued that success from the plaintiff's perspective cannot be judged in isolation from the larger system, the individual lawyer's overall financial success depends on that lawyer's portfolio of cases and obtaining returns from individual cases may be greatly influenced by reputations created by prior cases. Thus, while the self-interested broker may choose to view the work case by case, the best view of *long-term* self-interest may have to take into account the formal background of the professional.

APPENDIX 9A

Multivariate Analyses

TABLE 9A-1. Multivariate Analysis of Lawyer Success

Variable	All Cases		Excluding Outliers		Excluding Losers and Outliers	
	b	Standard Error	b	Standard Error	b	Standard Error
Log of stakes	70.69***	9.43	26.40***	3.41	44.83***	3.60
Complexity	−15.44	8.52	−.56	2.97	−1.69	2.69
Nontort/noncontract	−44.71	32.52	−35.79***	11.12	−18.35	11.34
Federal/state court	16.34	24.03	−6.11	8.33	−.85	7.46
Log of number of events	−.22	16.23	−1.08	5.58	−6.63	5.00
Trial/no trial	−29.46	31.56	−7.65	10.87	−10.70	11.55
Log of duration	−4.19	12.89	0.77	4.53	4.80	4.19
Proportion of time devoted to:						
Conferring with client	19.08	92.04	19.75	30.93	11.07	27.21
Discovery	−92.41	79.75	−8.19	27.71	−11.66	25.47
Other factual investigation	71.59	94.54	−24.94	32.22	−21.52	28.37
Settlement discussions	−70.53	87.62	24.39	30.01	−33.09	26.58
Pleadings and motions	−97.44	117.89	−48.03	41.65	50.93	40.15
Legal research	−109.19	113.72	−26.35	40.07	−17.67	39.28
Log of hours worked	−72.71***	11.02	−26.70***	4.08	−51.30***	4.40
Number of bargaining exchanges	21.68	11.44	5.25	3.93	−5.88	3.95
Strategic bargaining[a]	27.85	15.65	8.67	5.29	11.36*	5.76
Percentage of practice devoted to litigation	0.25	0.41	−.20	0.14	−.16	0.13
Years of experience	−1.23	1.10	−.41	0.40	0.12	0.35
Specialization	22.25	12.45	9.66*	4.42	12.86	3.83
Size of law firm	0.79	6.83	−.63	2.37	−3.28	2.20
Commitment to craft	−33.44*	13.47	−3.05	4.76	−2.95	4.29
Expectation of future cases against current opposing party	14.79	18.78	1.29	6.53	−3.35	5.92
Past representation of client	−15.15	26.84	−11.37	9.26	−14.53	8.62
Constant	−184.71		−59.55		−121.69	
Coefficient of determination (R^2)	.32		.33		.55	
Adjusted coefficient of determination	.26		.26		.50	
n	274		255		209	

[a]Log of the ratio of first demand to highest stakes evaluation.

  *$p<.05$.

  **$p<.01$.

  ***$p<.001$.

TABLE 9A–2. Multivariate Analysis of Defendant Success

Variables	All Variables		Omitting Stakes	
	b	Standard Error	b	Standard Error
Log of stakes	0.04	0.10	—	—
Complexity	−.03	0.13	0.03	0.12
Torts	0.19	0.52	0.63	0.41
Contracts	0.06	0.48	0.33	0.40
Both torts and contracts	−.20	0.75	0.45	0.65
Federal/state court	0.29	0.35	0.21	0.31
Log of number of events	−.38	0.26	−.14	0.21
Trial/no trial	−.63	0.51	−.76	0.48
Log of duration	−.28	0.23	−.23	0.21
Proportion of time devoted to:				
Conferring with client	1.30	1.45	0.46	1.32
Discovery	0.32	1.05	0.25	0.95
Other factual investigation	−1.46	1.40	−.09	1.27
Settlement discussions	−1.47	1.39	−1.23	1.26
Pleadings and motions	1.82	1.50	3.71**	1.19
Legal research	0.57	1.79	−.42	1.45
Log of hours worked	0.16	0.19	0.09	0.14
Number of bargaining exchanges	−.40	0.24	−.48	0.20
Strategic bargaining[a]	1.12***	0.15	1.03***	0.14
Percentage of practice devoted to litigation	0.00	0.01	−.00	0.01
Years of experience	0.00	0.01	0.00	0.01
Specialization	0.43*	0.20	0.40**	0.15
Size of law firm	−.08	0.10	−.09	0.09
Commitment to craft	−.08	0.24	−.01	0.20
Expectation of future cases against current opposing party	0.16	0.56	−.15	0.45
Past representation of client	0.24	0.30	0.15	0.26
Constant	3.59		2.72	
Coefficient of determination (R^2)	.52		.48	
Adjusted coefficient of determination	.36		.35	
n	103		127	

[a]Log of the ratio of first offer to highest stakes evaluation by opposing party.

*$p < .05$.

**$p < .01$.

***$p < .001$.

TABLE 9A-3. Multivariate Analysis of Plaintiff Success[a]

Variables	Model 1 b	Model 1 Standard Error	Model 2 b	Model 2 Standard Error	Model 3 b	Model 3 Standard Error
Log of stakes	0.01	0.02	-.01	0.02	-.02	0.02
Complexity	-.01	0.02	-.01	0.02	-.00	0.02
Federal/state court	0.00	0.05	0.01	0.05	0.01	0.05
Log of number of events	-.07*	0.03	-.07	0.04	-.07	0.04
Trial/no trial	-.00	0.08	0.02	0.08	0.01	0.08
Log of duration	0.04	0.03	0.04	0.03	0.04	0.03
Nontort/noncontract	-.11	0.08	-.11	0.07	-.11	0.07
Contingent fee	-.18**	0.06	0.61*	0.31	0.64*	0.31
Proportion of time devoted to:						
Conferring with client	-.00	0.21	0.00	0.20	0.03	0.21
Discovery	-.24	0.17	-.21	0.17	-.21	0.17
Other factual investigation	0.22	0.21	0.19	0.21	0.16	0.21
Settlement discussions	-.22	0.19	-.22	0.19	-.21	0.19
Pleadings and motions	-.09	0.23	0.05	0.23	-.09	0.23
Legal research	-.43*	0.21	-.38	0.21	-.39	0.21
Log of hours worked	-.03	0.02	-.03	0.02	-.02	0.02
Number of bargaining exchanges	0.01	0.03	0.01	0.03	0.01	0.03
Strategic bargaining[b]	0.17***	0.04	0.16***	0.04	0.16***	0.04

	Model 1		Model 2		Model 3	
Percentage of practice devoted to litigation	0.000	0.001	0.000	0.001	0.000	0.001
Years of experience	0.002	0.003	0.002	0.002	0.002	0.003
Specialization	0.02	0.03	0.02	0.03	0.02	0.03
Size of law firm	0.02	0.02	0.01	0.02	0.02	0.02
Commitment to craft	-.03	0.03	-.03	0.03	-.03	0.03
Expectation of future cases against current opposing party	0.04	0.04	0.03	0.04	0.03	0.04
Past representation of client	-.03	0.06	-.02	0.06	-.03	0.06
Interaction: stakes for hourly lawyers	—	—	0.08**	0.03	0.10**	0.04
Interaction: effort (hours) for hourly lawyers	—	—	—	—	-.05	0.05
Constant	0.69		0.09		0.07	
Coefficient of determination (R^2)	.18		.20		.20	
Adjusted coefficient of determination	.11		.13		.13	

[a]Sample size for all three models is 313.

[b]Log of the ratio of first demand to highest stakes evaluation.

*$p < .05$.

**$p < .01$.

***$p < .001$.

V

CONCLUSIONS

10

Lawyers and Litigation: Images and Implications

RIDGEON:	. . . . And thats the medical profession!
SIR PATRICK:	And a very good profession, too, my lad. When you know as much as I know of the ignorance and superstition of the patients, you'll wonder that we're half as good as we are.
RIDGEON:	We're not a profession: we're a conspiracy.
SIR PATRICK:	All professions are conspiracies against the laity.

George Bernard Shaw,
The Doctor's Dilemma (1913)[1]

While Shaw never wrote a play about the legal profession, he might, if writing today, direct the preceding sentiment to lawyers rather than physicians. Although few people would agree fully with the cynicism evidenced by this quotation, most knowledgeable observers of the legal profession would agree that there *is* a substantial gap between the professional ideal[2] and the actual experience of lawyers and their clients. Popular scorn of lawyers is by no means a new phenomenon (see Roth and Roth, 1989; Kupferberg, 1978). Shakespeare often made lawyers the target of his scorn and wit; while the line from *Henry VI* (Part II, Act IV, Scene 2) may be best known (appearing on a T-shirt sold by the Folger Shakespeare Library in Washington, D.C.), "The first thing we do, let's kill all the lawyers," two other lines may be more relevant for the present discussion[3]: the Fool's line from *King Lear* (Act I, Scene 4), "then 'tis like the breath of an unfee'd lawyer"; or Mercutio in *Romeo and Juliet* (Act I, Scene 4), "O'er lawyers' fingers, who straight dream on fees."

At least part of the popular antipathy may be due to the nature of advocacy itself. That is, given the role of lawyers to present their client's position in the best possible light, such a presentation is inevitably going to be seen by others, who do not share the perspective of the client being represented, as attempting to circumvent justice rather than as serving the ends of justice. John Stuart Mill is quoted (in Mellinkoff, 1973: 12) as describing a lawyer as being ready to "frustrate justice with his tongue."[4] This is consistent with contemporary research that shows that while people are critical of lawyers for manipulating the legal system "without any concern for right or wrong" or for filing "too many unnecessary lawsuits," they want lawyers who put clients first and can get

165

things done on behalf of clients (*National Law Journal*, 1986). Lawyers are praised when they work for you and damned when they work against you.

If lawyers do have an image problem, it reflects in substantial part the contradictions inherent in the professional ideal that the profession has laid out for itself. While ideals are seldom attainable (they would not be ideals if they were), the standards associated with the professional ideal are fundamentally contradictory when applied to the situation of the lawyer handling litigation. This creates a situation in which failure and disappointment are inevitable. Calling for more rigorous enforcement of codes of professional conduct or for increased attention to the ethical component of legal education (American Bar Association, 1986) will not solve the problems of professionalism among legal practitioners. Furthermore, the dilemma of practitioners is not helped by research that relies solely on a framework built around a concept that carries substantial normative implications in addition to defining a set of analytic dimensions;[5] empirical research based on such frameworks inevitably will lead to findings that show a gap between theory and practice.

Instead of looking to idealizations of professionalism, the analysis in the preceding chapters makes it clear that lawyers must arrive at an understanding of their work — at least the part of their work that comprises what I have called ordinary litigation — that acknowledges the contradictions and pressures inherent in what they are called on to do. The two images of professional and broker that have guided my analysis demonstrate one way to reconcile the unrealistic idealization of the professions with what has long been recognized as the economics that govern the work of lawyers (see, e.g., Hurst, 1950: 306). Applying the concept of the *professions*, as developed by sociologists,[6] to lawyering in ordinary litigation fails in many respects to account for what occurs in the everyday cases that make up the vast bulk of the work of America's civil courts. The alternative conception I proposed, that of the *broker*, in some ways complements that of the professional and in other ways provides a contrast to the more traditional image.

At the outset of my research, I viewed the broker image as possibly supplanting the professional image; the conceptual framework that I had developed would, I believed, provide a better account of the realities of the world of ordinary litigation as seen from the lawyer's perspective. However, as the analysis progressed, I realized the professional/broker distinction actually captured the conflicts that confront lawyers in their day-to-day work and thus provided complementary rather than alternative images. Lawyers work in a world that involves large elements of schizophrenia, regarding both the expectations of lay clients and observers and the economic realities that impinge on the routine work most nonelite lawyers perform most of the time. Recognizing these contradictory pressures is the first step toward coping with the resulting dilemmas.

Professionals and Brokers

The analysis I have presented demonstrates that in some ways the broker image works much better as an explanatory framework than does the professional image. The role of the fee-paying relationsh¡p has no place in the traditional concept of the professional;[7] on the other hand, it is very prominent in the idea of the broker. As I have shown in the preceding pages, the way the lawyer is to be paid impacts substantially on the lawyer's decisions to allocate time to litigation, both in terms of what influences those decisions and on the actual amount of effort allocated; interestingly, the fee-paying relationship seems to have little direct impact on the content of the lawyer's work, at least in terms of the categories used in my analysis.[8] The analysis of the results achieved through litigation showed that the fee-paying relationship had important implications for the outcome from the plaintiff's perspective; again, there is nothing in the theory of the professions that would lead one to expect such relationships, but it is not at all surprising in the context of the broker image. Likewise, the specific patterns of success for contingent fee lawyers, and their clients, make sense within this alternate image.

However, despite the better fit of the brokerage image in these areas, there are other ways in which the professional image seems more consistent with some of the findings. It is ironic that the component of the professionalism concept that originally led me to turn to the brokerage alternative – the autonomy (or what I had expected to be the lack of autonomy) of the lawyer vis-à-vis the client – seems to fit well with the traditional professional image. In contrast to prior work reporting less autonomy than the theory of professions suggests (e.g., Cain, 1979: 335), at least in explicit terms, lawyers handling ordinary litigation carry out their work with a large degree of autonomy.

There is little evidence of significant control of the lawyer by the client, regardless of whether the client is an individual or an organization (even if that organization is a large insurance company on which the lawyer is highly dependent). It may be that with clients from whom the lawyer expects (or hopes) to receive future work, there are self-imposed restrictions on autonomy. However, one would expect that such reductions in autonomy would be most likely to show up in efforts to minimize the cost of the litigation to clients with whom the lawyer has an ongoing professional relationship and, for hourly fee lawyers, there is no indication that an ongoing professional relationship with the client affects the amount of effort one way or the other. Thus, with regard to ordinary litigation, my findings are consistent with Heinz and Laumann's observation (1983: 360–365) that personal services lawyers have significant autonomy vis-à-vis their work, and it seems that this autonomy extends to lawyers who handle routine work for large corporations such as insurance companies, at least in terms of the daily conduct of litigation activities. One question I cannot answer regarding the autonomy possessed by lawyers in litigation is whether it reflects that clients defer to their lawyers as professionals, or simply that ordinary litigation is so unremarkable that there is little need for significant client input into the process.

When one looks at the content of the day-to-day work of ordinary litigation, the picture presented in the preceding chapters is a blend of the professional and broker images with, as I will argue in the next section, a heavy tendency toward the broker image. I divided the work of litigation into activities that draw on what I termed the formal legal and the informal legal skills, with most litigation requiring a mixture of the two. Some kinds of cases, particularly in the federal courts, draw very heavily on the formal legal skills (e.g., legal research and analysis) around which legal education is centered, and it is clear that for those areas the lawyer as portrayed by the professional image makes the most sense. However, in the most typical areas of ordinary litigation, torts and contracts, the lawyer must draw much more heavily on the informal, insider kinds of legal skills than on the formal skills. I will suggest in the next section that this heavy weighting away from the formal legal skills that form part of the core of the professional image of the lawyer raises the possibility of considering alternative approaches to representation in the handling of ordinary disputes.

The Role of Lawyers in Litigation:
The Implications for Change

In the last few years, participants and observers from various areas have begun to question the legal profession's monopoly on delivery of legal services in the United States.[9] The milder proposals have called for permitting nonlawyers to perform routine legal services such as drafting and probating simple wills, handling real estate closings, or preparing the paperwork for uncontested divorces (American Bar Association, 1988: 52; Luban, 1989a: 269; Public Protection Committee, 1988[10]). The most extreme proposals advanced by, among others, the former chairman of the Legal Services Corporation, seek the complete "deregulation" of who may practice law (*National Law Journal*, February 23, 1987; Abel, 1989a: 245;[11] Morrison, 1976).[12]

The legal profession has been vigorous in obtaining and enforcing laws against the "unauthorized practice" of law by nonlawyers (see Christensen, 1980; Rhode, 1981), but the evidence that (1) it reflects the desires of consumers, or that (2) it can be justified in terms of the quality of services delivered is no where to be found. In her study of complaints known to the chairs or heads of unauthorized practice enforcement committees and agencies, Rhode (1981: 33) found that only 27 out of 1,188 known "inquiries, investigations, and complaints" "arose from consumer complaints and involved specific customer injury."

There has been virtually no research on the qualitative differences between lawyer and nonlawyer advocacy. In its decision in Walters *v* National Association of Radiation Survivors (473 US 305), a case that challenged the statutory limits on fees paid to lawyers representing veterans involved in disputes with the Veteran's Administration concerning veterans' benefits, the Supreme Court cited figures comparing the relative success rates of claimants represented by lawyers, claimants represented by volunteers from veterans' organizations, and claimants who were unrepresented (at 327); these figures provided no indication of major differences contingent on type of (or presence of) representation;[13] the Supreme Court noted (and rejected) the District Court's conclusion that the number of claimants represented by lawyers was so low that comparisons were dubious. The trial judge who initially struck down the fee limitations (National Association of Radiation Survivors *v* Walters [589 F.Supp 1302]) quoted statistics comparing the success of veterans seeking to have their discharges from the armed services upgraded (from dishonorable or general discharge to honorable discharge—the latter being a condition for obtaining most types of veterans' benefits); those statistics (at 1318) showed differential success rates, with veterans represented by lawyers more likely to obtain the desired upgrade (73 percent) than those with lay representatives from one of the veterans' organizations (49 percent). It is unclear whether these differences reflect case selection by lawyers (lawyers may have rejected cases with little chance of success) or differences in the quality of advocacy. The discrepancy between the effect of type of representation on service discharge upgrades compared to veterans' benefits appeals may also reflect that the former was not a part of a highly routinized process while the latter was; the more *ad hoc* nature of discharge cases may be exactly the area where the ability to carry out legal research and to frame case-specific legal arguments is most important.

Other evidence concerning the impact of representation by an attorney in the dispute settlement process is reported by Ross (1980) in his study of the disposition of insurance claims. Ross observed that the presence of a lawyer representing the claimant increased the amount of the settlement.[14] He attributes this to a variety of factors (1980: 116–121), but the most prominent is that the lawyer is able to include in the claim evaluation factors that may not have occurred to the client. Insurance officials may insist that they want to settle claims fairly and quickly and that the presence of lawyers (or other kinds of representatives for the claimant) is irrelevant with regard to the final result; however, it is hard to imagine representatives of insurance companies telling people who claim far below what they might be "entitled" to that they are requesting too little in settlement (see Genn, 1988: 132).

Thus, the evidence concerning the impact of legal representation, as opposed to other forms of representation, is fragmentary at best. As noted, there has been virtually no research that rigorously compares cases utilizing different kinds of representation,[15] although there has been some consideration of the conditions under which various types of representation may be efficacious (see Menkel-Meadow, 1985b). In considering lawyers' virtual monopoly on paid representation in adversary settings, it would be ideal to have systematic comparative data on the effectiveness of different types of representatives. Given that there is little such information available, on what basis might a judgment be formed concerning whether nonlawyer advocacy should be an option available to potential and actual litigants?

There is little doubt, either from the analysis of ordinary litigation in the preceding chapters or from the other research discussed throughout this book, that expert assistance is valuable in dealing with contentious matters. However, does such representation, in routine disputes, require formal legal training? The image of the solo lawyer presented by Carlin (1962) casts doubts on the role played by what I have called formal legal knowledge in many of the disputes of the type that most frequently lead to ordinary litigation. Why not allow nonlawyers to assist persons making third-party claims against insurance companies? Might it even be possible for nonlawyers to initiate and handle some of the earlier stages of the litigation process in such cases? Could this kind of "opening up" make the process of resolving the cases that arise out of everyday motor vehicle accidents (and other kinds of common events that result in injuries and property damage) more economical? Rhode (1981: 78) reports that 20 out of 50 Workers' Compensation Boards permit lay representation, and the issues before those boards are probably comparable in complexity to those involved in other kinds of routine injury cases.

And what about cases arising outside of areas where one of the interested parties is not an insurance company? Would a similar line of argument apply? As I said in the last section, the analysis presented in the preceeding chapters indicates clearly that there are a number of areas of litigation, particularly in the federal courts, where the person handling the case must draw heavily on formal legal skills. Cases involving issues such as business regulation, civil rights/discrimination, government action, and government benefits stand strongly apart from the areas that are often very routine such as torts, contract, and domestic relations; however, while cases in the former categories represent a substantial fraction of the work of the federal courts, they are relatively rare in the state courts where most civil litigation takes place. Moreover, it may be that at least part of the reason that such cases draw heavily on skills such as legal research is that they arise in relatively new fields of law, where many questions remain to be settled; it may be that, over time, some or all of these areas will become more settled legally and will come to resemble torts and contracts in the skills that are required. It is also possible that some of the areas will remain such that significant formal legal skills will be needed; for example, it may well be that by the time government benefits claims reach the stage of litigation, the issues involved are almost exclusively legal as opposed to factual. Nonetheless, nonlawyer representatives are used in a variety of administrative tribunals, such as Public Utility Commissions (Rhode, 1981: 78), the federal Patent Office (Quigg, 1985; Rhode, 1981: 79), the Social Security Administration (Wolf, 1985), federal immigration agencies (Holmes, 1985), and state unemployment compensation commissions (Freedman, 1985). Despite the fact that cases in some of these agencies can frequently involve technical interpretations of complex legal issues, there is no evidence that nonlawyer advocates fare any differently than licensed attorney advocates.[16]

The areas of divorce, contract, and real property probably fall somewhere between torts and the more frontier areas to be found largely in the federal courts. The issues in divorce, contract, and real property cases are more likely to go beyond effectively presenting a client's claim. This is probably least true for divorce, where the issues may be simply knowing what entitlements the client has under existing law and being sure that all such entitlements are reasonably asserted; it is probably most true for contracts, where there may be a substantial element of interpretation of contract provisions involved. Even in the contracts area, it is difficult to judge the degree to which this is correct for the more mundane cases that fall within what I have termed ordinary litigation (the extreme example being cases where one party has failed or refused to make agreed-on payments); in such cases the law is usually fairly well settled, and the issues are primarily factual in nature.

We can now begin to see a basis of classification relevant to the kind of representation a case might require: to the degree that a case raises factual issues (which need to be resolved through factual investigation), the skills of the "legal broker" are most relevant; on the other hand, if a case raises significant issues of law (which require systematic legal research and analysis), the formal legal skills of the "legal professional" are more relevant. I recognize that it is dangerous to try to distinguish too sharply between law and fact; the framework established by the law determines which facts are relevant, and the particular facts influence the applicability of different legal principles. Nonetheless, for *most* cases there is a clear predominance of one side or the other of the fact/law distinction; only in a much smaller subset of cases does a greater deal of blending and ambiguity arise.

The use of the terms "legal broker" and "legal professional" is intended to take into account this interrelationship, while being sensitive to the question of the relative balance between law and fact in the issues that must be dealt with. I use the term "legal broker" to suggest a person who is knowledgeable about the law and draws on that knowledge to frame the development and presentation of a client's position. The "legal professional," on the other hand, must apply a combination of formal legal knowledge and formal legal skills in a more creative way. Thus, in cases where the task is primarily one of effectively evaluating and presenting a "claim" within a legal framework, it is the legal broker whose skills are most relevant (i.e., a person knowledgeable about the relevant law but also able to evaluate the claim accurately, drawing on the insider knowledge of "going rates," etc.). Where the issues presented involve more subtle questions of law, or areas of unsettled law, then the skills of the legal professional must be drawn on.

The alternative roles that I have described raise the possibility of alternative kinds of "legal" careers. I have in mind the kind of differentiation that exists within the medical sphere (although not necessarily the kinds of subordinate relationships that exist between physicians and other health practitioners). A lot of what goes on in health care does not require the level of training and expertise possessed by a fully qualified physician. Day-to-day care, including treatment of many minor problems, can be handled by someone with particular medical knowledge and a recognition of the limitations of that knowledge.

The term "professional" has come to be used for many of the persons working in the health-care field, but not in the sense that I have used the more specific sociological concept of the "profession." The level of training possessed by nurses, medical assistants, midwives, X-ray technicians, inhalation therapists, and so forth, is substantially less than that of the physician; for purposes of discussion, let me refer to this level of personnel as "paraprofessionals." My point, then, is that much of the work of health care is carried out on a daily basis by persons working at the paraprofessional level, and this reflects the level of expertise necessary to complete the tasks involved. In fact, there are numerous situations where the paraprofessional in the medical field does not even work under the direct supervision of a physician: the school nurse, the physical therapist, the medical dietitian, and so on.[17] One might argue that there are very stringent limits on the kinds of things that the paraprofessionals are permitted to do, but this may be more true in theory than in reality; while a physician may be required to sign a prescription form, if a well-trained and reliable nurse practitioner has determined that the medication is required, it is unlikely that the physician is going to think twice before handing over the prescription. One could require that all medical care be provided by fully qualified physicians, justifying that on the grounds that personnel with lesser qualifications might fail to recognize a medical situation that was beyond their skills; in fact, the opposite is the case—the trend is toward increasing reliance on paraprofessionals in the medical context.

This last kind of argument—the ability of someone with less training than the fully qualified professional to recognize all of the subtleties of a situation—has been used by the legal profession in its effort to control the delivery of law-related services. Yet the parallels between health care and legal services concerning the level of training and expertise required for routine areas are clear. Certain kinds of legal knowledge are necessary to carry out many law-related tasks; however, that legal expertise does not require the extensive training of a lawyer. One example might be a routine contract to purchase houses; a knowledgeable real estate broker is likely to be able to prepare a contract just as well as a person who has completed a full 3 years of law school (in fact, given a choice of an experienced real estate broker and a freshly minted law school graduate, I would have an overwhelming preference for the experienced broker!). Similarly, the preparation of a tax return must be done in conformance with the tax laws; one could turn to a lawyer for such work, but it is much more common to turn to a tax accountant or even, for the simplest returns, to a tax preparation service. A tax accountant, more so than a person working for a storefront tax preparation service, has specific legal knowledge that is used in the preparation of the return.[18]

How might a lawyer respond to proposals that the practice of law in routine cases needs to be "deprofessionalized" (again, I am using the term "professional" in the technical as opposed to common parlance)?[19] It is hardly necessary to point out that such a proposal would represent a potential threat to the livelihoods of a substantial number of lawyers, and that the organized profession would almost certainly move to ban, as the unauthorized practice of law, nonlawyers offering services as legal brokers. While the profession has been prepared generally to look the other way when activities that might be construed as the practice of law[20] are such that they do not represent an economic threat to members of the bar,[21] one of the major roles played by professional organizations has been to fend off potential competitors (see Hurst, 1950: 319–322; Christensen, 1980; Rhode, 1981).[22]

There are two obvious lines of attack. First would be the position that there is simply too much danger of someone who is not fully qualified in the law failing to recognize subtleties that need to be taken into account. Given the description of the solo practice lawyer as developed by Carlin (1962), it is hard to sustain this argument as a basis of distinguishing between the legal professional and the legal broker. But even presuming that most legal professionals would have the training and skill to recognize the kinds of legal subtleties that might be missed by legal brokers, I question the likelihood of this arising in the context of most cases that fall into my category of ordinary litigation (outside the "more legal" areas in the federal courts). Furthermore, the risks associated with this potential problem might well be reduced by the existence of good working relations between legal brokers and legal professionals whereby a legal broker could draw on the legal professional as a check against such potentialities. In a sense, there might be a relationship between the legal broker and the legal professional such as exists in England between the generalist solicitor and the specialist barrister, whereby the barrister can be brought in to give an expert opinion on legal issues or, in line with the more common image of the barrister, to argue the case in court if need be.[23]

The second line of criticism of the legal broker would be that the broker is at a severe disadvantage vis-à-vis negotiation. I argued in Chapter 9 that it was not possible to separate the results achieved outside of litigation from those achieved through litigation (and, likewise, one could not truly separate results achieved through settlement before trial to those achieved through trial) because the potential for litigation (and the experience of litigation in similar cases) sets the framework for all results achieved, regardless of the ultimate mode of resolution. The legal broker, unless empowered to carry a claim through to adjudication,[24] would not be in a position to threaten a recalcitrant opponent with litigation. Opponents would be able to take advantage of this to reduce the payment below that which might be achieved if the threat of litigation was perceived as real and immediate.[25]

This argument has force only if the potential payers of claims (i.e., the potential defendants) perceive it as being in their interest to resist the efforts of the legal broker. If the legal broker has a good working relationship with a legal professional who can be expected to bring suit on behalf of the client if that becomes necessary, then the negotiating disadvantage of the legal broker becomes moot.[26] Furthermore, if the potential costs to the defendant of forcing a case to litigation are greater than the effective penalty the legal broker suffers by not having the ability to turn to the courts, it would clearly be in the defendant's interest not to exploit this potential disadvantage of the legal broker.[27]

There are two potential justifications for considering the alternative of legal brokers as a paraprofessional group to handle substantial amounts of what is now ordinary litigation.[28] First, it is likely that an experienced legal broker could be more effective in handling claims than a generalist lawyer would be. The legal broker would not be at an advantage, in terms of gross results, over the specialist lawyer, who would essentially combine the skills of the legal broker with those of the legal professional. Given that the analysis presented in Chapter 4 shows that most ordinary litigation seems to be handled by lawyers who could be described fairly as litigation specialists, this argument cannot stand on its own.

The second justification starts from the presumption that legal brokers could, in most cases of ordinary litigation, achieve gross results comparable to those now obtained by the litigation specialists who handle most of this work. From the client's perspective, the question is not so much gross results as net results (i.e., what is obtained after all expenses have either been subtracted for the claimant or added for the defendant). If legal brokers could handle the work at a lower expense than legal professionals while maintaining the same level of gross results, the client would come out ahead of what would be achieved by a legal professional. Take, as a starting point, the defendant's representative, who would probably be paid on an hourly basis. The typical hourly rate charged by lawyers handling ordinary litigation is $75 to $100 per hour; if a legal broker could handle the work for $50 per hour (perhaps reflecting a combination of a lower level of overhead and a lower level of income), this would be a savings of at least 33 percent. Even at $50 per hour, the representation would not be cheap, but any kind of skilled service (plumbers, mechanics, etc.) is expensive. Greater savings would be achieved by the defendant if the use of legal brokers reduced the incidence of litigation, keeping in mind that only about 10 percent of disputes even now lead to the filing of a lawsuit (see Miller and Sarat, 1980–1981), because many of the routine but time-consuming (and thus costly) steps required by the formalities of litigation would be avoided.

The analysis is more complex on the claimant's side, presuming that the legal broker would be paid on a percentage (i.e., contingent) fee basis, as is the typical plaintiff's lawyer. Recall that the incentives for someone working on a percentage basis are governed by effective hourly rates achieved. That rate is, in turn, determined by the combination of the amount recovered, the percentage charged, and the hours worked. When one combines these three factors for the contingent fee lawyer, it immediately becomes clear that it is in the interest of the lawyer to settle the case quickly, even if the settlement is less than optimal from the client's viewpoint. If one were to assume that the savings obtained by using a legal broker rather than a legal professional (i.e., a contingent fee lawyer) would result from the former charging a significantly lower percentage (for illustration, let us assume 10 to 20 percent rather than 25 to 40 percent), the incentive for the broker to settle the case with minimum effort would be even greater than that for the lawyer. As with the contingent fee lawyer, the incentives for quick settlements would be greatest for the smaller cases, and it is precisely these cases that would be most likely to go to the legal broker. But, at the same time, the legal broker would begin with a strong presumption against litigation and would be much less likely to have to incur the costs (i.e., devote time) of preparing the legal documents associated with the court process itself.

Despite the nature of these economic incentives, the analysis of outcome for the contingent fee lawyers suggested that, at least in the more modest cases, the lawyers were able to obtain most of what they estimated to be a fair settlement from the viewpoint of their clients. Recall that I suggested that this probably meant that in smaller cases lawyers wanted to be quite certain of both the size and likelihood of recovery before accepting the case. If one presumes that this would be equally true of legal brokers, there is no reason to suspect that they would be any more affected, in terms of results achieved, by the economic incentives of the working situation.

On first glance the proposal that the lawyer's monopoly of representation in contentious matters be ended may seem to be very radical.[29] However, let me suggest that while it may be radical in appearance, it is not radical in reality. First, there has been substantial and very general movement toward the use of paralegal personnel to handle many types of matters that previously had been seen as the exclusive preserve of fully credentialed lawyers;[30] while some of these changes may be more cosmetic than real (reflecting a shift of work from experienced clerical staff to persons with the title of "paralegal"), other shifts reflect the recognition that routine and repetitive legal tasks can be handled by persons with particular legal knowledge and skills (as opposed to what might be characterized as the general knowledge and skills imparted by law school). As part of this general movement toward the use of paralegal personnel, there has been a more specific phenomenon of using paraprofessionals to assist clients of public sector legal service organizations with a variety of kinds of contentious legal problems (see Zemans, 1986: 57–62; but see Menkel-Meadow, 1985b); however, once a dispute reaches the stage of actual litigation, there must be at least some formal involvement on the part of a licensed lawyer. One might belittle this as just another example of cut-price justice for poor persons, but there is no specific evidence that paralegals working in legal clinics are any less effective than lawyers handling similar problems (Zemans, 1986: 60–61).

A second example where there is evidence of litigation-like work being done effectively by nonlawyers is in the debt collection field. Strictly speaking, as I have been using the idea of "dispute," uncontested debt cases fall outside my sphere of analysis. Still, the roles of the lawyer and the nonlawyer handling debt cases are instructive for the point I am making. Some law practices depend heavily on routine debt work as a major source of income. Up until the stage of filing suit, the work of the lawyer handling debt cases is really no different than the work of the nonlawyer debt collector. The threat of being faced with a court action for nonpayment may be more potent when it comes on the letterhead of a law firm, but whether or not it makes any difference in actual results is unknown. I suspect that law firms handling general debt cases obtain those cases because their fees do not differ significantly from other kinds of debt collection agencies, and the client has nothing to lose by paying a lawyer rather than a nonlawyer a percentage of what is recovered.

Finally, until a lawsuit is actually filed, the normal procedure for handling claims by an insurance company is to rely on the expertise of nonlawyer claims adjusters (see Ross, 1980; Carlin, 1962). There is no evidence to indicate that these adjusters are any less effective in dealing with the lawyers representing claimants than are lawyers who eventually are retained to handle cases that result in litigation. Why should claimants not be permitted to rely on nonlaw-yers to negotiate on their behalf? In fact, if one is involved in a claim against one's own insurance company (e.g., concerning a casualty loss arising from a house fire), it is possible to retain a private "claims adjuster" to evaluate the claim and negotiate with the insurance company. Why should this not be extended to claims against someone else's insurance company, and even to money damage disputes arising from contracts or other areas of law?

In England, a group of persons exists who function in this kind of role, although they are limited to claims against insurance companies (either claims against one's own insurance company or claims against a tort-feasor's insurance company); in a very real sense, these persons are essentially what I have described as legal brokers, but they do not have the ability to pursue cases into court. The legal profession is very critical of "claims assessors," as they are called (Law Society, 1970; Zander, 1978: 194–196), and I have heard insurance claims people in England refer to them disparagingly as "ambulance chasers." However, absolutely nothing is known about the effectiveness of their work, either as compared to representation by a solicitor or as compared to no representation at all. Furthermore, in England many kinds of contentious matters are dealt with outside the courts through an extensive system of tribunals (see Jackson, 1977: 110–177; Bell, 1969), and representation before such bodies is not restricted to lawyers. While there has been some examination of the frequency of representation before such tribunals, both by lawyers and by others (see Frost and Howard, 1977; Benson Commission, 1979b: 91–101), there has been no evaluation of the effectiveness of various types of representation.[31] A systematic comparison of what various kinds of advocates are able to achieve for their clients would provide a very important base for considering the implications of ending the monopoly of representation currently held by lawyers in the United States.

Finally, regardless of whether or not legal brokers are as effective as licensed lawyers in handling contentious work, opening up such work to other types of practitioners will immediately increase competition. The impact of such competition is likely to be a reduction in fees charged to the consumers of such services. The potentially dramatic effect of ending monopolies held by the legal profession can be seen in what happened in England after the solicitor's monopoly on "conveyancing" (the processing of transfers of ownership of real property) was ended. In the late 1970s, conveyancing fees for residential property ranged from 1 to 2 percent of the value of the transaction (Selinger, 1987; see also, Benson, 1979: 269–276);[32] these fees had changed little during the 1970s, even after what amounted to a minimum fee schedule was abolished in 1973 as the result of the action of the Monopolies Commission. However, estimates of the drop in typical conveyancing fees after the passage of legislation creating a paraprofessional group of government-licensed conveyancers ranged from 25 percent (see Abel, 1989b: 292) to 50 percent (*Guardian*, January 14, 1987, p. 4),[33] *even before the first conveyancers entered practice in 1987!*[34] While part of this effect is probably unique to the particulars of real estate transaction in England, the impact of competition among different types of advocates is almost certain to reduce the costs of representation to substantial numbers of consumers. This will only increase the average person's access to justice.

Notes

Chapter 1

1. While the organized legal profession is concerned about how it is perceived by the American public (see "ABA Study Says Lawyers' Professionalism Has Declined," National Law Journal, August 4, 1986, p. 10), the legal profession has been the subject of disdain throughout American history, and as far back as ancient Rome and Greece (see Rhode, 1985: 589; Pound, 1953: 137; Roth and Roth, 1989).

2. Over the last 2 decades, research on the criminal justice system has provided a picture of the role of lawyers in the processing of persons charged with criminal conduct. This is in no small part the result of the research funding provided by LEAA.

3. In the federal trial courts during 1984, 261,485 civil cases were filed (230,378 excluding prisoner petitions, which are typically filed on a *pro se*—without representation—basis) compared to only 18,587 criminal cases (Administrative Office, 1985: 133, 166). In the state courts, figures collected by the National Center fc State Courts suggest that in courts of general jurisdiction, over 70 percent of the caseload is civil, and in all trial courts, omitting traffic cases, it is over 55 percent civil (Flango, Roper, and Elsner, 1983: 25–27). For 1981, the National Center estimated that a total of 14,800,000 civil cases were filed in state trial courts compared to 10,500,000 criminal (including juvenile) cases (National Center for State Courts, 1985: 47).

4. Divorce is one area of litigation conspicuous by its absence from the preceding list; while any area of litigation has its unique features, it is likely that within the broad contours of ordinary litigation, divorce differs more than other areas. In the discussion and analyses that follow, I will deal with divorce litigation only marginally, both because of its unique aspects and because of its intentionally low representation within the data set from which I will work.

5. Abel's efforts are a part of a much larger, comparative effort by the Working Group for Comparative Study of Legal Professions of the Research Committee on Sociology of Law of the International Sociology Association. The descriptive and theoretical efforts of this collective endeavor are reported in Abel and Lewis (1988a, 1988b, 1989; see also, Abel, 1985; Rueschemeyer, 1986; Arthurs, Weisman, and Zemans, 1986).

6. Abel (1989a: 14) describes his own work as "a sociology of the legal *profession*, not of lawyers' *work* [emphasis in original]."

7. One "selected" bibliography, now over 15 years old, is over 50 pages long (Moore, 1970: 245–301).

8. The topic headings in Abel's (1980) bibliography on the legal profession include things such as "demographics," "professional ethics," "recruitment, socialization, and allocation," "professional associations," and "lawyers and social change." Maru's recent bibliographic essay on *Research on the Legal Profession* (1986) considers "historical studies," the "work of lawyers," "career development and career patterns," "regulating the profession," "the organized bar," and "extraprofessional activities."

9. There are many discussions of the problems and issues involved in defining what is meant by the notion of a profession; see, for example, Rueschemeyer (1983: 40f); Geison (1983: 4); Greenwood (1957); Cogan (1953); Hughes (1963: 656f); Barber (1963: 672); Parsons (1968: 536); Dingwall (1976: 336f); Gyarmati (1975: 629); Goode (1957: 194f); Ritzer (1973: 62–63); Millerson (1964); see Bucher and Strauss (1961) or Johnson (1972: 24–25) for critiques of efforts to identify the distinguishing characteristics of professions.

10. Even the most minimal definitions include some reference to specialized knowledge; for example, in his recent analysis of competing professions, Abbott eschews the need for rigorous definition (1988: 318) but uses as his "loose definition – professions are somewhat exclusive groups on individuals applying somewhat abstract knowledge to particular cases."

11. As noted previously, Abel's major work on the legal professions in England and the United States, (1986; 1988a, 1988b, 1988c, 1989a) emphasizes another dimension that some sociologists (e.g., Larson, 1977; Freidson, 1986) have suggested as an alternative approach to looking at the role and impact of professions in society: the control of the market, both in terms of entry into the profession and in terms of services provided, by the profession itself, usually through professional organizations. Abbott's work (1986, 1988) on lawyers and the professions more generally deals with similar issues.

12. As Rueschemeyer (1986: 442) pointed out, this "idealizing character" of the concept of profession "was used to state occupational ideals in capsule fashion [and] it became the centerpiece of a rosy self-presentation."

13. This view of the advocate's fee as a voluntary payment goes back at least as far as ancient Rome (see Pound, 1953: 54, 68).

14. One element of the autonomy of the professional is the control of the norms of behavior and performance of members of the professional group by the profession itself through professional organizations.

15. A second important dimension distinguishes between lawyers who work on "contentious" matters (i.e., civil litigation, arbitration, criminal defense) from those who focus on more "cooperative" matters (corporate law, trusts and estates, property transfers, etc.).

16. This finding leads Heinz and Laumann to draw on Johnson's (1972) distinction between patronage and collegial control. Ironically, the earliest professionals (e.g., artists, architects, physicians, clergy) were entirely dependent on "patrons" for their livelihood (Johnson, 1972: 68). It was only with the growth of first an entrepreneurial class and then a well-paid middle class that professionals were able to "sell" their services to a broad clientele and escape direct dependence on a patron (Johnson, 1972: 52).

17. A more general analysis of the work of lawyers provides little evidence that most of their work effort is devoted to highly technical tasks drawing on formal legal expertise. Landon reports that lawyers in rural Missouri spend almost two thirds of their time

conferring with clients (1982: 483). Those practicing in a more urban setting spend much less time conferring with clients, but less than a third of their time is spent on technical legal tasks such as researching and preparing legal documents.

18. More generally, the system of payment for the lawyer can create a variety of potential conflicts of interest between lawyer and client; see Kritzer (1989) for a discussion of the impact of economic incentives on the behavior of solicitors handling personal injury claims in England.

19. In the report of the earlier study (Kritzer, 1984a), I used only three dimensions, combining the first two listed here into what I labeled the "professional" dimension.

20. I am by no means the first to question some of the key components of the professionalism framework. Legal historian Lawrence Friedman, in his discussion of the development of the profession in the United States, observed that "most lawyers always served, mainly themselves, next their clients, and last of all their conception of that diffuse, nebulous thing, the public interest (1973: 554)."

21. Galanter (1985a: 549) links the brokerage image directly to negotiation: "To posit the centrality of bargaining characterizes lawyers less as masters of a body of recondite knowledge than as brokers and middlemen." While brokering may be related to negotiation, my argument goes well beyond the point suggested by Galanter.

22. There is a third role that falls somewhere between that of the self-interested broker and the alter ego professional: the ombudsman. One associates with the ombudsman role the intermediary position and insider knowledge of the broker and the altruism of the professional. It is worth noting that the distinction between the broker and the ombudsman has important implications for the study of a variety of political phenomenon. Recent writing on the constituency service aspects of the work of legislators has typically characterized that work in terms of an ombudsman function (Gellhorn, 1967; Verkuil, 1975; Hill, 1976; VUWLR, 1982), where a better conceptualization would be a brokerage function, given that there is an expectation of an exchange relationship (see Homans, 1958; or Waldman, 1972, for discussions of the exchange theory perspective).

23. Anthropologists have used the broker concept most extensively (starting with Wolf, 1956; and Geertz, 1960) in the study of what is called "culture brokers": "[an] individual who stands between two . . . cultural traditions, and assumes the task of fostering the spread of one into the domain of the other" (Hopkins et al., 1977: 30); however, while this use of the concept of broker captures the intermediary aspects of the role, it fails to incorporate the other central aspects of brokerage.

24. Boissevain develops this concept of brokerage in the context of a discussion of patronage that he defines in terms of the distribution of first-order resources. He is seeking to distinguish brokerage from patronage (see the work on patronage by Mayer, 1967; Blok, 1969).

25. Boissevain's ideas have been used previously in the study of law-related activities; in particular, Flood's study of barristers clerks (1981, 1983) is, in part, built around this conceptualization.

26. In an examination of political leadership in Canada, Aucoin (1986: 18) has applied the notion of brokerage to understanding the relationships among elites, with a particular emphasis on the importance of *transactions* as the binding force in cabinet government. In a study of American political executives, Ries (1969: 105f) used the idea of broker similarly. Neither study, however, systematically explicates what is included in the broker concept (although Ries seems to be using the term as essentially synonymous with that of a simple intermediary).

27. Bailey notes (1969: 173) that the broker in the village where his Indian fieldwork was based (Bisipara) "is despised by those at both ends of his transactions. His fellow-villagers think of him as a liar and a cheat and a hypocrite, a man who has made a fortune out of their predicaments with the administrators, a renegade who pretends to serve his fellow villagers but in fact serves no-one but himself. Officials and politicians see him as a villager with ambitions far above his education and his abilities, an unreliable man, at the behest of the highest bidder and hypocritical in his protestations of concern for the public interest." *This is strikingly similar to often expressed contemporary views of lawyers!*

28. An alternate argument may be made that brokers, in fact, enhance the value of transactions by bringing their expertise to the situation; that is, the transaction is more valuable as a result of the broker's work than it would be without that work. See Gilson (1984) for an application of this argument to the work of business lawyers.

29. The exchange theory perspective (see Homans, 1958) can be seen as asserting the centrality of transactional ties in all social interactions. My position is that such ties are a significant element in the phenomenon I am considering, but I would not go so far as to assert that such ties are the central element (see Kritzer, 1984a).

30. Hughes (1977: 288) speaks of the "moral division of labor," which refers to "the processes by which differing moral functions are distributed among members of society." I am using "moral" to refer not to the basis of distribution of roles by society but to the basis of acceptance of roles by individuals (i.e., the acceptance of a "calling").

31. Compare my distinction between technical knowledge and insider knowledge to Freidson's distinction between "formal knowledge" and "nonformal specialized knowledge" (Freidson, 1986: 3).

32. Note that in some circumstances the position dimension for the professional could be filled in rather than being left as "[specified]." For example, in the medical sociology literature (see, e.g., Mechanic, 1978: 350–375), the role of the doctor as the professional is sometime portrayed as what might be described as a team leader, either in a large group practice context (where the other players are nurses, nurse practitioners, physician assistants, laboratory and X-ray technicians, etc.) or in the hospital setting (where the other players are nurses, laboratory staff, therapists, etc.). A similar view of lawyers is advanced by Fitzpatrick (1989).

33. One area of criminal defense work that has been considered within a fairly broad professionalism framework is the relatively elite field of white-collar defense (see Mann, 1986).

34. Interestingly, Carlin describes the actors who refer clients to lawyers as "brokers" (1962: 135f)—the person who gets the lawyer and client together (i.e., serves as an intermediary between the lawyer and the potential client). At several junctures Carlin speaks of lawyers serving as brokers between their clients and other lawyers to whom they refer clients (1962: 141) or between their clients and vendors of other services or commodities such as banking, real estate, and insurance, "possibly mediating between them" (1962: 114–115). Similarly, an early study of public interest legal practice (Marks with Leswing and Fortinsky, 1972) devotes an entire chapter to a similar brokerage function: the matching of clients or causes with lawyers prepared to handle public interest work; most of the brokers are themselves lawyers.

35. The notion of "client control" as used by lawyers in speaking of clients clearly refers to the lawyer controlling the client rather than vice versa. For example, in his study of lawyers in rural Missouri, Landon (1985: 104) quoted one lawyer as saying "Lawyers here tend to control their clients in subtle ways, even with tone of voice, in order to avoid too aggressive confrontation." See Reed (1969), Hosticka (1979), Blum-

berg (1967), Flemming (1986), or Sarat and Felstiner (1986, 1988) for other discussions of the problem of client control (or perhaps, more appropriately, "controlling clients").

36. In his important study of "Lawyers and Consumer Protection Laws," Macaulay (1979) points out that lawyers often represent their clients in a nonadversarial fashion, either serving as "information brokers" (p. 125, 152), as mediators between represented and unrepresented parties (p. 117), or as "counsel for the situation" (p. 128, 159). Macaulay uses the term "broker" (and its derivatives "brokering" and "brokerage") several times in several different ways in his article, all of which draw on the notion of the intermediary, but none of which involve the concept I have fully developed here.

37. One theme that I will not deal with in this book but that is interesting in terms of the larger implications is the applicability of the broker/professional distinction for understanding the work of other occupations. For example, the role of the primary care physician in the relationship between patients and the medical system could be considered in this framework. The medical sociology literature deals with this issue: the case management model. Intagliata (1982: 659) describes case management as "the human link between the client and the system," which fits nicely with the point with which I opened the chapter, that lawyers are the link between clients and the legal system. Often, however, case managers deliver care services as well as serving a brokering function (see Lamb, 1980), and the theoretical issues raised in the case management literature (see Dill, 1987, for a good summary of these issues) are very different from those that form the core discussion of this book.

The only explicit discussion of brokerage I could find in the medical literature concerned the role of nurses in countries where there are parallel systems of biomedical health care and ethnomedical health care (traditional healers relying on spiritual, herbal, or similar approaches). Barbee (1986, 1987) describes the nurse in Botswana as occupying a brokerage role between the traditional culture (in which most nurses were brought up and that emphasizes ethnomedicine) and biomedicine (in which the nurses have been trained): "In their formal and informal dealings with the people, nurses share the same *baTswanna* cosmology about health and illness as do the people in the community. At the same time they also hold the biomedical beliefs about health and illness. When the two come into conflict, it is the nurses who act as the buffers between the two systems" (1986: 78).

Chapter 2

1. Because of the contracting process used by the research sponsor, many of the design decisions were dictated by the requirements imposed by the Justice Department. The data are available from the Interuniversity Consortium for Political and Social Research at the University of Michigan.

2. The overall design of the data collection effort is described in Kritzer (1980–1981); a partial evaluation of the results of that effort is in Kritzer (1984b).

3. The overall study also included cases from alternative third-party dispute-processing institutions and from cases that were handled bilaterally without third-party involvement, but those cases are not included in the analysis presented here. For information on those cases see Kritzer and Anderson (1983); Trubek, Kritzer, Holst, and Felstiner (1985); Kritzer (1980–1981: 515); Miller and Sarat (1980–1981; see also Miller, 1983).

4. The specific courts were: Richland County (Columbia, South Carolina, and the surrounding area) Court of Common Pleas; District Court for the Second Judicial

District (Albuquerque, New Mexico, and the surrounding area); and Los Angeles County Superior Court (Downtown Branch).

5. In eastern Pennsylvania the two courts were the Philadelphia Court of Common Pleas and the Chester County Court of Common Pleas; in Wisconsin the two courts were the Milwaukee County Circuit Court and the Dodge County Circuit Court.

6. Where possible a simple random sample was drawn based on a list of terminated cases; in some courts it was necessary to resort to a cluster sampling procedure, which is described in Kritzer (1980–1981: 515–516). The only bias in the sampling procedure that became evident was that "old" cases (i.e., those filed in 1974 or before) were not represented in the sample for the Los Angeles County Superior Court.

7. Lawyers directly employed by governmental agencies or departments were not included in this survey.

Part II

1. A condensed version of the chapters in this part appear in a companion study based on these same data (Kritzer, forthcoming).

2. Some additional detail on the cases can be found in Trubek et al. (1983a, 1983b).

Chapter 3

1. See, for example, the civil cover sheet, form JS-44, that is used in the federal district courts.

2. This is the same method used by the authors of the Federal Judicial Center's District Court Study: "The cases coded were categorized by the coders, rather than by reliance on the JS-44 form filled out by the attorney at filing. . . . This process was more useful for research purposes because it permitted cases to be categorized based on a substantive judgment concerning what the case actually involved, in contrast to . . . what is essentially an attorney's prediction, at filing, concerning the issues a newly filed case would present. Also, attorneys occasionally categorize a case in ways that seem to reflect strategic considerations. If a case is shaky on jurisdiction, a lawyer may categorize it as antitrust, or patent, or some other federal jurisdiction, when in reality it is an ordinary diversity case involving personal injury or a contract dispute" (Flanders, 1977: 115).

3. The 130 categories available allowed the coders to be very specific; in fact, the categories are so detailed that it was necessary to combine them into a much smaller set in order to perform any type of meaningful analysis.

4. Because of the nature of the sampling design (described in Chapter 2), this category of cases will be used only selectively in the analysis. All domestic relations cases in the interview sample involved some dispute over property division, alimony, child support, or child custody.

5. A list of individual categories, showing how the broad categories were formed, can be found in Appendix 3.A at the end of this chapter.

6. I have excluded domestic relations from the discussion in this section because the sampling design cannot provide an accurate representation of the relative role of such cases in the courts' caseloads.

7. The civil docket of the federal court for the Eastern District of Pennsylvania is clearly dominated by diversity of citizenship cases (i.e., cases that could be filed either

in state or federal courts). This is confirmed by a recent analysis of the potential impact of abolishing the diversity jurisdiction of the federal district courts. Using data for the 1987 fiscal year, Flango (1989: 7) reports that more cases would have been shifted from federal to state courts in Pennsylvania than in any other state.

8. From the defendant's perspective, this initial statement of claim may define what is potentially at risk and may have some relevance for what action that defendant takes in response to the suit.

9. This image of stakes contains an important dynamic element: the stakes may change over the life of a case, either going up or down (or both). Moreover, the perception of stakes may depend on which party one is talking to; the plaintiff and defendant are likely to see the stakes as somewhat different. This definition of stakes also incorporates attitudes toward risk (a risk-averse party may be willing to settle for less than the actual damages in order to be certain of obtaining something), uncertainty (a party involved in multiple cases will be willing to settle a case at something around an average value, even if that is more or less than what the case is "worth"), and the time value of money (a party may be prepared to settle a case for an amount less than could be obtained at some point in the future because that amount constitutes the "present value" of what could be obtained by waiting). I believe that this conceptualization of stakes captures the notion of "case worth" as that idea is commonly used by lawyers, and it is consistent with several well-known analyses of the settlement process (Posner, 1973; Friedman, 1969).

10. Where the response was monetary but was expressed in terms of a periodic payment, the periodic payment was converted to a lump sum by figuring the present value of those payment streams using the average prime interest rate in 1978 (9.06 percent) as a discount factor and establishing a duration based on case type. Case types were determined by visual inspection of the court record coding form. Duration was then figured by applying the following rules:

(a) Divorce – 9 years (median of 0–18 years) unless only alimony, in which case 2 years was used.
(b) Social Security, retirement, or black lung benefits – life expectancy (by sex) at age 65.
(c) Disability payments – life expectancy (by sex) based on actual age (if known) or 43 (median of 21 and 65).
(d) Mortgage payments – 10 years (median of 0 and 20).
(e) Consumer credit – 2 years.
(f) Unemployment benefits – 1 year.
(g) Tenant debt - 2 years.

11. In fact, there were several larger cases in the sample, one involving a settlement of $10,000,000, where the respondent had been unable or unwilling to answer the stakes questions.

12. These figures can be compared to those reported by Peterson and Priest in their study of jury verdicts in Cook County, Illinois. That study drew on the *Cook County Jury Verdict Reporter*, which reports virtually every jury verdict handed down in Cook County. One should note that the universe of cases in the two studies is quite different: "all" civil cases versus civil cases resulting in jury verdicts. The median jury verdict in Cook County, in 1979 dollars, was $7,900, and this figure excludes the cases where the jury found for the defendant (Peterson and Priest, 1982: 8–9).

13. All of these figures are based on cases terminated in 1978, and it is likely that they would be somewhat higher today; however, I doubt that the rise would fully reflect increases in the cost of living since 1978.

14. I should point out here, as I noted previously, that only four of the cases that were excluded from the sample because they were too complex to code came from the state courts; all four were from the Los Angeles Superior Court.

15. While accurate figures exist on the number of federal court cases, comparable figures for state courts are difficult to acquire (but see National Center for State Courts, 1978, and Flango, Roper, and Elsner, 1983). Lieberman (1982: 12–18) suggests that there may be as many as 350 to 500 times as many state court cases filed as federal court cases. This figure includes courts of both general and limited jurisdiction. He feels that about 20 percent of state cases are in courts of general jurisdiction. This would mean, then, that about 70 to 100 times as many state general jurisdiction cases as federal cases are filed each year.

16. This would be consistent with a comparison of jury verdicts that Rand did for San Francisco County, California, and Cook County, Illinois. That comparison reported a median of $21,000 for San Francisco (Shanley and Peterson, 1983: x) versus the $7,900 I mentioned previously; however, when cases in a limited jurisdiction division of the Cook County Court (the Municipal Division) were excluded, the Cook County median rose to $15,000 (Shanley and Peterson, 1983: x). In 1978, 78.7 percent of the state civil cases in Cook County were processed by the Municipal Department (*1978 Annual Report to the Supreme Court of Illinois*, p. 182). See Peterson (1987) for updates of the figures for both California and Cook County into the 1980s.

17. In Wisconsin, the limited jurisdiction county court was consolidated with the general jurisdiction court on August 1, 1978; most of the cases in the Wisconsin sample would have been filed when both courts were in operation. In South Carolina, the limited jurisdiction County Court, which was permitted by the state constitution but authorized on a court-by-court basis, was abolished by the legislature in 1979; the $15,000 figure is for the County Court in Richland County, where our data were collected ("South Carolina Law Digest," *Martindale Hubbell Law Directory 1979, Volume VII, Law Digests*, p. 2286).

18. For information on the limited jurisdiction courts, see the *National Survey of Court Organization* (LEAA, 1973, 1982).

19. In 1988, the minimum for diversity cases was raised to $50,000.

20. One often hears this kind of argument with regard to the on-again, off-again medical malpractice crisis. Take, for example, a statement by the secretary of the Wisconsin State Medical Society: " . . . nuisance settlements [in which insurance carriers settle a claim that has no merit because it is cheaper than fighting the claim] encourage claims in cases without merit in the anticipation of some financial award to the patient and a financial award to an attorney" (Madison *Capital Times*, February 17, 1984, p. 9).

21. In the following discussion, I have excluded from consideration domestic relations cases since, by definition, they involve two individuals; furthermore, the sampling design was such that were no domestic cases from some jurisdictions, and where there were such cases, their proportion had arbitrarily been limited to 20 percent of the sample.

22. As noted by White (1985: 148), this has been true in Wisconsin for more than 50 years and is based on judicial precedent (*Oertel v. Williams*, 214 Wisc. 68 [1934]) rather than legislative action (as was the case in Louisiana, which is the other state White identifies as permitting direct suits against the tort-feasor's insurance company).

23. These findings differ substantially from those reported by Wanner in his study of Milwaukee, Baltimore, and Cleveland. That study reported a far greater proportion of organizational plaintiffs and suggested that the dominant pattern of litigation was an organizational plaintiff suing an individual defendant (1973, 1974). Here, individuals

are the most frequent plaintiff; furthermore, organizations suing individuals constitute a very small portion of the caseload of the courts in this study's samples. The apparent differences reflect two factors. First, Wanner may have taken at face value the nominal participants in the cases in his study; I have argued that this may lead to a false picture, particularly as it pertains to defendants in tort cases. Second, and probably more important, the definition of what was to be examined differs substantially between the two studies: CLRP excluded uncontested collections cases and cases involving a claim of under $1,000 (unless some other substantial, nonmonetary issue was raised) and substantially limited the number of domestic relations cases that could occur in any sample; Wanner's study imposed no such limitations, and it is likely that his findings reflect the numerical dominance of routine, uncontested collections cases (many of which involve sums of less than $1,000) and divorce actions.

24. As I write this, news reports (Chicago *Tribune*, June 21, 1989, p. 5) feature the settlement for $81.28 of a lawsuit filed by a high school sophomore against a boy who had broken their date to attend a high school prom. To settle the case, Marlon Chadd, 17, reimbursed Tomontra Mangrum, 15, for expenses she had incurred (including the cost of having her hair done and purchasing a pair of shoes).

Chapter 4

1. It is always helpful to be able to place any set of descriptive statistics into some kind of perspective. In this chapter I will compare to other published data for various groups and subgroups of lawyers. Through footnotes I will draw several internal comparisons where noteworthy differences appear. I will use three criterion variables in drawing these internal comparisons: *income* from the practice of law ("typical"—under $75,000, "high"—$75,000 to $100,000, and "very high"—over $100,000), *size of law firm* ("small"—under 20 lawyers, "medium"—20 to 49 lawyers, and "large"—50 or more), and *percent of time spent on litigation* ("minimal" litigators—25 percent or less of their time on litigation, "semilitigators"—25 to 50 percent of their time on litigation, and "regular" litigators—more than 50 percent of their time on litigation). One might object that I have not really isolated sharply divergent groups (i.e., incomes over $250,000 or law firms with 200 or more lawyers), but those very extreme groups form such a small percentage of the sample that such comparisons are not possible. One might also object that the law firm size and income variables are so closely related that distinguishing between them is pointless; in fact, there is only a slight relationship between income and firm size, as shown in the following table.

	Firm Size		
Income	Small	Medium	Large
Typical	850	92	33
High	120	21	12
Very high	76	9	12

2. This classification of law schools is based partly on the Cartter Report (1977) rankings. I have followed the convention (see Zemans and Rosenblum, 1981: 232) of labeling the top six schools as "elite" and the next nine as "prestige." I have not at-

tempted to distinguish between "regional" and 'local" schools but have simply divided the remaining schools between "public" and "private." There is a residual category consisting of proprietary (for-profit) law schools, foreign law schools, and law schools no longer in existence; only about 1 percent of the lawyers in the sample attended law schools in this category.

3. As one might expect from the literature on the elite law firms (e.g., Smigel, 1964; Nelson, 1983, 1985, 1988; Slovak, 1979, 1980, 1981a, 1981b), the formal educational background of the lawyers is clearly related to the size of firm in which they practice. Only 6 percent of the lawyers in small firms (or not in firms at all) attended an elite law school (11 percent prestige) compared to 15 percent elite (20 percent prestige) in medium firms, and 23 percent elite (35 percent prestige) in large firms. There is a smaller relationship between income and formal legal education: 19 percent of the average-income lawyers went to elite or prestige schools compared to 28 percent of the high-income lawyers and 36 percent of the very-high-income lawyers.

4. Large-firm lawyers were more likely to report service on law review (48 percent) than either small- or medium-firm lawyers (34 percent).

5. I have been told anecdotally of surveys of law students that find that considerably more than 50 percent of the respondents claim to be in the upper half of their class; I have not been able to find actual published examples of this phenomenon.

6. Recall that none of the lawyers in this sample were direct employees of government agencies, since those lawyers were interviewed in a separate survey.

7. In terms of background, experience distinguishes lawyers in the high- and very-high-income groups: 37 percent of the former and 34 percent of the latter had been in practice for 20 years or more compared to only 15 percent in the typical income group (under $75,000). Forty-two percent of the lower-income lawyers had been practicing 5 years or less versus only 7 percent of the higher-income lawyers.

8. Higher-income lawyers bring not only years of experience to their cases but also case-specific experience. Two thirds of the very-high-income group reported having handled 100 similar cases or more previously, and over one third reported 500 or more prior cases. The lawyers in the high-income group ($75,000 to $100,000) also reported substantial amounts of case-specific experience: slightly less than two thirds had reached the 100-case plateau, but only 22 percent had handled 500 similar cases or more. Less than 50 percent of the lower-income group reported 100 prior cases or more, and only 12 percent reported 500 or more.

9. The level of self-perceived expertise is much higher for the high-income lawyers. Seventy-nine percent of the very-high-income group and 61 percent of the high-income group rated themselves as experts; this compares to only 36 percent for the lawyers outside these income groups. The higher expertise is also reflected in the numbers of outside activities related to the field the various groups of lawyers report. Only 23 percent of the typical income lawyers reported involvement in three or more of the various activities compared to 50 percent for the two higher-income groups taken together.

10. Defendants' lawyers were more likely *not* to be in private practice (7 percent) than were plaintiffs' lawyers (3 percent).

11. Compare this to Carlin's report 25 years ago that "half the lawyers in Chicago, as in practically all the other cities of the United States, are individual practitioners" (1962: 17).

12. Of those in firms of two or more, about two-thirds were partners or senior partners; the remainder were associates or employed by the law firm under some other title.

13. Not surprisingly, plaintiffs are more likely to use a solo practitioner (23 percent of the plaintiffs' lawyers in private practice were solo practitioners) than were defendants (12 percent of defendants' lawyers in private practice were solo).

14. It should not be surprising that lawyers in large firms are more likely to encounter legal problems requiring tailor-made responses. Forty-one percent of the large-firm lawyers reported that more than three quarters of their cases required custom-made responses compared to 25 percent for medium-firm lawyers and 16 percent for small-firm lawyers. Only 11 percent of the large-firm lawyers reported that one quarter or less of their cases required such responses compared to 29 percent of the medium-firm lawyers and 37 percent of the small-firm lawyers.

15. Spangler (1986: 48–49) reports that even the most elite law firms "have developed routines and forms called 'boilerplate,' which standardize some aspects of their written work. [This involves] an elaborate menu of forms and documents that attorneys consult to organize deals and business matters." She describes the "universal consensus" as "we never do anything from scratch." At the same time, she describes a very strong emphasis on initial drafting and custom drafting, particularly by associates in their years of apprenticeship. Nelson (1988: 171; see also 188–189) makes much the same point, noting that "rather than seeking to reduce the level of skill in legal work, the elite of firms have actively sought to cultivate the specialized skill base necessary to attract the business of corporate clients in a rapidly changing and uncertain legal environment."

16. Lawyers were also asked whether they used standardized procedures for estimating the value of cases; 58 percent reported that they did. Also, 50 percent of the lawyers who did not use preprinted forms for pleadings, motions, or discovery said that they did have a standard procedure for estimating the value of cases; thus, overall, only 12 percent of the lawyers did not use one or more of the types of standard procedures that were asked about.

17. One way to look at the relationship among these eleven items is to employ a statistical technique called factor analysis. Factor analysis shows how the items are related by suggesting broad dimensions that can be seen as underlying the individual items. For these eleven items, such an analysis does not suggest an easily interpretable set of dimensions.

18. There were some modest but interesting variations in attitudes related to firm size or income: large-firm lawyers are more likely to rate intellectual challenge and working with pleasant and interesting people as very important. Small-firm and solo lawyers were substantially more likely to rate "being your own boss" as very important. Small-firm and solo lawyers seem to be more "service oriented," rating both serving the community and helping individuals as very important substantially more often than do large-firm lawyers.

As for income-related variations, the two items that stand out are "making a lot of money" and "having a high standing in the community." High-income lawyers viewed both of these as more important than did lawyers with more typical incomes. All of these variations are more or less what common sense would lead one to expect. The lesser importance placed on "being one's own boss" by large-firm lawyers and the lesser importance of "making a lot of money" or having "high status" by lower-income lawyers may simply reflect rationalizations of the lawyers' situations. That is, rather than leading the lawyers in particular career directions (i.e., attitudes causing behavior), the attitudes toward legal practice largely may represent accommodations to the situations in which the lawyers find themselves. Expressed in terms of accommodation rather than rationalization, this explanation is consistent with the greater weight put on service by the small-firm lawyers; since they are less likely to obtain satisfaction from the intellectual aspects of their work, they derive their satisfaction from a sense that they are helping people.

19. There are some interesting variations in likes and dislikes related to income and amount of litigation a lawyer does. As income goes up, lawyers seem to be slightly more inclined toward arguing and trying (52 percent to 59 percent to 66 percent) at the expense of planning and research (20 percent to 14 percent to 10 percent). More striking, however, is the sharp increase in preferences for arguing and trying that is associated with the proportion of practice comprised by litigation: 27 percent of those spending a quarter or less of their time on litigation most liked arguing and trying compared to 63 percent of those who spent more than half of their time on litigation.

20. There are some slight variations in attitudes about what makes a good litigator related to firm size. The lawyers in the large firms are less likely (by 10 to 15 percentage points) to rate all factors except thoroughness as being "very important."

Part III

1. This need not be the case; one of the justifications for many of the privileges (e.g., immunity from liability for negligence in the conduct of a case) enjoyed by English barristers—the branch of the legal profession in England and Wales with a monopoly on advocacy in the higher courts—is that their first commitment is to the system of justice, including the judges and their barrister colleagues, and their commitment to their clients is constrained by that higher responsibility (see Committee on the Future of the Legal Profession, 1988: 39–40, 165).

Chapter 5

1. The specific problem involved in distinguishing between individual and organizational clients (as applied to analyses based on the lawyer survey) is that the interview itself did not record this information and the information in the court record is ambiguous (as I noted in Chapter 3); the ambiguity arises in tort litigation involving insurance companies as effective defendants (i.e., the insurer hires the lawyer and controls the defense in all respects), but the court record usually shows the tort-feasor and not the insurance company as the defendant. As it turns out, a crude but surprisingly accurate distinction can be drawn between individual clients and organizational clients in the way that the lawyer is to be paid; as I will discuss, virtually no individuals paid their lawyers on an hourly basis and virtually no organizations paid their lawyer on a percentage (or contingency) basis (this point is considered on pp. 58–59; see Table 5–2). Thus, in the preceding discussion, hourly fee lawyers are treated as representing organizations and contingent fee lawyers are treated as representing individuals; lawyers paid on some other basis are omitted. The biggest problem with this classification scheme would be with domestic relations cases, where contingent fees are not used; however, domestic relations cases tend to be handled on a flat fee basis and hence are excluded from the analysis.

2. To understand why lawyers did and did not take specific cases, one would have to have a sample that included cases that were not taken; no such cases are included in the sample available for analysis here.

3. Organizational and individual clients are again distinguished by the fee arrangement used; see note 1 for more detail. In addition, for likely organizational clients, lawyers reported discussing fees before sending a bill with about 45 percent of their

clients when $50,000 or less was involved; this rises to over 70 percent when more than $50,000 was at stake. This probably indicates that lawyers and organizational clients acted on assumptions concerning fee arrangements for relatively routine cases. For likely individual clients, there was no systematic variation by stakes in the proportion of lawyers reporting fee discussions with their clients.

4. Abel referred to "the widespread convention that lawyers and physicians do not discuss fees in advance."

5. Note that information on fee arrangements from the litigants is available only when the litigant reported having discussed fees prior to receiving a bill from the lawyer or (in the case of organizational litigants) there was a standing agreement on how the lawyer would bill for his or her time.

6. However, it is worth noting that organizations do occasionally use contingent fees as well, particularly when they are plaintiffs in tort or contract (most likely debt collection) cases.

7. As I will show in Chapter 9, even contingent fee plaintiffs can incur out-of-pocket expenses, so this arrangement is not really a no-risk situation. Out-of-pocket expenses arise in cases where the costs other than lawyer fees (for which the client is, at least in theory, liable, regardless of the outcome of the case) exceed the amount of the award after deducting the share for the lawyer's fee itself.

8. Recall that each case can involve multiple areas of law. For this reason, a respondent may appear in more than one column of Table 5-2*b*.

9. I have excluded domestic relations cases from the table because contingent fees are not normally used in such cases due to strictures in codes governing lawyer behavior (see Center for Professional Responsibility, 1987: 40–45); this reflects an "acknowledgment of the lawyer's duties in a domestic relations case with regard to reconciliation, the integrity of the family, and other issues involving the children" (Center for Professional Responsibility, 1987: 41).

10. Even in contingent fee cases where the defendant usually makes the settlement check payable jointly to the lawyer and the client, the client must consent to the settlement before any check is written (and then must endorse it before the lawyer can be paid).

11. Even when the patient on whose behalf the physician's fee is being paid objects to some aspect of the fee (e.g., charges for services that were neither requested nor consented to), the insurer will make payment if the fee falls within its guidelines.

12. While there was a slight tendency for there to be more consistency for the likely organizational clients than for the likely individual clients, the difference was too small to be significant.

13. Controlling for area of law provides no indication that the organizational/ individual difference might simply reflect individual plaintiffs playing a small role in tort cases. The patterns, by inferred (from fee arrangement) type of client controlling for area of law and the presence of an understanding about the client's role, were remarkably similar.

14. While controlling for the area of law on this question does not account for the individual/organizational difference, there is a slight but consistent trend for clients in tort cases to be less involved in strategic planning than clients in other kinds of cases, with a difference of about 5 percentage points for organizations and 12 for individuals. There was a similar, but less consistent, trend for the more general involvement question discussed previously.

15. About 44 percent of the organizations that did not report explicit discussions regarding allocation of responsibilities but had used the lawyer previously had a standing fee arrangement with the lawyer; particularly where there was a standing fee ar-

rangement, there was likely to be some standing agreement about allocation of responsibilities.

16. The pattern that I describe is generally consistent with that reported by Reed (1969: 77) based on his survey of lawyers in Duval County, Florida.

Chapter 6

1. See Mohr (1976) and Clynch and Neubauer (1981) for critiques of these "organizational" approaches.

2. It would have been interesting to have available information on the lawyer's assessment of the likelihood of representing the current client in future cases (because the possibility of repeat "business" could certainly shape the actions of the lawyer in the present case). Unfortunately, an error in questionnaire design resulted in questions about future representation not being asked when the lawyer represented only a single client and did not have a prior personal, nonbusiness relationship with that client (or an employee of the client if the client was an organization); the result was that the future representation question was asked only of an unrepresentative group of lawyers, a group that cannot really be used for analysis.

3. Private defense attorneys have been portrayed by some research as suggesting to their clients that their (the lawyers') relations with other actors in the system can be used to the client's benefit (see Blumberg, 1967; Casper, 1972). I know of no systematic evidence that supports this advantage of the insider; there is some anecdotal evidence, such as Clarence Earl Gideon's preference to be represented by a local attorney at his retrial after the Supreme Court overturned his conviction in the landmark case *Gideon v. Wainwright* (see Lewis, 1964: 223–238).

4. Lawyers were also asked the following question.

> [Either] before you took on this case, did you know the opposing party on a personal basis outside of business? [Or] before you took on this case, did you know anyone in [the opposing organization] who would have been in a position to influence the organization's of handling of disputes such as this one?

This question has the same kinds of wording problems discussed in relationship to the parallel question regarding the opposing lawyer (i.e., "Did it refer to any kind of personal acquaintance or only to a social acquaintance?"). Only 7 percent of the lawyers reported a prior personal, nonbusiness relationship with the opposing party or, with an employee of the opposing party, when the opposing party was an organization; this percentage is constant across different areas of law. This low frequency of such relationships is not surprising since, given the wording of the question asked, the existence of such a relationship might, in fact, represent a potential conflict of interest; it is unfortunate that the question was not worded in a fashion that had not excluded a prior business acquaintanceship.

5. Much of this section draws on analyses previously published (Kritzer, 1986).

6. The role of adjudication in the cases that were not terminated through adjudication is reinforced by the fact that in 10 percent of them a written opinion was issued.

7. There is yet another 6 percent of the cases in which motions listed in Table 6–2 were filed, but that were never ruled on (at least no ruling was indicated in the court record); in some fraction of those cases, it is likely that settlement occurred in anticipation of the adjudicatory decision that never came. The figures may, in fact, underestimate the role of adjudication (or other forms of judicial intervention) in disposing of cases. When the lawyers were asked about the way the case was processed, 44 percent

said that the case went to trial, (court-annexed) arbitration, was resolved by a judicial decision outside of trial, and/or the judge made one or more important rulings. An additional 8 percent said that the a judge had had "significant" involvement in the case. In other words, more than half the lawyers interviewed said that the case's resolution had involved some significant judicial involvement.

8. There were some interesting variations by area of law in the level of adjudicatory involvement by judges. The three "traditional" areas of torts, contract/commercial, and real property, plus a fourth area, business regulation, all had similar patterns where very few cases are tried, and most are not adjudicated (which I took to generally mean they were settled); the one figure for these four areas that seems to stand out is the high "nonadjudication" rate for torts, 75 percent. The other four areas—domestic relations, civil rights/civil liberties/discrimination, government action (taxation, zoning, political processes, public health and safety, Freedom of Information Act, etc.), and government benefits (welfare, black lung, disability, other social security)—differ sharply from the other areas, but in varying ways. A higher "trial rate" in domestic relations probably reflects the requirement of a formal resolution in divorce cases; while the court record may show an event that is labeled as a trial, it is typically nothing more than the ratification of a settlement agreed on by the parties. Two areas, civil rights and government action, have similar patterns, with nonadjudication rates around 45 percent. The most unique area is government benefits, which has a nonadjudication rate of only 10 percent and a "decided" rate of 70 percent, more than three times the decided rate of any other area of law. The variations here no doubt reflect the kinds of issues that the different cases present; most important is the point that the dominance of settlement, with the possible exception of torts, is far from clear in many areas and simply nonexistent in others. See Kritzer (1986) for a more extensive discussion of the variation in the amount of adjudication in ordinary litigation.

9. I have not sought to assess the level of judicial involvement in settlement here because lawyers were asked about such involvement only if a particular judge had been assigned to oversee the case from beginning to end. Elsewhere (Kritzer, 1982), I did examine the data on judicial involvement in settlement and found that almost two-thirds of the lawyers involved in cases where there was an assigned judge reported some settlement-related activities on the part of the judge.

Chapter 7

1. A recent book comparing the practice of medicine in England, the United States, France, and West Germany (Payer, 1988) suggests that there are substantial variations in the degree to which medical practice is based on empirical rather than theoretical knowledge. For example, medical practice in France is described as heavily "Cartesian" in orientation.

2. While the distinction between these two kinds of activities is important both conceptually and empirically, there are inevitable ambiguities. For example, while I classify negotiations as an informal legal activity, one can easily imagine negotiations focusing on highly technical points of law (e.g., arguments about potentially complex legal questions such as causation or duty in tort); likewise, while I classify brief writing as a formal legal activity, in many situations the actual preparation may be closely related to specific knowledge about the orientations of the judge to whom the brief is directed. Despite these ambiguities, the distinction between informal and formal legal activities is useful for describing and understanding the day-to-day work of lawyers in litigation.

3. Sixteen hundred and forty eight of the 1,649 cases in the sample have usable data for this analysis.

4. Court-annexed arbitration occurred only in the Pennsylvania state courts during the period of this study. Pennsylvania had a rule requiring that certain types of cases be submitted to nonbinding arbitration before the case could be brought to trial.

5. Multiple estimates of stakes were obtained when more than one lawyer in the case was interviewed and more than one of the interviewees provided a stakes estimate.

6. This information could have been missing for various reasons. For some of the cases in the sample, no interviews were conducted (either because the cases were filtered out of the interview process or because the lawyer respondents declined to be interviewed). For other cases involving lawyers who handled more than one case in the sample, no stakes information was obtained from abbreviated interviews conducted with "multiple-case" lawyers. For still other cases the respondents were not able to express stakes in clear monetary terms.

7. If one transposes Table 7–3 so that each row represents one category of event count within a court, the largest range within any row is only 13 percentage points if the government benefits category is omitted from the comparisons.

8. I also examined breakdowns for specific event types; the results were consistent with the preceding statement.

9. The idea of "judge centeredness" is similar to the idea of "managerial judging" (see Resnik, 1982; Elliott, 1986) or the continental practice of judges taking a more active role in investigation (see Langbein, 1985). However, as I use the term, it implies less a notion of judicial control and more the idea that the advocates defer to and respond to the judge.

10. One other hypothesis that might be advanced is that the federal/state difference reflects formal differences in the procedural rules. In order to test this explanation, I looked at variations by location. If the federal/state differences are determined by the procedural rules governing civil cases in the various courts, I expected that the state with rules most similar to federal rules (i.e., Wisconsin) would evidence a pattern similar to the federal courts while the state with rules most dissimilar (i.e., Pennsylvania) would have a pattern substantially different (see Oakley and Coon, 1986, for a recent discussion of the use of the federal rules in state courts). In fact, the most similar state was fairly distant from the federal courts while the most dissimilar state was one of state courts that was relatively close to the federal courts (see Kritzer et al., 1984b: 10–11, for more detail).

11. It does not make sense to use the arsenal of statistical tools that I will employ on the quantity question at this juncture because, in light of the results I will present later, the results I would obtain here would be highly misleading. The particular problem here is one of statistical misspecification. If I were to fit a single regression equation for effort to the complete set of data, I know that the equation would suffer from severe misspecification (resulting in parameter estimates that are highly suspect) because the analysis in Chapter 8 shows clearly that different equations are appropriate for hourly and contingent fee lawyers.

12. The quantity question is also important if one is concerned about the "cost of litigation," particularly the costs associated with lawyers working on an hourly fee basis. In an analysis of these data dealing with the cost question (Kritzer et al., 1984a; see also, Kakalik and Pace, 1986), it has been shown that lawyers' fees make up the vast bulk of the cost of litigation, even when that cost includes the value of the time of the litigants themselves. The issue of the cost of litigation is an important one, but I will not digress onto that particular subject here, since it has been treated extensively elsewhere.

13. If a typical case involves 100 hours of lawyer time on each side, and 10 percent of that time is devoted to legal research, that suggest a somewhat different image than if the typical case involves only 10 hours of lawyer time (and thus only 1 hour is devoted to legal research).

14. Part of the reason for the stakes difference between federal and state courts is the requirement that in a major portion of the federal court's jurisdiction (i.e. diversity of citizenship cases – cases involving parties from different states) be limited to controversies with at least $10,000 at stake (in 1988, this minimum was raised to $50,000).

15. In fact, the best description of the form of the relationship between stakes and effort is that effort rises proportionally to the square root of stakes.

16. I do not mean to suggest that this triage – the initial assessment of a problem and the appropriate course of action to deal with it – is unimportant. As in the medical world (see Lewis, Fein, and Mechanic, 1976: 24), it requires considerable sophistication and experience, both about the technical problem and about the individuals involved or potentially involved.

17. I have used the label "informal legal" activities in preference to two other possible labels: "insider" activities or "nonlegal" activities. My choice is intended to emphasize that I am not presuming that these activities are less legal than what I label "formal legal activities" but, instead, that they rely on a different kind of preparation.

18. Although during the time that lawyers were working on the cases in my sample, Lexis and Westlaw were not as widely used as they are today (and the latter may not even have existed during the early stages of some of the cases in the sample).

19. Recent observational studies of lawyer–client interaction seem to suggest that very little time is devoted to discussing legal or technical issues; if anything, the education of the client draws more on the informal, insider knowledge of the lawyer than it does on the formal knowledge (see Sarat and Felstiner, 1986; Berends, 1981).

20. The figures given by the lawyers during the interview were normalized to add to 1.0.

21. There are actually two ways one might look at the question of concentration of effort: in aggregate terms (i.e., Does any one area tend to dominate the work of the group of lawyers taken as a whole?), and in individual terms (i.e., Do lawyers tend to spend at least half of their time on one particular type of activity, with very small portions of their time on the remaining areas?). The discussion here focuses on the former. As for the latter, when I looked at the individual case level by determining the proportion of time spent on the most time-consuming activity for the specific case (regardless of what that activity was), I found that the median proportion of time spent on that area was .25, and only 14 percent of the respondents reported spending more than half of their time on one area.

22. In the discussion in this section I will rely on the means of the proportions rather than on the medians because the restricted range of a proportion (from 0.0 to 1.0) eliminates the distorting effect of extreme outliers.

23. For this analysis, I have eliminated the "other" category and renormalized the proportions to add to 1.0.

24. I have omitted time spent on appeals since so few cases involved any such time.

25. There were no meaningful differences in the other two areas (pleading and motions, and trial/hearing).

26. An alternate interpretation of the lower proportion on conferring with clients in federal cases is that since those cases tend to involve more work in total, particularly on activities that consume little if any time in state cases, client consultation forms a smaller overall proportion.

27. There is also a statistically significant difference between federal and state courts for the means of stakes within the two lower categories. However, the magnitude of the differences in the federal and state averages are not large enough, \$3,821 versus \$3,150 in the low category and \$25,050 versus \$20,510 in the middle category, to raise major problems for analyses within those categories.

28. Because the areas of law are not mutually exclusive (meaning that a single case can appear under two or more different areas of law), I did not perform statistical tests of significance to compare the areas of law; however, as the results show, the differences are so clear that the absence of such tests presents no problem for the analysis.

29. The very low proportion of time spent on negotiation in cases where the opposing party is a government agency is confirmed by the responses of government lawyers in a separate survey; those lawyers also reported spending a very small proportion of their time on discussions aimed at settling the cases.

30. Recall that uncontested divorce, probate, and debt cases have been excluded from the study, and contested divorce cases have been included in only a limited fashion.

31. It is worth noting that applying the proportions of .32 and .39 for tort and contract cases, respectively, to the median numbers of hours, 20 and 17, yields almost identical values of 6.6 and 6.4.

32. That questioning is fueled in part by the experience of one of my research colleagues. In the very beginning of a study of lawyers, this colleague was trying to convince a number of lawyers to participate in the study. That process involved a lot of handholding and reassurance. One of the lawyers that he was trying to persuade to participate called my friend while we were attending a conference of the Law and Society Association in Toronto for help with a specific legal question regarding a routine case the lawyer was handling. My friend, who was not a lawyer, spent several hours trying to find someone at the conference who could answer the question. The impression that was left by this was that the lawyer, who normally handled the kinds of ordinary cases just discussed, was so unaccustomed to doing legal research or dealing with any but the most routine legal questions, that he did not hesitate to call on a layperson for help with a question that a little legal research should have been able to resolve.

33. Note that I am also omitting from consideration cases filed by prisoners in state and federal prisons—cases that are part of the federal courts' *civil* caseload but that are usually brought *pro se*, that is, without the assistance of a lawyer.

Chapter 8

1. The analysis described here is a revision and recasting of that presented in Kritzer et al. (1985). The results here are consistent with those presented previously. The major difference is the identification of a group of variables under the label "the lawyer's relationships," including the addition of the "future cases against the current opposing party" variable. A second difference is the correction to the mean of the stakes variables for the two groups of lawyers and the resulting difference in the values shown in Tables 8-2 and 8B-1 (as compared to the equivalent Table 4 in the earlier presentation) although none of the interpretations change.

2. While a direct question was asked, an error in the questionnaire resulted in data being available only for a small fraction of the respondents, those representing multiple clients.

3. Again there was a question about this, but it was only asked of lawyers reporting a prior "personal" relationship with the opposing lawyer.

4. The impact of payment system on the behavior of workers in professional occupations is not limited by any means to lawyers. Goldmann (1952), Roemer (1962), and Glaser (1970) consider the impact of payment systems on the delivery of medical care by physicians, and Lees (1966) describes more generally how private professional markets differ from what would be expected under systems of perfect competition. One study (Epstein, Begg, and McNeil, 1986) reported that physicians in prepaid group practices ordered fewer laboratory tests than physicians in fee-for-service groups; the explanation for such a pattern is that the former group has no economic incentive for performing such tests while the latter group (which presumably receives a share of the profits from the laboratory operation) does. These kinds of issues have been very prominent in England recently in light of proposals by the Conservative government led by Margaret Thatcher to tie compensation to general practitioners to their utilization of hospital services and medication; physicians would have financial incentives *not* to order drug therapies or hospital services (see "Doctors in Rebellion as Thatcher Moves to Alter National Health," *Chicago Tribune*, June 27, 1989, p. 4).

5. Another criticism of the contingent fee is that by making representation too easily available, the contingent fee will tend to encourage litigation.

6. The analysis will be restricted to hourly and contingent fee arrangements; the argument could be extended to the flat fee as well, with the expectation that lawyers working on a flat, fixed fee should try to minimize their effort because once the fee is set, there is no immediate financial gain from putting in any more time than is absolutely necessary.

7. It was complications introduced by the structuring effect that led me to defer any extensive examination of the factors influencing the amount of lawyer effort until now.

8. See note 2 *supra*.

9. The statistical problem referred to here is that of specification error. Omitting relevant variables may lead to incorrect conclusions about the variables included in the model.

10. Because of the importance of stakes in predicting lawyer effort, lawyers who were unable to provide a statement of stakes in unambiguously monetary terms were excluded from the analysis. Recall that in Chapter 3, I reported that most respondents who could not give a specific dollar figure for stakes were nonetheless mostly concerned about a monetary outcome; consequently, most of the respondents omitted from this analysis were, in fact, involved with monetary cases.

11. One case characteristic that is conspicuously missing is area of law; in Chapter 7 I showed that area of law seemed to have little influence on amount of effort once court was controlled for. The analyses described here were repeated including indicators of the area of law. The analysis suggested that there might be some effects for certain areas in certain circumstances.

Hourly fee lawyers seemed to spend more time on property cases.

Contingent fee lawyers seemed to spend more time on nontraditional areas such civil rights/discrimination and government action (and perhaps business regulation and government benefits, as well).

However, the numbers of cases falling into the categories outside torts and contracts were so small that the specific effects were too unstable to be able to make statements with any confidence. More important for the analysis described here, the *inclusion of area of law effects did not appreciably change any of the other coefficients in the model.*

Consequently, since the omission of those effects does not seem to affect the analysis that I will report, I excluded them from the model on grounds of parsimony.

12. There were not enough lawyers paid in other ways in the sample to permit their inclusion.

13. There were a number of major technical problems that had to be considered before this analysis could be carried out. The first had to do with missing data, and particularly missing data on stakes. Because of its importance as an explanatory variable, I did not make any effort to adjust for stakes if it was missing. A comparison of cases with and without stakes information indicated that those for which monetized stakes information was available were more likely to involve tort and contract issues and were more likely to be in the state courts. For some of the variables in the analysis, it was possible to replace missing data with a mean value adjusted by a normal random deviate (to avoid depressing the variation in the variable); this was done for all of the factor score variables (normally making the replacement on the components of the score rather than on the final score itself) and for complexity. (In Kritzer et al. [1984a: 571] it was erroneously reported that missing data for all variables other than stakes was replaced in this way.)

All of the variables in the analysis were examined for curvilinearity problems. The only one for which this seemed to a problem was stakes; the best description of the relationship between stakes and effort was that effort was directly related to the square root of stakes; consequently, the square root of stakes was used in the analysis.

All of the predictor variables were examined for possible problems created by high intercorrelations (multicollinearity). This was a problem only for the original standard operating procedure variables; the two factor scores were created from the original four standard operating procedure variables (one each for pleadings, motions, discovery, and estimating case value) to eliminate this problem.

Outliers (i.e., cases with extreme values on one or more variables) can create major problems for regression analysis. While the focus of the research was on "ordinary" cases, the sampling design was such that a few atypically "big" or extreme cases were likely to be included. To examine the impact of outliers on the results of the analysis, the regressions were performed with and without the outliers included. Outliers were defined as cases requiring more than 500 hours of lawyer time, involving more than $250,000, taking more than 1,500 days from filing to termination, or having more than 20 discovery events, 10 motions, or 10 briefs filed by the opposing party. For the hourly fee lawyers, the inclusion or exclusion of the outliers had minimal impact on the regression results but, for the contingent fee lawyers, the impact was clearly noticeable. For consistency, outliers were omitted entirely from the analysis.

The last problem that had to be considered was that of heteroscedasticity, a violation of the assumption in regression analysis that the variance of the equation error term (i.e., the difference between the observed and predicted values of the dependent variable) be constant for all systematically identifiable subsets of observations. Heteroscedasticity tends to lower severely the power of significance tests. Common sense suggests that one should expect a greater range of predictive error for big cases than for small cases; this is consistent with the idea that stakes serve to limit the level of lawyer effort. To correct for heteroscedasticity in the data, I applied an adjustment factor to each observation; this yielded a "corrected" regression equation. The specific adjustment I used was to divide all of the variables for each case by the square root of stakes (see Hilton, 1976: 95–100, for more details on this procedure). For most analytic purposes, the "corrected" results are reported; I will make explicit any situations where this is not the case.

14. A statistical test of the global hypothesis that the coefficients differ for the two groups indicates that they do, indeed, differ; this test, which is known as the Chow test, yielded an F ratio of 2.05 (with 32 and 585 degrees of freedom).

15. The planning variables, other than that related to settlement negotiations, seem to work in the opposite direction to what was hypothesized. This may indicate that planning was associated with intensive activity rather than efficiently conducted activity (see Kritzer et al., 1984a: 586–587).

16. In one sense this probably reflects something of a *craft effect*, which is also seen in the commitment to craft variable that is significant for hourly fee lawyers (who can expect to be compensated for responding to their inclination to do a well-crafted job on a piece of legal work) compared to the contingent fee lawyer (who will receive no compensation unless that extra effort leads directly to an improved outcome). To the degree to which the greater time on federal cases discussed in Chapter 7 reflects specific demands created by or reflected in the choice of court environment (e.g., the need to prepare and file briefs or the greater complexity of cases), the other factors in the model account for them for the contingent fee lawyer (since that lawyer's effort is determined solely by the needs of the case). The hourly fee lawyer, on the other hand, is free to respond in a less cost-constrained fashion to the expectations of the federal court environment; that is, the federal court can be treated as the "big time," where judges expect greater preparation and care by the lawyers, even where that preparation and care may have little direct impact on case outcome.

17. This finding should be treated cautiously because the actual number of contingent fee lawyers with organizational clients is very small.

18. These lawyer characteristic variables do have some effect on the hourly rates lawyers charge (see Kritzer et al., 1984a: 590–592) or, in the case of contingent fee lawyers, the rates they are able to obtain (see Chapter 9).

19. One potentially confounding factor for this analysis is the fact that contingent fee lawyers represent plaintiffs while hourly fee lawyers represent either plaintiffs or defendants (in this sample 71 percent of the hourly fee lawyers represent defendants). To what extent do the differences described represent the effect of side rather than that of fee arrangement? This question was considered in some detail in Kritzer et al. (1985). The conclusion that was reached was that while one should be cautious in attributing specific differences to fee arrangement effects or to side effects, fee arrangement definitely has a significant impact over and above any impact that might be attributed to side.

20. One must also add to this sum the regression constant, which is shown at the bottom of Table 8B-1.

21. These values can be obtained from Table 8-1 by computing the weighted average of the two means for each variable; the weights are equal to the proportion of each type of lawyer (i.e., 374/647 for hourly fee lawyers and 273/647 for contingent fee lawyers).

22. The larger values in this table compared to the comparable one in Kritzer et al. (1985: 266) reflect an error in the calculation of the mean value of stakes; the means used before were the squares of the mean of the square root of stakes. Despite the larger values in the table here, the pattern among the values remains essentially unchanged.

23. The values here may seem substantially larger than those discussed in previous chapters because the ones here are based on means rather than on medians and thus reflect the skew in variables such as stakes.

24. If one were to put confidence limits around the lines to represent the sampling errors, those limits would be in the form of bands fanlike in appearance, narrowest at the mean stakes value and widening out as stakes got smaller or larger than that mean.

25. "Statistically," this is the proper conclusion to be drawn. It does not mean that the pattern shown in Figure 8-1 (i.e., hourly fee lawyers putting in more time in smaller cases, and contingent fee lawyers putting in more time in bigger cases) is not correct; it simply means that the statistical evidence does not permit us to draw a conclusion that the gap for the larger cases is anything more than sampling error. The lack of significance of the larger cases may mean either that there really is no difference (and all that is going on is sampling error), or it may mean that because of the concentration of cases at the lower end of the spectrum, the estimates at the higher end are insufficiently reliable to draw a conclusion of difference even though there really is a difference there.

26. If most of the contingent fee cases accepted because of prior representation came from organizational clients, it might be that this result, combined with the finding that contingent fee lawyers spend *more* time on cases from organizational clients, reflects a multicollinearity problem. An examination of the correlation between these two variables indicates that this is not the case.

27. While only 15 percent of the contingent fee lawyers reported having previously represented their current client, the fairly substantial effect could arise if those cases deviate substantially in terms of effort as compared to contingent fee cases where there was no prior representation.

28. Compare this finding to Macaulay's comment (1979: 122) about a lawyer's willingness to handle a regular client's minor consumer problem as "a kind of 'loss-leader' service . . . in order to keep a client's good will."

29. This would not necessarily be inconsistent with the interpretation of this variable as indicative of the possibility of future representation since, for the contingent fee lawyer particularly, such future representation is most likely where there is already a history of representation; furthermore, future representation is likely to be a strong (and perhaps the only) motivation for taking a minimal case on a contingency basis.

30. Area of law was entered into the equations as a series of dummy variables, with specific dummy variables for multiple-area cases and for cases not falling into one of the eight defined categories.

31. Because of the constrained range of the dependent variable, it was necessary to find a transformation of stakes that was appropriate to describe any relationship that might exist. Several transformations were examined, and the natural logarithm seemed to provide the best "fit." Consequently, the natural logarithm of stakes was used in the analyses reported in this section.

32. Fee arrangement was entered into the equations as a series of dummy variables using four categories: hourly, contingent, flat, and other. For a further discussion of how fee arrangement was handled, see note 33.

33. Preliminary analyses indicated that fee arrangement did not have the kind of structuring effect on work content that it had on lawyer effort; consequently, a single regression model was used for all fee arrangements (with fee arrangement it self-introduced as a series of three dummy variables). Analyses indicated that stakes had an influence on work content (higher stakes led to more factual investigation, including discovery, while lower stakes led to a higher proportion of time spent on conferring with the client and settlement discussions); however, since the effect of stakes on content was less important than on effort, and the inclusion of stakes as a variable required that cases without monetized stakes information had to be omitted, the analysis was repeated omitting stakes from the regression equation.

34. Because of the sparseness of the relationships, I have omitted any tabular presentation of the results, which would inevitably be quite complex.

35. This section was previously published (Kritzer, 1986) and appears in similar form in my book on negotiation (Kritzer, forthcoming).

36. It is highly instructive that the example of Ms. Brown and Mr. Snead is based on a hypothetical case developed by the Legal Services Corporation, Office of Program Support, for training legal services attorneys (Menkel-Meadow, 1984: 772n).

37. There are, in fact, a variety of alternative compensation schemes that might be created: fee shifting, whereby the defendant pays the plaintiff's attorney for time or, perhaps, a central fund, created by "taxing" monetary contingent fees, to which the lawyer could apply for compensation.

38. The apparent inability of large-firm corporate lawyers (described as depending on small numbers of large-scale clients for their livelihood—see Heinz and Laumann, 1982) to see problems of legality and ethics in what they are asked to do by their clients (see Heinz, 1984; Nelson, 1985) is another example of the inability of the professionalism image to cope with the realities of the world in which lawyers must work.

39. Given the retrospective nature of the surveys, one might argue that the lack of correlation between the content indicators and the relationship variables simply shows that the content measures contained too much error for reliable analysis. This position ignores the very strong relationships between the content indicators and area of law that were discussed in Chapter 7; if the content measures were heavily contaminated with error, those relationships would not have appeared in the way they did.

40. The numbers in parentheses index the specific variables to the references in the tables in this chapter.

Chapter 9

1. The study (Wanner, 1974, 1975) from which Galanter drew his now widely referred to distinction between "one-shot" and "repeat" players was based heavily on routine collections cases. However, while the typical collections case might involve an organization as plaintiff (a "repeat player") and an individual as defendant (a "one shotter"), in ordinary litigation as I have defined it the most common configuration is exactly the reverse, with the individual as plaintiff and the organization (frequently an insurance company) as defendant.

2. One feminist writer has argued that the "deconstruction of binary oppositions by many feminist theorists can be applied to the legal paradigm by noting the limitations and futility of win/loss litigation results . . . " (Menkel-Meadow, 1989: 315). My point is that the image of binary oppositions—winners and losers—does not hold even in the ordinary litigation process.

3. At the time of the study, the minimum for federal diversity cases was $10,000; it has since been raised to $50,000.

4. I include in this expense category fees paid by the lawyer on behalf of the client such as filing fees, witness fees, reporter fees, and so forth. To simplify the discussion in this section, I will simply lump these expenses in with the lawyer's fee and refer to the combined as the "fee."

5. One potential complication that needs to be considered here is the situation where a defendant counterclaims in a lawsuit. This kind of counterclaim is probably most likely to occur in a tort case in which there is a dispute over who was at fault; however, in terms of who is at risk for payment, there usually really are two separate "cases" in these kinds of disputes, one where the nominal plaintiff is suing the defendant's insurance company and one where the nominal defendant is suing the plaintiff's insurance compa-

ny. Counterclaims can also arise in contract cases, particularly where payment has been withheld; one party might sue for payment while the other counterclaims for damages related to nonperformance (or vice versa). In cases where there is a counterclaim, the notion of who is the plaintiff and who is the defendant, other than in purely nominal terms in the court record, is more or less arbitrary. For purposes of the analysis in this chapter, I have treated the party that recovered as the plaintiff and the party that paid as the defendant; where there was no recovery, I have used the designation in the court record.

6. About a third of those plaintiffs who suffered net losses and were paying their lawyers on a contingency basis had fee agreements that involved some mixed arrangement (e.g., a flat fee plus a percentage); still, over two thirds were paying on a pure percentage (plus expenses) basis. About 15 percent of the contingent fee plaintiffs that ended up with net losses did recover some amount of money from the other side, but it was less than the expenses that they had to pay to their lawyers.

7. I should note that this strong relationship is at least partly due to the influence of the small number of large cases in the sample. If I restrict the analysis to cases under $100,000, the correlation for unadjusted outcome drops off to .62 (.64 for adjusted outcome). Furthermore, the regression coefficients (i.e., the indicator of how the predicted outcome would change for a unit change in stakes), drop as well.

Dependent Variable	Regression Coefficient (Stakes)	
	All Cases	Cases Under $100,000
Adjusted outcome	.82	.57
Unadjusted outcome	.79	.54

8. Conflicts of interest between lawyers and clients are by no means limited to contingent fee situations. Hourly fee lawyers have an incentive to devote excessive time to a case in order to increase the billable hours (see Johnson, 1980–1981; Wessel, 1976). Public interest lawyers may want to pursue a case well beyond the point that is satisfactory to the named plaintiff or may want to refuse a settlement offer that does not include payment of attorneys' fees (Luban, 1989: 320).

9. For hourly fee lawyers "success" may be of interest, either out of empathy for the client or because of concerns about professional reputations (and the possible long-run implications for the lawyer's ability to attract clients and the resulting fees), but "success" for them will closely parallel success for their clients.

10. Here I am using *fee* to refer only to that part of the payment to the lawyer that is for time spent; in the typical contingent fee case, the fee is computed by the lawyer first taking the percentage specified in the retainer agreement and then adding to that fee the expenses that the lawyer incurred (filing fees, reporter fees, etc.). In the analysis in this section, *fee* refers only to the first component of the amount the lawyer receives.

11. The amount of time that a law firm has to "sell" can always be increased by simply adding more lawyers to the firm.

12. The $50 figure is from an analysis of the hourly rates obtained by hourly fee lawyers (Kritzer et al., 1984a: 587–592) and is the effective hourly rate (fee divided by hours) rather than the quoted hourly rate. The analysis of the hourly rates charged by hourly fee lawyers showed relatively little variation in those rates; as I will show in the

following discussion, this is not true of contingent fee lawyers, whose effective hourly rates vary widely.

13. Luban (1989: 246) points out that the Model Rules of Professional Conduct state that a "lawyer's fee shall be reasonable" (Rule 1.5(a)); however, the explication of what constitutes a reasonable fee provides no guidance ("a fee is clearly excessive when, after a review of the facts, a lawyer of ordinary prudence would be left with a definite and firm conviction that the fee is in excess of a reasonable fee"). There is no history of reviewing contingent fees that use standard percentage rates, even where such fees when viewed on an hourly basis could readily be construed as excessive.

14. In one sense, these figures *overstate* the return lawyers can expect from contingent fee cases when stakes are low. Another way of computing aggregate return is to combine all cases that meet a given set of conditions and then compute the return on the average hour of effort for those cases by dividing the total fees earned by the total hours worked. For cases involving less than $10,000, the average hour of effort returned only $25 in 1978. When this calculation is carried out on all cases, the average return per hour is $47 (the increase over the $42 median effective hourly rate reflecting the skew from a small number of cases with very large hourly rates), and when it is done on all tort cases the average return is $51.

15. As an extreme example, Philip Corboy is reported to have earned a $20,000 contingent fee for 4 hours work (see Jenkins, 1989: 315). A similar fee, based on a combination of $250 per hour and a 25 percent contingency, is reported to have been earned by an Illinois attorney in a postdivorce case; Harold Collins received $42,800 based on the hours worked plus $800,000 as a contingent fee, which works out to $4,923 per hour, assuming that the case took 171.2 hours of Mr. Collins' time (*National Law Journal*, September 18, 1989, p. 13). Interestingly, this fee was disallowed by the courts, but on the grounds that contingent fees could not be applied in a divorce-related matter and not on the grounds that the fee was excessive; one might suspect that it was, in fact, the excessive nature of the fee that actually accounted for the court's decision, although the court did not want to justify its decision on those grounds because of the precedent that would be established.

16. For representative information on the fees charged by top law firms, see the *National Law Journal*'s survey on billing (published as a supplement to the November 7, 1988 issue). Also, in the study of big-time litigators cited previously, one defense lawyer is quoted as stating that he had "*discounted* [his] rate to $150 an hour for major clients" (Jenkins, 1989: 317).

17. The highest single effective hourly rate reported in the sample was $2,500 in a case that took only 1 hour of a lawyer's time and yielded a $7,124 settlement. Of the 15 cases with effective hourly rates of $300 or more, four involved outcomes of under $10,000, and four involved outcomes of over $50,000. Five involved less five hours or less of lawyer time.

18. Very high hourly rates are rare in the sense that only a tiny proportion of cases generate them; given the large numbers of cases handled on a contingency basis, there are substantial numbers of such cases in absolute terms.

19. One of the most vocal critics of contingent fees in recent years has been the medical profession; physicians have been quick to blame the "medical malpractice crisis" on fee-hungry lawyers in general and contingent fees in particular. With this in mind one might imagine a cap on lawyers' effective hourly rates equal to the highest effective hourly rates charged by the medical profession. Given the physicians' fees (the following figures are only for the fees charged by the physician; they exclude hospital charges) charged for certain medical procedures (e.g., $8,000 for a 4-hour heart bypass

operation, $800 for a cardiac catheterization procedure taking approximately 1 hour, $400 for a gastroscopic examination of the stomach requiring less than 1 hour of a physician's time – all these examples are taken from recent family medical bills), I doubt if many lawyers would object to such a limitation.

20. The difference between the likelihood of no fee in federal tort cases and state tort cases is statistically significant ($Z=2.60$).

21. See Cecil and Douglas (1987) for an empirical study of the use of summary judgment in three federal district courts.

22. Given the lack of any strong theory guiding the selection of variables for inclusion in the model, there is no way of being certain that I have included all relevant variables. However, I believe that I have included all potentially important variables, at least those available in the data set. For this analysis, and for the parallel analyses in later sections of this chapter, I have replaced missing data for predictor variables other than stakes with means adjusted by a random normal deviate; for variables transformed by taking the logarithm, the replacement was done based on means and standard deviations obtained after transformation. For those respondents who reported making no specific demands in negotiation, the log of the demand ratio (labeled "strategic bargaining" in the tables in this chapter) was set to zero.

23. One troubling aspect of the complete set of coefficients shown in Table 9A-1 is that many of the coefficients seem strangely large (e.g., stakes and hours worked); this is at least partly attributable to high intercorrelations between stakes and some of the other variables. I reran the analysis omitting stakes; that decreased some of the very high coefficients but also substantially decreased the coefficients of determination. As a result, it is best to treat the specific values of the coefficients with some caution, since the reality of holding hours constant as stakes increases (or holding stakes constant as one moves from state to federal court) is difficult to imagine in reality.

24. One question that might be raised about the negative impact of effort on effective hourly rate concerns something known in the statistical literature as the "ratio variable problem." Given two independent random variables (A and B), if a third variable (C) is created by dividing B by A, A and C will tend to have a negative correlation. The issues concerning this problem have been heavily debated (see the extensive citations in Kritzer, 1990) but, in fact, reflect more substantive theoretical questions than statistical questions (see Kritzer, 1990). In fact, for the analysis presented here, the zero-order correlations between the hourly rate and the number of hours worked are modestly negative ($-.09$, $-.13$, and $-.11$ for the three sets of results shown in Tables 9-3 and 9A-1 – only the second of these correlations is statistically significant), while the zero-order correlations between fee (hourly rate times number of hours worked) has a much stronger positive correlation (.29, .36, and .72). Computing hourly rate removes an artifactual correlation related to amount at stake (as indicated by the sharply reduced magnitude of the correlations).

25. One variable conspicuous by its absence here is success from the client's perspective. I did include in one version of the model an indicator of client success (net recovery divided by stakes). The results indicated that client's success was not related to the contingent fee lawyer's effective hourly rate; this was true regardless of the subset of cases included in the analysis. I ultimately excluded client success from the analysis reported here because missing data for the client success variable required that a fairly substantial number of cases be omitted from the analysis.

26. One of the implicit assumptions of this analysis is that extra dispute goals (i.e., goals beyond the instant case), such as precedence and creating a reputation as a hardball player, are not to be considered in evaluating success. In fact, without a

detailed, case-by-case analysis, there would be no way of incorporating such "extra" goals into an analysis of success.

27. There are 202 cases in which there are stakes estimates from both plaintiff and defense lawyers; in 69 percent of these cases, the plaintiff's estimate exceeds the defendant's.

28. See Trubek et al. (1983*b*: 116–119) for an analysis based on the third indicator (defendant's estimate of stakes). The major difference in the analysis is the simple likelihood of "success." Using the defendant's stakes estimate, the savings achieved exceed the lawyer's fee for 24 percent of the respondents; using the plaintiff's estimate of stakes, savings exceed fee for 67 percent of respondents. The earlier analysis found no strong relationships between success and the other variables that are discussed next. The earlier analysis relied on a slightly larger group of respondents, 191 versus the 143 that I am using here.

29. The mathematical relationship between the two measures of defendant's success is:

$$ds = 1 - \frac{1}{DS}$$

30. Success for the plaintiff will be measured by:

$$PS = \frac{\text{Recovery} - \text{Fees}}{\text{Plaintiff's Stakes}}$$

If one rewrites the two equations using "adjusted outcomes" in place of "recovery + fees" or "recovery − fees," the two formulas are the inverse of one another.

$$PS = \frac{\text{Adjusted Outcome}}{\text{Plaintiff's Stakes}}$$

$$DS = \frac{\text{Plaintiff's Stakes}}{\text{Adjusted Outcome}}$$

Even though there are some asymmetries between the two equations (for plaintiffs and defendants) — only the plaintiffs can have negative values — I chose to work with the second defendant success indicator because of the similarity to the plaintiff's formula.

31. This calculation ignores internal costs to the defendant (i.e., the value of the defendant's time or the value of the time of the defendant's employees); this will be discussed later in this chapter.

32. If the respondent reported making no offers, the log of the offer ratio was set to zero.

33. Preliminary analyses indicated that including the small number of cases with success ratios exceeding 10 produced unstable results; consequently, I report only the results where these outliers have been omitted.

34. Table 9A–2 shows results with and without the stakes variable included in the analysis, since omitting stakes substantially increases the number of cases available for analysis (from 103 to 127); in fact, there is little difference between the two sets of results, and I will focus on the results with stakes in the equation in my textual discussion. The one exception is that with stakes omitted, the proportion of time on pleadings and motions has a statistically significant impact on defendant success (success goes up as the proportion of time on pleadings and motions goes up).

35. Because the number of variables in the equation is fairly high relative to the number of observations used for the analysis, the adjusted coefficients of determination

provide a better indicator of the fit of overall explanatory power of the equation. The unadjusted R^2 is .52; with stakes omitted from the equation, the adjusted and unadjusted R^2's are .35 and .48, respectively. The adjusted coefficients of determination (R^2's) are shown in Tables 9-3 and 9A-1 as well; because of the larger number of cases in that analysis, the adjusted values are much closer to the unadjusted values. The R^2's for defendant success are comparable to those for the first two subsets of cases used in the lawyer success analysis (i.e., both subsets that included cases where the lawyer received no payment).

36. When stakes were omitted from the equation, proportion of time on pleadings and motions also seemed to have a significant effect on defendant success.

37. The R^2 for all cases is .30.

38. The F ratios are 0.93 and 1.46 for the models with stakes and without stakes, respectively.

39. Keep in mind that this analysis uses only the cases in which results were monetary. Nonetheless, the strength of the bargaining ratio indicator casts some question on the arguments for moving away from adversary bargaining (see Menkel-Meadow, 1984).

40. For example, the most common defendant in the study is an insurance company. Most of the internal processing costs for an insurance company involve the work of the adjuster who is responsible for settling the case, and this work goes on regardless of whether or not a court case is filed. In fact, very often, most of the adjuster's work is completed before the case is filed; once a lawsuit starts, the responsibility tends to shift to the lawyer handling the case.

41. This observation alludes to the problem of selection bias. The statistical techniques used throughout this study were designed to try to assess the results that might be obtained through a truly random experimental situation. Yet, while the sample was designed to be a random subset of the cases in the courts studied, the internal dynamics of individual cases do not involve random assignment of things such as lawyers. To answer properly the question of whether or not relative skill of the opposing lawyers makes a difference, it would be necessary to assign randomly lawyers of differing skills to cases. Needless to say, this is not going to happen in the real world.

42. This hypothetical case is based on a similar case described by Vidmar (1985).

43. This can be seen clearly in a recent case in England. In 1987 it was discovered that a pathologist in Liverpool had incorrectly diagnosed smear tests for cervical cancer for almost 1,000 women. Despite the devastating consequences of these errors, the women affected "are unlikely to receive large amounts of compensation" because the English courts have valued injuries of the type many women suffered at only $3,000 to $5,000 (see the *Guardian*, September 25, 1987, p. 3; see Quam, Dingwall, and Fenn, 1987, for a general discussion of medical malpractice issues in England in light of the American experience).

Another example drawing on litigation in England that demonstrates the important role played by the potential for recovery through the courts in affecting out-of-court resolutions can be found in the products liability area. In the United States the pharmaceutical company Eli Lilly (and/or its insurer) has had to make substantial payments to persons who have claimed injuries related to taking Opren, an arthritis medication that Lilly produced and marketed for a brief time. The payments in the United States reflect the awards and anticipated awards that would be forthcoming in U.S. courts. In the United Kingdom, Lilly resisted settling claims because its situation is much more ambiguous under English law and because the size of judgments that might be forthcoming from the High Court judges who might decide any lawsuits would be substantially smaller than in the United States (see articles in the *Guardian*, June 5, 1987, p. 19; July 1, 1987, p. 29).

44. A good illustration of the ambiguity in stakes evaluation is to be found in Rosenthal's study of lawyers and clients in personal injury cases (1974). Given his interest in assessing what affected the outcome of cases, Rosenthal had to have some independent estimate of the value of each of the cases in his sample against which to compare the result. To accomplish this, he had a panel of five "experts" independently evaluate each case. The results of those evaluations, which are published in his book (1974: 202–207), demonstrate the inherent difficulty in any such evaluation process: in 52 of the 59 cases for which evaluations were made, the ratio of the highest to the lowest evaluation was 2; in 19 the ratio was 4. Given that these were experts who should be able to agree on valuations of cases, one is forced to question how good anyone's evaluation is. Furthermore, if the stakes are ambiguous in relatively straightforward cases, how much more difficult is it in cases involving nonmonetary issues? Clearly, "objective" assessments of success, relative to some independently arrived at standard of comparison, are dubious.

45. A number of years ago while bicycling to the university campus I was struck by a car turning left across my path. I was banged up a bit and suffered an injury to my wrist that necessitated wearing a brace for a couple of months. Very soon after the accident the driver's insurance company contacted me, anxious to settle my claim. I was not sure how much I should ask for; my first inclination was about $300; in any case, I put off the insurance company in order to be sure that my wrist would mend without further complications. While I was wearing the brace, I ran into an acquaintance who was a lawyer; since I knew that he handled personal injury claims, I asked him what he thought my wrist injury was worth. He responded that his firm was getting around $750 for injuries of that sort and suggested that I ask for $1750 (because it sounded like a figure that had been carefully thought through, rather than a round number such as $2,000). I wrote to the insurance company asking for this amount, indicating my desire to reach a settlement "without having to turn the matter over to my attorney." We settled for $1,000.

46. When one looks systematically at the ratio of outcome to fees, one finds relatively little variation where the lawyer is paid on a contingency basis; the median ratio is 2.9, and the first and third quartiles are 2.5 and 3.5, respectively. Likewise, there is relatively little variation related to amount at stake or whether the case was in federal or state court. The picture is very different when the lawyer is retained on an hourly fee basis; the median is similar to that for contingent fee lawyers (3.6 versus 2.9), but the quartiles are sharply different (first quartile 0.0, third quartile 15.2). Additionally, there are significant variations related to stakes (0.5 for cases under 10,000, 7.5 for cases of $10,000 to $50,000, and 18.0 for cases over $50,000) and, to a lesser degree, to court (3.0 for federal cases versus 4.9 for state cases).

47. Recall that each case could involve multiple areas of law, so that there are a small number of cases in the table that involve both torts and contracts (and appear in both sets of columns). The median for all tort cases combined (including one that was handled under an arrangement other than hourly or contingent) was .50 (the first and third quartiles were .25 and .67, respectively).

48. There are an additional six contracts cases handled under some arrangement other than contingent or hourly fees; the median for the complete set of contract cases is .65 (first and third quartiles are .20 and .83, respectively).

49. Four nontort/noncontract cases were handled under fee arrangements other than hourly or contingent fees; the median for all nontort/noncontract cases combined is .33 (the first and third quartiles are .00 and .62, respectively).

50. See note 44 for a discussion of the ambiguities associated with determining what is at stake in a personal injury case.

51. Another point of evidence that supports the interpretation that the success achieved on behalf of the tort clients decreases as stakes goes up is that other studies have found similar results. For example, Viscusi (1986: 338–340) found lower levels of success as stakes increased in product liability cases. A number of studies of tort cases arising from automobile accidents (Conard et al., 1964: 251; Department of Transportation, 1970: 29; Landes, 1982: 259; All-Industry Research Advisory Committee, 1979: 73) have reported that recoveries as a percentage of economic loss decline as the amount of the measured loss went up.

52. While in the tables and text I report results only for contingent and hourly fee lawyers, the basic model was estimated for all fee arrangements as well. This added only 10 observations to the analysis, and the results were essentially identical to those excluding other fee arrangements.

53. One outlier with a success ratio exceeding 10 was excluded from the analysis.

54. This figure was arrived at by dividing the coefficient for contingency fee lawyers by the interaction term representing the specific impact of stakes for hourly fee lawyers; this result was then exponentiated to yield 1,768.

55. A number of years ago I was involved as a consultant in a large class action case concerning possible side effects of a widely prescribed drug. My role was to assist in assessing the adequacy of the proposed settlement on the presumption that the drug had the alleged side effect. On that presumption, it quickly became clear that the amount proposed was grossly inadequate to provide any meaningful compensation to more than a tiny fraction of the affected class. It seemed strange that the plaintiff's attorneys would advance the settlement proposal under these circumstances, but then it became clear that some of those attorneys had begun to realize that the case had relatively little chance of succeeding (the accumulating medical evidence was running strongly against the plaintiffs); while the settlement would not have yielded a great deal to the plaintiff class as a whole, it would have provided a good bit of compensation for the attorneys. My interpretation was that it was an effort by a part of the plaintiffs' committee (other members of that committee strongly opposed the proposed settlement and eventually succeeded in getting an appeals court to overturn a key provision, which effectively scuttled the proposal) to get whatever they could to cover their sunk costs.

56. I replicated this analysis as much as possible for contingent fee lawyers only (i.e., omitting lawyers paid on some basis other than a contingency basis); the results were generally consistent with those reported here. One interesting difference, at least in terms of significant coefficients, was that the log of the number of court events was negatively related to plaintiff's success (note that the coefficient for the log of the number of events was negative in the other analyses as well); this seems to suggest further the importance of a quick, easy resolution to the success achieved by the contingent fee lawyer. Compare this to Conard et al.'s (1964) study of automobile accident victims in Michigan, which reported that those who filed suit and then settled quickly (i.e., before pretrial conferences or trial) had the highest probability of receiving some payment and had the highest mean recovery.

57. Lind et al. (1989) also found little relationship between objective outcomes and litigant satisfaction.

58. I should acknowledge that I have measured outcomes in a very narrow way in this analysis. There are many other kinds of issues that could, and should, be considered in assessing the quality of resolutions achieved in litigation and other kinds of dispute processing procedures (see Galanter, 1988, 1989; Bush, 1989; Luban, 1989; Tyler, 1989; Esser, 1989).

59. One possible challenge to these results, particularly the apparent link between success and strategic bargaining, is that the indicators of these two concepts contain a

common element (an estimate of stakes); as mentioned in note 24 *supra* there is an extensive literature on this the ratio variable problem (see Kritzer, 1990). I do not believe that these results can be explained away by reference to the ratio variable problem. First, while there is a strong link between success and strategic bargaining, it is nowhere near as strong as the link between outcome and initial offer or demand; that is, the creation of the ratio dampers the relationship between two not particularly interesting (from a theoretical perspective) variables. Second, the sign of the relationship between success and strategic bargaining is positive for both plaintiffs and defendants, even though stakes appear in the numerator of the success ratio for one and in the denominator for the other (while stakes stay in the denominator of the strategic bargaining indicator for both sides).

60. Elsewhere (Kritzer, forthcoming) I have reported data that suggests that plaintiff's lawyers are less likely to engage in strategic bargaining that are defendant's lawyers. It may be that this is because contingent fee lawyers (representing plaintiffs) have come to know that success from their own perspective is not enhanced by such bargaining.

Chapter 10

1. This quotation can be found on p. 116 of the Penguin Books Edition of *The Doctor's Dilemma* (1954), or on p. 515 in *The Complete Plays of Bernard Shaw* (London: Odhams Press, 1934).

2. See Pound (1953) for a statement of this ideal as applied to lawyers.

3. *The Harvard Concordance to Shakespeare* lists eleven explicit references of lawyers (Spevack, 1973: 690); nine of these are scornful. Whether this actually reflected the level of scorn directed to lawyers during the Elizabethan period or simply reflected Shakespeare playing to an audience that contained many lawyers and law students (the Globe was just across the Thames from one of the Inns of Court) is unclear.

4. See Post (1987) for a number of similar comments from popular literature.

5. It would be unfair to suggest that researchers are unaware of the problems associated with concepts that carry double meanings of this type (see Nelson, 1988: 18).

6. Strictly speaking, I have been applying what has been described as the functionalist perspective on the professions (see Nelson, 1989: 18–22 for a brief summary of this perspective). I have generally ignored some of the alternative perspectives, such as the focus on professional monopoly developed by Larson (1977), which has been extensively applied by Abel (1985a, 1986a, 1986b, 1988a, 1988b, 1988c, 1989a), and some of the other approaches that have focused on professions as institutions (Freidson, 1986; Abbott, 1986, 1988; Rueschemeyer, 1986; Suleiman, 1987). The analysis I have presented has substantial implications for the legal profession as an institution, and I will discuss these implications in the later sections of this chapter.

7. An exception to this is the theory of the professions focusing on market control referred to in note 6. It has not gone unrecognized in earlier writing on the professions; Freidson (1970: *xvii*), in pointing out the double meaning in the word *profession*, contrasted the idealization the word suggests to the occupational implications—the fact that a profession is a job that generates a livelihood.

8. Cf. Feinberg (1986: 623): "Attorneys who work for contingent fees budget their time and efforts differently than if they were billing on an hourly basis."

9. In other countries, such as England (see Abel, 1988a: 177–188), the limitations on what would in the United States be considered the practice of law is much more narrowly drawn.

10. The California Bar went into a turmoil over the proposals advanced by Public

Protection Committee that would have permitted nonlawyers to encroach on areas of work currently reserved for licensed attorneys. Ironically, the committee was charged with investigating consumer abuses by nonlawyers, but shocked the legal community by returning recommendations that called for recognizing a status quo in which various kinds of service providers handle matters that can be construed as the practice of law. After attacks by opponents within local bar associations and specialty bar associations, the committee's proposals for the recognition, licensing, and regulation of "legal technicians" by the state of California were, in the words of the *National Law Journal* (September 11, 1989, p. 6) "gutted." The Bar did decide to proceed to have a ten-member commission to draw up standards for training, licensing, and regulation of legal technicians, but it seems to oppose any move that would allow such persons to appear in court (The State Bar of California, press release dated September 8, 1989).

11. There is an irony in Abel's advocacy of opening legal practice to nonlawyers. In considering alternative mechanisms for dispute resolution, type of representation can be viewed as one of the key dimensions (the other two being type of resolution process — adjudication, arbitration, mediation, etc. — and type of forum — court, administrative agency, private third party, etc.). In earlier work Abel (1982, 1985b) was very critical of "informal justice," even though nonlawyer representation constitutes the "informal" end of the representation dimension.

12. During the 1970s, an organization that called itself HALT (Help Abolish Legal Tyranny) was established to lobby for legal reforms that would reduce the role of the legal profession. In the early 1980s it was reported to have a membership of about 30,000 (Rhode, 1981: 4–6). The organization has since changed its name to HALT-Americans for Legal Reform (HALT-ALR).

13. The success rate for appellants represented by an attorney was 18 percent compared to 16 to 17 percent for those with veteran organization (American Legion, Disabled American Veterans, Veterans of Foreign Wars) representation and 15 percent for those with no representation.

14. There is some evidence that the likelihood of attorney representation in auto injury claims is rising (see All-Industry Research Advisory Council, 1988).

15. Interestingly, the best study comparing the work of those with and without formal legal training focused on judges and found no empirical evidence of significant differences between lay and law-trained judges in the lower courts (Provine, 1986b).

16. Rhode (1981: 79) quotes a U.S. Patent Office report to the Hoover Commission that found "no significant difference between lawyers and nonlawyers either with respect to their ability to handle the work or with respect to their ethical conduct."

17. For example, nurse practitioners and physician's assistants have been used to provide primary care in rural areas not served by a doctor. One recent news article on the use of paraprofessional medical personnel in rural areas quoted the head of the National Rural Health Association as saying that such physician's assistants "can do roughly 80 percent of the work doctors do, and . . . [that] they are extremely cost effective" ("Medical Assistants Heal Shortage of Doctors in Many Rural Areas," *Chicago Tribune*, January 15, 1989, p. 1:5). Use of paraprofessionals to deliver primary care is also growing in the context of cost-conscious health maintenance organizations (see "Demand for Physician Assistants Growing," Madison *Capital Times*, October 16, 1989, p. 1).

18. When I posed a tax law question to my own attorney (who specializes in trusts and estates and the tax consequences of them), he suggested that an accountant familiar with the specific area in question would be able to advise me on the tax consequences of what I was considering more efficiently (i.e., at less cost to me) than he would.

19. In a speech before the Board of Governors of the American Bar Association, the chairman of the Legal Services Corporation under the Reagan administration proposed abolishing the Corporation. As an alternative means of providing representation to the poor he proposed breaking up the "legal cartel" by repealing all state unauthorized practice-of-law statutes and opening up legal practice to all comers (*National Law Journal*, February 23, 1987, p. 2).

20. The problem of defining exactly what constitutes the practice of law is shown by what is general doctrine applied in litigation on the matter: "The practice of law comprises those services customarily rendered by lawyers" (Christensen, 1980: 192).

21. This usually occurs in situations where the work will not yield a reasonable fee. This can arise for one or more of several reasons: legal limitations on the fee that can be paid, inability of the potential client to pay a fee, or the amount at stake is too small to yield a percentage fee that is commensurate with the amount of effort that will be required. A good example is the use of volunteer lay advocates before the tribunal in Wisconsin that considers contested claims for unemployment compensation: lawyers have not resisted the use of such advocates because the amount at stake is usually fairly modest and the law limits any fee that can be paid to a maximum of 10 percent of the compensation that is granted.

22. As mentioned in note 10 *supra*, the Public Protection Committee that proposed permiting nonlawyers to perform tasks now reserved for licensed attorneys was in fact appointed to investigate consumer abuses by nonlawyers.

23. The English legal profession is undergoing substantial change that might lead to a lessening of the division of work between solicitors and barristers. However, from my own observations of the English system of litigation, at least in the nonmetropolitan areas of England, barristers appear as advocates even in the lower county courts where solicitors have rights of audience!

24. One could make a case that lay advocates, such as legal brokers, should be permitted to appear in court, possibly with some restrictions on the kinds of cases or kinds of courts (see Rhode, 1981: 76–77); while I would probably be prepared to support that position, it is not central to the argument I am advancing here.

25. In England, the Law Society (the professional association of solicitors), attacked "claims assessors" (laypersons who serve a function much like what I have termed legal brokers, but only in cases involving insurance companies) in precisely these terms (1970: 3): "The negotiation of personal injury claims concerns the question of legal liability, and the power of the claimant or his representative to negotiate a just settlement depends entirely on the ability to back the claim with the threat of legal proceedings." I should note that the Law Society forbids its members from working in conjunction with claims assessors. Interestingly, Gilb (1956: 232–233) reports that in the early 1930s the California Bar succeeded in putting out of business independent claims adjusters (who would represent claimants in negotiations with third-party insurance companies) by disciplining lawyers who worked with those companies (Gilb describes the bar's efforts as "a scathing onslaught").

26. In England legal professionals do not have a monopoly of the representation of injured persons making claims against the tort-feasor's insurance company, at least up until the point that formal court action is initiated. A group of specialists, called "loss assessors" or "claims assessors," will represent injured persons in negotiations with an insurance company (for a percentage of the amount recovered). The Law Society challenged the ability of loss assessors to obtain full value for claims because of their inability to threaten to file suit (Law Society, 1970), and practice rules for English solicitors forbid them from working in conjunction with loss assessors. However, con-

versations I had, both with insurance claims officials and with loss assessors, make it clear that loss assessors have no trouble handing cases over to a solicitor when negotiations are unsuccessful, and the insurance companies deal with loss assessors in full knowledge that a solicitor is always somewhere in the background. Interestingly, loss assessors frequently are persons who spent years working for insurance companies as "claims inspectors" (what Americans refer to as "claims adjusters") and know both what injuries are worth and how the insurance companies operate.

27. It is sometimes said by plaintiff's lawyers that they have to file suit in order to convince the defendant that they are serious about the case. This might be interpreted as an effort on the part of the defendant to force the plaintiff's lawyer to incur some costs as a means of discouraging certain kinds of claims. There is no evidence as to how often this happens; most modest disputes result in settlement without the filing of a lawsuit, even when the claimant retains a lawyer. I suspect this reflects the recognition by defendants that the potential expense to them of imposing this kind of cost on the plaintiff's lawyer is greater than the return.

28. A third possible reason might be thought of as a form of deregulation on principle: if there is no absolute necessity for creating barriers to lay advocacy and representation, then those artificial bars should be removed.

29. Some commentators might see the proposal as fundamentally conservative in that it represents just one more of the many alternatives that comprise systems of "informal justice" that really constitute second-class measures for the subordinate classes in society; this critique advances the position that only by empowering fully the segments of society outside the elite to deal on an equal footing with disputing opponents can there be any hope of something resembling true justice (see Abel, 1981, 1982).

30. In England this is reflected in the ending of the conveyancing monopoly whereby only solicitors could handle the transfer of ownership of real property (see Abel, 1988a: 178–185; Selinger, 1987).

31. A recent report issued by the Lord Chancellor's Department (1987) has suggested that lay advocates should be integrated more fully into the working of the court system, particularly at the lower level.

32. Abel (1988a: 194) reports that fees changed little after "scale" fees were abolished by the Law Society in 1972. The fees, both before and after the fee schedule was abolished, were tied to property values in a way that bore little relationship to the amount of work lawyers had to perform in connection with the property transfer.

33. The *Guardian* reported that conveyancing fees were 0.4 to 1.0 percent of house prices after the passage of the legislation. Selinger (1987) refers to fees of .05 to .07 percent, but these figures represent either a misprint or a miscalculation. See Domberger and Sherr (1989) for a far more sophisticated analysis of changes in conveyancing charges.

34. I should note that during much of this period, house prices in southern England (particularly in and around London) were going up very rapidly. Also, the Law Society during this time changed its rules to permit solicitors to advertise; part of the drop in the cost of conveyancing no doubt reflected intraprofessional competition as well as the threat of external competition.

References

Abbott, Andrew. 1986. "Jurisdictional Conflicts: A New Approach to the Development of the Legal Professions." 1986 *American Bar Foundation Research Journal* 187–225.

_____. 1988. *The System of Professions: An Essay on the Division of Expert Labor.* Chicago: University of Chicago Press.

Abel, Richard. 1979a. "Socializing the Legal Profession: Can Redistributing Lawyers' Services Achieve Social Justice?" 1 *Law & Policy Quarterly* 5–51.

_____. 1979b. "The Rise of Professionalism." 6 *British Journal of Law and Society* 82–98.

_____. 1981. "Conservative Conflict and the Reproduction of Capitalism: The Role of Informal Justice." 9 *International Journal of the Sociology of Law* 245–267.

_____. 1982. "The Contradictions of Informal Justice." In Richard Abel (ed.), *The Politics of Informal Justice: The American Experience.* New York: Academic.

_____. 1985a. "Comparative Sociology of Legal Professions: An Exploratory Essay." 1985 *American Bar Foundation Research Journal* 1–80.

_____. 1985b. "Informalism: A Tactical Equivalent to Law?" 19 *Clearinghouse Review* 375–383.

_____. 1986a. "The Decline of Professionalism?" 49 *Modern Law Review* 1–41.

_____. 1986b. "The Transformation of the American Legal Profession." 20 *Law & Society Review* 7–18.

_____. 1988a. *Lawyers in England and Wales.* London: Basil Blackwell.

_____. 1988b. "United States: The Contradictions of Professionalism." Pp. 186–243 in Richard L. Abel and Philip S.C. Lewis (eds.), *Lawyers in Society: The Common Law World.* Berkeley: University of California Press.

_____. 1988c. "England and Wales: A Comparison of the Professional Projects of Barristers and Solicitors." Pp. 23–75 in Richard L. Abel and Philip S.C. Lewis (eds.), *Lawyers in Society: The Common Law World.* Berkeley: University of California Press.

_____. 1989a. *American Lawyers.* New York: Oxford University Press.

_____. 1989b. "Between Market and State: The Legal Profession in Turmoil." 52 *Modern Law Review* 285–325.

Abel, Richard L. and Philip S.C. Lewis (eds.). 1988a. *Lawyers in Society: The Common Law World*. Berkeley: University of California Press.

———. 1988b. *Lawyers in Society: The Civil Law World*. Berkeley: University of California Press.

———. 1989. *Lawyers in Society: Comparative Theories*. Berkeley: University of California Press.

Abel-Smith, Brian and Robert Stevens. 1968. *In Search of Justice: Society and the Legal System*. London: Allen Lane.

Administrative Office. 1985. *Report of the Administrative Office of the United States Courts, 1984*. Washington, D.C.: U.S. Government Printing Office.

Aldisert, Ruggero J. 1968. "A Metropolitan Court Conquers Its Backlog—Part II, From Pure Pretrial to Compulsory Settlement Conferences." 51 *Judicature* 247–252.

All-Industry Research Advisory Committee (AIRAC). 1979. *Automobile Injuries and Their Compensation in the United States*. Chicago: AIRAC.

———. 1988. *Attorney Involvement in Auto Injury Claims*. Chicago: AIRAC.

Allison, Graham T. 1971. *Essence of Decision: Explaining the Cuban Missile Crisis*. Boston: Little, Brown.

Alschuler, Albert. 1986. "Mediation with a Mugger: The Shortage of Adjudicative Services and the Need for a Two-Tier Trial System in Civil Cases." 99 *Harvard Law Review* 1808–1859.

American Bar Association. 1986. " . . . *In the Spirit of Public Service: A Blueprint for the Rekindling of Lawyer Professionalism*." Chicago: American Bar Association, Commission on Professionalism.

Arthurs, H.W., R. Weisman, and F.H. Zemans. 1986. "The Canadian Legal Profession." 1986 *American Bar Foundation Research Journal* 447–532.

Aucoin, Peter. 1986. "Organizational Change in the Machinery of Canadian Government: From Rational Management to Brokerage Politics." 19 *Canadian Journal of Political Science* 3–27.

Bailey, Frederick George. 1963. *Politics and Social Change: Orissa in 1959*. Berkeley: University of California Press.

———. 1969. *Strategems and Spoils: A Social Anthropology of Politics*. New York: Schocken.

Barbee, Evelyn L. 1986. "Biomedical Resistance to Ethnomedicine in Botswana." 22 *Social Science and Medicine* 75–80.

———. 1987. "Tensions in the Brokerage Role: Nurses in Botswana." 9 *Western Journal of Nursing Research* 244–256.

Barber, Bernard. 1963. "Some Problems in the Sociology of the Professions." 92 *Daedulus* 669–688.

Batten, Jack. 1980. *Lawyers*. Toronto: Macmillan of Canada.

Baum, Lawrence. 1986. *American Courts: Process and Policy*. Boston: Houghton Mifflin.

Bedlin, Howard and Paul Nejelski. 1984. "Unsettling Issues About Settling Civil Litigation: Examining 'Doomsday Machines,' 'Quick Looks,' and Other Modest Proposals." 68 *Judicature* 9–29.

Bell, Kathleen S. 1969. *Tribunals in the Social Services*. London: Routledge & Kegan Paul.

Benson Commission. 1979a. *The Royal Commission on Legal Services: Final Report, Volume Two*. London: HMSO.

———. 1979b. *The Royal Commission on Legal Services: Final Report, Volume One (Surveys and Studies)*. London: HMSO.

Berends, Miek. 1981. "Modes of Lawyer-Client Interaction: Translation, Transformation, and Social Control." Paper presented at meetings of the Law & Society Association, Amherst, Mass., June 12–14.

Blok, A. 1969. "Variations in Patronage." 16 *Sociologische Gids* 365–378.

Blumberg, Abraham S. 1967a. "The Practice of Law as a Confidence Game: Organizational Cooptation of a Profession." 1 *Law & Society Review* 15–39.

_____. 1967b. *Criminal Justice*. Chicago: Quadrangle.

Boissevain, Jeremy. 1969. "Patrons as Brokers." 16 *Sociologische Gids* 379–386.

_____. 1974. *Friends of Friends: Networks, Manipulators and Coalitions*. Oxford: Basil Blackwell.

Bork, Robert H. 1976. "Dealing with the Overload in Article III Courts." 70 *Federal Rules Decisions* 231–239.

Brazil, Wayne. 1985. *Settling Civil Suits: Litigators' Views about Appropriate Roles and Effective Techniques for Federal Judges*. Chicago: American Bar Association.

Bucher, R. and A. Strauss. 1961. "Professions in Process." 66 *American Sociological Review* 325–334.

Burger, Warren E. 1982. "Isn't There a Better Way?" 68 *American Bar Association Journal* 274–277.

_____. 1984. Remarks at the Dedication of the American Bar Association's Headquarters, Chicago, August 5, 1984. Reported in *The New York Times*, August 6, 1984, p. 20 (Midwest Edition).

Bush, Robert A. Baruch. 1989. "Defining Quality in Dispute Resolution: Taxonomies and Anti-Taxonomies of Quality Arguments." 66 *Denver University Law Review* 335–380.

Cain, Maureen. 1979. "The General Practice Lawyer and the Client: Towards a Radical Conception." 7 *International Journal of the Sociology of Law* 331–354.

Carlin, Jerome E. 1962. *Lawyers on Their Own: A Study of Individual Practitioners in Chicago*. New Brunswick, N.J.: Rutgers University Press.

_____. 1966. *Lawyers' Ethics: A Survey of the New York City Bar*. New York: Russell Sage.

"Cartter Report." 1977. "The Cartter Report on the Leading Schools of Education, Law, and Business." 9(2) *Change* (February) 44–48.

Carty, R.K. 1981. "Brokerage and Partisanship: Politicians, Parties and Elections in Ireland." 14 *Canadian Journal of Political Science* 53–81.

Casper, Jonathan D. 1972. *American Criminal Justice: The Defendant's Perspective*. Englewood Cliffs, N.J.: Prentice-Hall.

Cecil, Joe S. and C.R. Douglas. 1987. *Summary Judgment Practice in Three District Courts*. Washington, D.C.: Federal Judicial Center.

Center for Professional Responsibility. 1987. *The Legislative History of the Model Rules of Professional Conduct: Their Development in the ABA House of Delegates*. Chicago: American Bar Association.

Christensen, Barlow F. 1980. "The Unauthorized Practice of Law: Do Good Fences Really Make Good Neighbors—or Even Good Sense?" 1980 *American Bar Foundation Research Journal* 159–216.

Civiletti, Benjamin R. 1986. "Zeroing in on the Real Litigation Crisis: Irrational Justice, Needless Delays, Excessive Costs." 46 *Maryland Law Review* 40–47.

Clermont, Kevin M. and J.D. Currivan. 1978. "Improving on the Contingent Fee." 63 *Cornell Law Review* 529–639.

Clynch, Edward and David Neubauer, "Trial Courts as Organizations: A Critique and Synthesis." 3 *Law & Policy Quarterly* 69–94.

Cogan, M.L. 1953. "Toward a Definition of Profession." 23 *Harvard Education Review* 33–50.

Committee on the Future of the Legal Profession. 1988. *A Time for Change*. London: The General Council of the Bar and The Law Society.

Connard, Alfred F., James Morgan, Robert Pratt, Charles Voltz, and Robert Bomgaugh. 1964. *Automobile Accident Costs and Payments: Studies in the Economics of Injury Reparation*. Ann Arbor: University of Michigan Press.

Cooter, Robert and Stephen Marks. 1982. "Bargaining in the Shadow of the Law: A Testable Model of Strategic Behavior." 11 *Journal of Legal Studies* 225–251.

Council on the Role of Courts. 1984. *The Role of Courts in American Society*. St. Paul, Minn.: West Publishing.

Curran, Barbara A. 1986. "American Lawyers in the 1980's: A Profession in Transition." 20 *Law & Society Review* 19–51.

Daniels, Arlene Kaplan. 1973. "How Free Should Professionals Be?" Pp. 39–57 in Eliot Freidson (ed.), *The Professions and Their Prospects*. Beverly Hills, Calif.: Sage.

Daniels, Stephen. 1984. "Ladders and Bushes: The Problem of Caseloads and Studying Court Activities over Time." 1984 *American Bar Foundation Research Journal* 751–796.

――――. 1985. "We Are Not a Litigious Society." 24(2) *The Judges' Journal* 18–22.

――――. 1986. "Civil Juries, Jury Verdict Reporters, and the Going Rate." Paper presented at 1986 Annual Meeting of the Law & Society Association, Chicago, May 29–June 1.

Danzon, Patricia M. 1982. *The Resolution of Medical Malpractice Claims: Research Results and Policy Implications*. Santa Monica, Calif.: The Rand Corporation.

――――. 1983. "Contingent Fees for Personal Injury Litigation." 14 *Bell Journal of Economics* 213–224.

De Jongh, M. 1982. "Black Urban Broker." 8 *Humanitas* 335–347.

de Tocqueville, Alexis. 1945. *Democracy in America*. New York: Knopf.

Department of Transportation. 1970. *Economic Consequences of Automobile Accident Injuries*. Washington, D.C.: U.S. Department of Transportation.

Dill, Ann E.P. 1987. "Issues in Case Management for the Chronically Mentally Ill." Pp. 61–70 in David Mechanic (ed.), *Improving Mental Health Services: What Can the Social Sciences Tell Us*. San Francisco: Jossey-Bass.

Dingwall, Robert. 1976. "Accomplishing Profession." 24 *Sociological Review* 331–349.

――――. 1983. "Introduction." Pp. 1–13 in Robert Dingwall and Philip Lewis (eds.), *The Sociology of the Professions: Lawyers, Doctors and Others*. New York: St. Martins.

Domberger, Simon and Avrom Sherr. 1989. "The Impact of Competition on Pricing and Quality of Legal Services." 9 *International Review of Law and Economics* 41–56.

Eisenberg, Melvin. 1976. "Private Ordering through Negotiations: Dispute-Settlement and Rulemaking." 89 *Harvard Law Review* 637–681.

Eisenstein, James. 1978. *Counsel for the United States: U.S. Attorneys in the Political and Legal Systems*. Baltimore: The Johns Hopkins University Press.

Eisenstein, James and Herbert Jacob. 1977. *Felony Justice: An Organizational Analysis of Criminal Courts*. Boston: Little, Brown.

Eisenstein, James, Roy B. Flemming, and Peter F. Nardulli. 1988. *The Contours of Justice: Communities and Their Courts*. Boston: Little, Brown.

Elliott, E. Donald. 1986. "Managerial Judging and the Evolution of Procedure." 53 *University of Chicago Law Review* 306–336.

Engel, David M. 1977. "The Standardization of Lawyers' Services." 1977 *American Bar Foundation Research Journal* 817–844.

Engel, G.V. 1970. "Professional Autonomy and Bureaucratic Organization." 15 *Administrative Science Quarterly* 12–21.

Epstein, Arnold, Colin B. Begg, and Barbara J. McNeil. 1986. "The Use of Ambulatory Testing in Prepaid and Fee-for-service Group Practices." 314 *New England Journal of Medicine* 1089–1094.

Erlanger, Howard S. 1978. "Young Lawyers and Work in the Public Interest." 1978 *American Bar Foundation Research Journal* 83–104.

Erlanger, Howard S. and Douglas A. Klegon. 1978. "Socialization Effects in Professional School." 13 *Law & Society Review* 11–35.

Esser, John P. 1989. "Evaluations of Dispute Processing: We Do Not Know What We Think and We Do Not Think What We Know." 66 *Denver University Law Review* 499–562.

Etheridge, Carolyn F. 1973. "Lawyers Versus Indigents: Conflict of Interest in Profession-Client Relations in the Legal Profession." Pp. 245–265 in Eliot Freidson (ed.), *The Professions and Their Prospects*. Beverly Hills, Calif.: Sage.

Eulau, Heinz and John D. Sprague. 1964. *Lawyers in Politics: A Study of Professional Convergence*. Indianapolis: Bobbs-Merrill.

Evan, William M. and Ezra G. Levin. 1966. "Status-Set and Role-Set Conflicts of the Stockbroker: A Problem in the Sociology of Law." 45 *Social Forces* 73–83.

Feeley, Malcolm M. 1982. "Plea Bargaining and the Structure of the Criminal Process." 7 *Justice System Journal* 338–354.

Feinberg, Kenneth R. and John S. Gomperts. 1986. "Attorneys' Fees in the Agent Orange Litigation: Modifying the Lodestar Analysis for Mass Tort Cases." 14 *New York University Review of Law & Social Change* 613–631.

Fine, Ralph Adam. 1986. *Escape of the Guilty*. New York: Dodd, Mead.

Fiss, Owen. 1984. "Against Settlement." 93 *Yale Law Journal* 1073–1090.

Fitzpatrick, James F. 1989. "Legal Future Shock: The Role of Large Law Firms by the End of the Century." 64 *Indiana Law Journal* 461–471.

Flanders, Steven. 1977. *Case Management and Court Management in the United States District Courts*. Washington, D.C.: Federal Judicial Center.

Flango, Victor Eugene. 1989. "The Effect of Proposed Changes in Federal Diversity Jurisdiction on State Courts." 1(2) *State Justice Institute News* 7–8.

Flango, Victor Eugene, Robert T. Roper, and Mary E. Elsner. 1983. *The Business of State Trial Courts*. Williamsburg, Va.: The National Center for State Courts.

Flemming, Roy B. 1986. "The Client Game: Defense Attorney Perspectives of Their Relations with Criminal Clients." 1986 *American Bar Foundation Research Journal* 253–277.

Flood, John. 1981. "Middlemen of the Law: An Ethnographic Inquiry into the English Legal Profession." 1981 *American Bar Foundation Research Journal* 377–405.

———. 1983. *Barristers' Clerks: The Law's Middlemen*. Manchester: Manchester University Press.

Foster, James C. 1986. *The Ideology of Apolitical Politics: The Elite Lawyers' Response to the Legitimation Crisis in American Capitalism, 1870–1920*. Millwood, N.Y.: Associated Faculty Press.

Franklin, Marc A., Robert H. Chanin, and Irving Mark. 1961. "Accidents, Money and the Law: A Study of the Economics of Personal Injury Litigation." 61 *Columbia University Law Review* 1–39.

Freedman, Eric. 1985. "Non-Lawyers May Represent Clients at Michigan Job Hearings." *National Law Journal* (July 29, 1985), p. 11.

Freidson, Eliot. 1960. "Client Control and Medical Practice." 65 *American Journal of Sociology* 374–382.

_____. 1970. *Profession of Medicine: A Study of the Sociology of Applied Knowledge.* New York: Dodd, Mead.

_____. 1983. "The Theory of Professions: State of the Art." Pp. 19–37 in Robert Dingwall and Philip Lewis (eds.), *The Sociology of the Professions: Lawyers, Doctors and Others.* New York: St. Martins.

_____. 1986. *Professional Powers: A Study of the Institutionalization of Formal Knowledge.* Chicago: University of Chicago Press.

Fried, Charles. 1976. "The Lawyer as Friend: The Moral Foundations of the Lawyer-Client Relation." 85 *Yale Law Journal* 1060–1089.

Friedman, Alan E. 1969. "An Analysis of Settlement." 22 *Stanford Law Review* 67–100.

Friedman, Lawrence M. 1973. *A History of American Law.* New York: Simon and Schuster.

_____. 1985. *Total Justice.* New York: Russell Sage.

Freund, Paul A. 1963. "The Legal Profession." 92 *Daedulus* 689–700.

Frost, Anne and Coral Howard. 1977. *Representation and Administrative Tribunals.* London: Routledge & Kegan Paul.

Galanter, Marc. 1974. "Why the Haves Come Out Ahead: Speculations on the Limits of Legal Change." 9 *Law & Society Review* 95–160.

_____. 1981. "Justice in Many Rooms." 19 *Journal of Legal Pluralism* 1–47.

_____. 1983a. "Reading the Landscape of Disputes: What We Know and Don't Know (and Think We Know) About Our Allegedly Contentious and Litigious Society." 31 *UCLA Law Review* 4–71.

_____. 1983b. "Mega-Law and Mega-Lawyering in the Contemporary United States." Pp. 152–176 in Robert Dingwall and Philip Lewis (eds.), *The Sociology of the Professions: Lawyers, Doctors and Others.* New York: St. Martins.

_____. 1985a "The Legal Malaise; or, Justice Observed." 19 *Law & Society Review* 537–556.

_____. 1985b. "' . . . A Settlement Judge, Not a Trial Judge': Judicial Mediation in the United States." 12 *Journal of Law and Society* 1–18.

_____. 1986a. "The Emergence of the Judge as a Mediator in Civil Cases." 69 *Judicature* 256–262.

_____. 1986b. "The Day After the Litigation Explosion." 46 *Maryland Law Review* 3–39.

_____. 1988. "The Quality of Settlements." 1988 *Journal of Dispute Resolution* 55–84.

_____. 1989. "Judges and the Quality of Settlement." Working Paper JE-1, Center for Philosophy and Public Policy, University of Maryland.

Geertz, Clifford. 1960. "The Japanese Kijaji: The Changing Role of a Cultural Broker." 2 *Comparative Studies in Society and History* 228–249.

Geison, Gerald L. 1983. "Introduction." Pp. 3–11 in Gerald L. Geison (ed.), *Professions and Professional Ideologies in America.* Chapel Hill: University of North Carolina Press.

Gellhorn, Walter. 1967. *Ombudsmen and Others: Citizens' Protectors in Nine Countries.* Cambridge, Mass.: Harvard University Press.

Genn, Hazel. 1988. *Hard Bargaining: Out of Court Settlement in Personal Injury Actions.* Oxford: Clarendon.

Gilb, Corinne Lathrop. 1956. "Self-Regulating Professions and the Public Welfare: A Case Study of the California Bar." Unpublished Ph.D. Dissertation, Radcliffe College, Cambridge, Mass.

Gilson, Ronald J. "Value Creation by Business Lawyers: Legal Skills and Asset Pricing." 94 *Yale Law Journal* 239–313.

Glaser, William A. 1970. *Paying the Doctor: Systems of Remuneration and Their Effects*. Baltimore: The Johns Hopkins Press.

Goldmann, Franz. 1952. "Methods of Payment for Physicians' Services in Medical Care Programs." 42 *American Journal of Public Health* 131–141.

Goode, William J. 1957. "Community within a Community: The Professions." 22 *American Sociological Review* 194–200.

Goulden, J.C. 1972. *The Superlawyers: The Small and Powerful World of the Great Washington Law Firms*. New York: David McKay.

Grady, John F. 1976. "Some Ethical Questions About Percentage Fees." 2(4) *Litigation* 20–26.

Green, Mark J. 1975. *The Other Government: The Unseen Power of Washington Lawyers*. New York: Grossman.

Greenwood, Ernest. 1957. "Attributes of a Profession." 2 *Social Work* 45–55.

Grescoe, Paul. 1978. "The King of Torts." *Canadian Business* (May) 58.

Grossman, Joel B., Herbert M. Kritzer, Kristin Bumiller, and Stephen McDougal. 1981. "Measuring the Pace of Litigation in Federal and State Trial Courts." 65 *Judicature* 86–113.

Grossman, Joel B., Herbert M. Kritzer, Kristin Bumiller, Austin Sarat, Stephen McDougal, and Richard E. Miller. 1982. "Dimensions of Institutional Participation: Who Uses the Courts and How?" 44 *Journal of Politics* 86–114.

Gyarmati, Gabriel. 1975. "The Doctrice of the Professionals: Basis of a Power Structure." 27 *International Social Science Journal* 629–654.

Halliday, Terence C. 1987. *Beyond Monopoly: Lawyers, State Crises, and Professional Empowerment*. Chicago: University of Chicago Press.

Handler, Joel. 1967. *The Lawyer and His Community*. Madison: University of Wisconsin Press.

Handler, Joel, Ellen Jane Hollingsworth, and Howard S. Erlanger. 1978. *Lawyers and the Pursuit of Legal Rights*. New York: Academic.

Harrington, Christine. 1985. *Shadow Justice: The Ideology and Institutionalization of Alternatives to Court*. Westport, Conn.: Greenwood.

Heinz, John P. and Edward O. Laumann. 1982. *Chicago Lawyers: The Social Structure of the Bar*. New York: Russell Sage.

Hill, Larry. 1976. *The Model Ombudsman*. Princeton, N.J.: Princeton University Press.

Hilton, Gordon. 1976. *Intermediate Politometrics*. New York: Columbia University Press.

Holmes, David B. 1985. "Nonlawyer Practice Before the Immigration Agencies." 37 *Administrative Law Review* 417–419.

Homans, George C. 1958. "Social Behavior as Exchange." 63 *American Journal of Sociology* 597–606.

Hopkins, Nicholas S., Monday U. Ekpo, Janet Heileman, Maddy Michtom, Ann Osterweil, R.T. Sieber, and George H. Smith. 1977. "Brokers and Symbols in American Urban Life." 50 *Anthropolotical Quarterly* 65–75.

Horowitz, Donald L. 1977. *Jurocracy*. Lexington, Mass.: Lexington Books.

Hosticka, Carl J. 1979. "We Don't Care About What Happened, We Only Care About What Is Going to Happen: Lawyer-Client Negotiations of Reality." 26 *Social Problems* 599–610.

Hughes, Everett C. 1963. "Professions." 92 *Daedulus* 655–668.

———. 1971. "The Study of Occupations." Pp. 283–297 in *The Sociological Eye: Selected Papers on Work, Self, & the Study of Society*. Chicago: Aldine-Atherton.

Hurst, James Willard. 1950. *The Growth of American Law: The Law Makers*. Boston: Little, Brown.

Intagliata, J. 1982. "Improving the Quality of Community Care for the Chronically Mentally Disabled: The Role of Case Management." 8 *Schizophrenia Bulletin* 655–674.

Jackson, R.M. 1977. *The Machinery of Justice in England*. Cambridge: Cambridge University Press.

Jenkins, John A. 1989. *The Litigators*. New York: Doubleday.

Jennings, Diana. 1989. "King of Torts." *Chicago Tribune* (July 25) 2:1–2.

Johnson, Earl, Jr. 1978. *Justice and Reform: The Formative Years of the American Legal Services Program*. New Brunswick, N.J.: Transaction Books.

———. 1980–1981. "Lawyers' Choice: A Theoretical Appraisal of Litigation Investment Decisions." 15 *Law & Society Review* 567–610.

Johnson, Terence J. 1972. *Professions and Power*. London: Macmillan.

Kagan, Robert A. and Robert Eli Rosen. 1985. "On the Social Significance of Large Law Firm Practice." 37 *Stanford Law Review* 399–443.

Kakalik, James S. and Nicholas M. Pace. 1986. *Costs and Compensation Paid in Tort Litigation*. Santa Monica, Calif.: The Rand Corporation.

Katz, Jack. 1982. *Poor People's Lawyers in Transition*. Brunswick, N.J.: Rutgers University Press.

———. 1985. "Caste, Class, and Counsel for the Poor." 1985 *American Bar Foundation Research Journal* 251–292.

Kessler, Mark. 1987. *Legal Services for the Poor: A Comparative and Contemporary Analysis of Interorganizational Politics*. New York: Greenwood.

Kritzer, Herbert M. 1980–1981. "Studying Disputes: Learning from the CLRP Experience." 15 *Law & Society Review* 503–524.

———. 1982. "The Judge's Role in Pretrial Case Processing: Assessing the Need for Change." 66 *Judicature* 28–38.

———. 1984a. "The Dimensions of Lawyer-Client Relations: Notes Toward a Theory and a Field Study." 1984 *American Bar Foundation Research Journal* 409–425.

———. 1984b. "The Civil Litigation Research Project: Lessons for Studying the Civil Justice System." Pp. 30–36 in Alan Gelfand (ed.), *Proceedings of the Second Workshop on Law and Justice Statistics, 1983*. Washington, D.C.: U.S. Department of Justice, Bureau of Justice Statistics.

———. 1986. "Adjudication to Settlement: Shading in the Gray." 70 *Judicature* 161–165.

———. 1987. "Fee Arrangements and Negotiation: A Research Note." 21 *Law & Society Review* 341–348.

———. 1989. "A Comparative Perspective on Settlement and Bargaining in Personal Injury Cases." 14 *Law & Social Inquiry* 167–186.

———. 1990. "Substance and Method in the Use of Ratio Variables, or the Spurious Nature of Spurious Correlation." 52 *Journal of Politics* 243–254.

———. (Forthcoming). *Let's Make a Deal: Understanding the Negotiation Process in Ordinary Litigation*. Madison, Wis.: University of Wisconsin Press.

Kritzer, Herbert M. and Jill K. Anderson. 1983. "The Arbitration Alternative: A Comparative Analysis of Case Processing Time, Disposition Mode, and Cost in the

American Arbitration Association and the Courts." 8 *Justice System Journal* 6–19.

Kritzer, Herbert M., Austin Sarat, David M. Trubek, Kristin Bumiller, and Elizabeth McNichol. 1984a. "Understanding the Costs of Litigation: The Case of the Hourly Fee Lawyer." 1984 *American Bar Foundation Research Journal* 559–604.

Kritzer, Herbert M., Joel B. Grossman, Elizabeth McNichol, David M. Trubek, and Austin Sarat. 1984b. "Courts and Litigation Investment: Why Do Lawyers Spend More Time on Federal Cases." 9 *Justice System Journal* 7–22.

Kritzer, Herbert M., William L.F. Felstiner, Austin Sarat, and David M. Trubek. 1985. "The Impact of Fee Arrangement on Lawyer Effort." 19 *Law & Society Review* 251–278.

Kupferberg, Tuli. 1978. "An Insulting Look at Lawyers Through the Ages." 8 *Juris Doctor* 62 (October/November).

Lamb, H.R. 1980. "Therapist-Case Managers: More than Brokers of Services." 31 *Hospital and Community Psychiatry* 762–764.

Landes, Elisabeth M. 1982. "Compensation for Automobile Accident Injuries: Is the Tort System Fair?" 11 *Journal of Legal Studies* 253–259.

Landon, Donald D. 1982. "Lawyers and Localities: The Interaction of Community Context and Professionalism." 1982 *American Bar Foundation Research Journal* 459–485.

_____. 1985. "Clients, Colleagues, and Community: The Shaping of Zealous Advocacy in Country Law Practice." 1985 *American Bar Foundation Research Journal* 81–111.

_____. 1988. "Lasalle Street and Main Street: The Role of Context in Structuring Law Practice." 22 *Law & Society Review* 213–236.

Langbein, John H. 1985. "The German Advantage in Civil Procedure." 52 *University of Chicago Law Review* 823–866.

Larson, Magali Sarfatti. 1977. *The Rise of Professionalism: A Sociological Analysis.* Berkeley, Calif.: University of California Press.

Laumann, Edward O. and Jack P. Heinz, with Robert L. Nelson and Robert H. Salisbury. 1985. "Washington Lawyers and Others: The Structure of Washington Representation." 37 *Stanford Law Review* 495–502.

Law Enforcement Assistance Administration (LEAA). 1973. *National Survey of Court Organization.* Washington, D.C.: Department of Justice.

_____. 1982. *National Survey of Court Organization.* Washington, D.C.: Department of Justice.

Law Society. 1970. *Memorandum on Maintenance and Champerty: Claims Assessors and Contingency Fees.* London: The Law Society.

Le, Tang Thi Thanh Trai. 1982. "The French Legal Profession: A Prisoner of Its Glorious Past?" 15 *Cornell International Law Journal* 63–104.

Lees, D.S. 1966. *Economic Consequences of the Professions.* London: Institute of Economic Affairs.

Lewis, Anthony. 1964. *Gideon's Trumpet.* New York: Random House.

Lewis, Charles E., Rashi Fein, and David Mechanic. 1976. *A Right to Health: The Problem of Access to Primary Medical Care.* New York: Wiley.

Lieberman, J. 1982. "The Public Processing of America's Disputes: The Capacities and Capabilities of Our Courts and Other Formal Public Dispute Resolution Institutions." Paper presented at National Conference on the Lawyer's Changing Role in Resolving Disputes, Harvard Law School.

Lind, E. Alan, et al. 1989. *The Perception of Justice: Tort Litigants' Views of Trial, Court-Annexed Arbitration, and Judicial Settlement Conferences.* Santa Monica, Calif.: The Rand Corporation.

Lord Chancellor's Department. 1987. *Civil Justice Review: General Issues* (Consultation Paper Six). London: Lord Chancellor's Department.

Luban, David. 1989a. *Lawyers and Justice: An Ethical Study.* Princeton, N.J.: Princeton University Press.

_____. 1989b. "The Quality of Justice." 66 *Denver University Law Review* 381–418.

Lynch, Eugene F. 1978. "Settlement of Civil Cases: A View from the Bench." 5(1) *Litigation* 8–10, 57–58.

Macaulay, Stewart. 1979. "Lawyers and Consumer Protection Laws." 14 *Law & Society Review* 115–171.

MacKinnon, F. 1964. *Contingent Fees for Legal Services.* Chicago: Aldine.

Mann, Kenneth. 1986. *Defending White-Collar Crime: A Portrait of Attorneys at Work.* New Haven, Conn.: Yale University Press.

Marks, F. Raymond, with Kirk Leswign and Barbara A. Fortinsky. 1972. *The Lawyer, the Public, and Professional Responsibility.* Chicago: American Bar Foundation.

Maru, Olavi. 1986. *Research on the Legal Profession: A Review of Work Done* (2nd Ed.). Chicago: American Bar Foundation.

Mayer, Adrian C. 1967. "Patrons and Brokers: Rural Leadership in Four Overseas Indian Communities." Pp. 167–188 in Maurice Freedman (ed.), *Social Organization: Essays Presented to Raymond Firth.* London: Fran Cass & Co.

McIntosh, Wayne. 1980–1981. "150 Years of Litigation and Dispute Settlement: A Court Tale." 15 *Law & Society Review* 823–848.

_____. 1983. "Private Use of a Public Forum: A Long-Range View of the Dispute Processing Role of Courts." 77 *American Political Science Review* 991–1010.

_____. 1989. *The Appeal of Civil Law: A Political-Economic Analysis of Litigation.* Urbana: University of Illinois Press.

McThenia, Andrew W. and Thomas L. Shaffer. 1985. "For Reconciliation." 94 *Yale Law Journal* 1660–1668.

Megarry, R.E. 1962. *Lawyer and Litigant in England.* London: Stevens & Sons.

Mellinkopf, David. 1973. *The Conscience of a Lawyer.* St. Paul, Minn.: West.

Menkel-Meadow, Carrie. 1984. "Toward Another View of Legal Negotiation: The Structure of Problem Solving." 31 *UCLA Law Review* 754–842.

_____. 1985a. "Judges and Settlement: What Part Should Judges Play?" 21(10) *Trial* 24–29.

_____. 1985b. "Nonprofessional Advocacy: The 'Paralegalization' of Legal Services for the Poor." 19 *Clearinghouse Review* 403–411.

_____. 1989. "Exploring a Research Agenda of the Feminization of the Legal Profession: Theories of Gender and Social Change." 14 *Law & Social Inquiry* 289–319.

Menkel-Meadow, Carrie and Robert Meadow. 1983. "Resource Allocation in Legal Services: Individual Attorney Decisions in Work Priority." 5 *Law & Policy Quarterly* 237–256.

Miller, Arthur. 1984. "The Adversary System: Dinosaur or Phoenix." 69 *University of Minnesota Law Review* 1–37.

Miller, Richard E. 1983. "Erratum for 'Grievances, Claims, and Disputes: Assessing the Adversary Culture'." 17 *Law & Society Review* 653.

Miller, Richard E. and Austin Sarat. 1980–1981. "Grievances, Claims and Disputes: Asssessing the Adversary Culture." 15 *Law & Society Review* 525–566.

Millerson, Geoffrey. 1964. "Dilemmas of Professionalism." 3(88) *New Society* 15–16 (June 4, 1964).

Mnookin, R.H. and L. Kornhauser. 1979. "Bargaining in the Shadow of the Law: The Case of Divorce." 88 *Yale Law Journal* 950–997.

Mohr, Lawrence B. 1976. "Organizations, Decisions, and Courts." 10 *Law & Society Review* 621–642.

Moore, Nancy J. 1987. "Professionalism Reconsidered." 1987 *American Bar Foundation Research Journal* 773–790.

Moore, Wilbert E. 1970. *The Professions: Roles and Rules.* New York: Russell Sage.

Morgan, Thomas D. 1985. "The Fall and Rise of Professionalism." 19 *University of Richmond Law Review* 453–466.

Morrison, Alan B. 1976. "Breaking Up the Legal Monopoly." 1 *New Directions in Legal Services* 113.

Mungham, Geoff and Philip A. Thomas. 1983. "Solicitors and Clients: Altruism or Self-Interest." Pp. 131–151 in Robert Dingwall and Philip Lewis (eds.), *The Sociology of the Professions: Lawyers, Doctors and Others.* New York: St. Martins.

Nardulli, Peter F. 1978. *The Courtroom Elite: An Organizational Perspective on Criminal Justice.* Cambridge: Ballinger Publishing.

Nardulli, Peter F., James Eisenstein, and Roy B. Flemming. 1988. *The Tenor of Justice: Criminal Courts and the Guilty Plea Process.* Urbana: University of Illinois Press.

Nardulli, Peter F., Roy B. Flemming, and James Eisenstein. 1985. "Criminal Courts and Bureaucratic Justice: Concessions and Consensus in the Guilty Plea Process." 76 *Journal of Criminal Law & Criminology* 1103–1131.

National Center for State Courts. 1978. *State Court Caseload Statistics: The State of the Art.* Washington, D.C.: Law Enforcement Assistance Administration.

_____. 1985. *State Court Caseload Statistics: Annual Report 1981.* Williamsburg, Va.: National Center for State Courts.

National Law Journal. 1986. "What America Really Thinks About Lawyers." *National Law Journal* (August 18, 1986).

Naythons, Edwin E. 1973. "The Civil Settlement Conference." 9 *Forum* 75.

Nelson, Robert. 1981. "Practice and Privilege: Social Change and the Structure of Large Law Firms." 1981 *American Bar Foundation Research Journal* 95–140.

_____. 1985. "Ideology, Practice and Professional Autonomy: Social Values and Client Relations in the Large Law Firms." 37 *Stanford Law Review* 503–555.

_____. 1988. *Partners in Power: Bureaucracy, Professionalism, and Social Change in the Large Law Firm.* Berkeley: University of California Press.

Oakley, John B. and Arthur F. Coon. 1986. "The Federal Rules in State Courts: A Survey of State Court Systems of Civil Procedures." 61 *Washington Law Review* 1367–1434.

Parsons, Talcott. 1939. "The Professions and Social Structure." 17 *Social Forces* 457–67. Reprinted as pp. 34–49 in *Essays in Sociological Theory* (1954). New York: Free Press.

_____. 1954. "A Sociologist Looks at the Legal Profession." Pp. 370–385 in *Essays in Sociological Theory.* New York: Free Press.

_____. 1968. "Professions." Pp. 536–547 in David Sills (ed.), *International Encyclopedia of the Social Sciences*, Vol. 12. New York: Macmillan.

Paulson, Beth A. 1987. *Alternative Dispute Resolution: An ADR Primer.* Washington, D.C.: American Bar Association, Standing Committee on Dispute Resolution.

Payer, Lynn. 1988. *Medicine and Culture*. New York: Holt.

Perry, J.A.G. 1973. "The Broker in a Rural Lesotho Community." 32 *African Studies* 137–152.

Peterson, Mark A. 1987. *Civil Juries in the 1980's: Trends in Jury Trials and Verdicts in California and Cook County, Illinois*. Santa Monica, Calif.: The Rand Corporation.

Peterson, Mark A. and George L. Priest. 1982. *The Civil Jury: Trends in Trials and Verdicts, Cook County, Illinois, 1960–1979*. Santa Monica, Calif.: The Rand Corporation.

Podmore, David. 1980. *Solicitors and the Wider Community*. London: Heinemann.

Posner, Richard A. 1973. "An Economic Approach to Legal Procedure and Judicial Administration." 2 *Journal of Legal Studies* 399–455.

Post, Robert C. 1987. "On the Popular Image of the Lawyer: Reflections in a Dark Glass." 75 *California Law Review* 379–389.

Pound, Roscoe. 1953. *The Lawyer from Antiquity to Modern Times*. St. Paul: West Publishing.

Powell, Michael J. 1988. *From Patrician to Professional Elite: The Transformation of the New York City Bar Association*. New York: Russell Sage.

Priest, George L. 1985. "Reexamining the Selection Hypothesis: Learning from Wittman's Mistakes." 14 *Journal of Legal Studies* 215–243.

Priest, George L. and Benjamin Klein. 1984. "The Selection of Disputes for Litigation." 13 *Journal of Legal Studies* 1–55.

Provine, D. Marie. 1986a. *Settlement Strategies for Federal District Judges*. Washington, D.C.: Federal Judicial Center.

———. 1986b. *Judging Credentials: Nonlawyer Judges and the Politics of Professionalism*. Chicago: University of Chicago Press.

Public Protection Committee. 1988. *Report of the Public Protection Committee*. San Francisco: Office of Professional Standards, State Bar of California.

Quam, Lois, Robert Dingwall, and Paul Fenn. 1987. "Medical Malpractice in Perspective." 294 *British Medical Journal* 1529–1532, 1597–1600.

Quigg, Donald J. 1985. "Nonlawyer Practice Before the Patent and Trademark Office." 37 *Administrative Law Review* 409–411.

Rabin, Robert L. 1976. "Lawyers for Social Change: Perspectives on Public Interest Law." 28 *Stanford Law Review* 207–263.

Rathjen, Gregory J. 1976. "The Impact of Legal Education on the Beliefs, Attitudes and Values of Law Students." 44 *Tennessee Law Review* 85–116.

Reed, John. 1969. "The Lawyer-Client: A Managed Relationship?" 12 *Academy of Management Journal* 67–80.

Resnik, Judith. 1982. "Managerial Judges." 96 *Harvard Law Review* 374–448.

Rhode, Deborah. 1981. "Policing the Professional Monopoly: A Constitutional and Empirical Analysis of Unauthorized Practice Prohibitions." 34 *Stanford Law Review* 1–112.

———. 1985. "Ethical Perspectives on Legal Practice." 37 *Stanford Law Review* 589–652.

Ries, John C. 1969. *Executives in the American Political System*. Belmont, Calif.: Dickenson Publishing.

Ritzer, George. 1973. "Professionalism and the Individual." Pp. 59–73 in Eliot Freidson (ed.), *The Professions and Their Prospects*. Beverly Hills, Calif.: Sage.

Roemer, Milton I. 1962. "On Paying the Doctor and the Implications of Different Methods." 3 *Journal of Health and Human Behavior* 4–14.

Rosen, Robert Eli. 1988–1989. "The Inside Counsel Movement, Professional Judgment and Organizational Representation." 64 *Indiana Law Journal* 479–554.

Rosenberg, Maurice. 1980–1981. "Civil Justice Research and Civil Justice Reform." 15 *Law & Society Review* 473–483.

_____. 1984. "The Federal Rules After Half a Century." 36 *Maine Law Review* 243–251.

Rosenthal, Douglas. 1974. *Lawyer and Client: Who's in Charge?* New York: Russell Sage.

Rosett, Arthur and Donald R. Cressey. 1976. *Justice by Consent: Plea Bargains in the American Courthouse*. Philadelphia: J.B. Lippincott.

Ross, H. Laurence. 1980. *Settled Out of Court: The Social Process of Insurance Claims Adjustment* (Rev. 2nd Ed.). New York: Aldine.

Roth, Andrew and Jonathan Roth. 1989. *Devil's Advocate: The Unnatural History of Lawyers*. Berkeley, Calif.: Nolo Press.

Rotunda, Ronald D. 1987. "Lawyers and Professionalism: A Commentary on the Report of the American Bar Association Commission on Professionalism." 18 *Loyola University of Chicago Law Journal* 1149–1180.

Rueschemeyer, Dietrich. 1964. "Doctors and Lawyers: A Comment on the Theory of the Professions." 1 *Canadian Review of Sociology and Anthropology* 17–30.

_____. 1973. *Lawyers and Their Society. A Comparative Study of The Legal Profession in Germany and in the United States*. Cambridge, Mass.: Harvard University Press.

_____. 1983. "Professional Autonomy and the Social Control of Expertise." Pp. 38–58 in Robert Dingwall and Philip Lewis (eds.), *The Sociology of the Professions: Lawyers, Doctors and Others*. New York: St. Martins.

_____. 1986. "Comparing Legal Professions Cross-Nationally: From a Professions-Centered to a State-Centered Approach." 1986 *American Bar Foundation Research Journal* 415–446.

Ryan, John Paul, Allan Ashman, Bruce D. Sales, and Sandra Shane-DuBow. 1980. *American Trial Judges: Their Work Styles and Performance*. New York: Free Press.

Sander, Frank E.A. 1976. "Varieties of Dispute Processing." 70 *Federal Rules Decisions* 111–134.

Sander, Richard H. and E. Douglass Williams. 1989. "Why Are There So Many Lawyers? Perspectives on a Turbulent Market." 14 *Law & Social Inquiry* 431–479.

Sarat, Austin. 1981. "The Role of Courts and the Logic of Court Reform: Notes on the Justice Department's Approach to Improving Justice." 64 *Judicature* 300–311.

Sarat, Austin and William L.F. Felstiner. 1986. "Law and Strategy in the Divorce Lawyer's Office." 20 *Law & Society Review* 93–134.

_____. 1988. "Law and Social Relations: Vocabularies of Motive in Lawyer/Client Interaction." 22 *Law & Society Review* 737–770.

Schiller, Lawrence and James Wall. 1981. "Judicial Settlement Techniques." 5 *American Journal of Trial Advocacy* 39–61.

Schneyer, Ted. 1989. "Professionalism as Bar Politics: The Making of the Model Rules of Professional Conduct." 14 *Law & Social Inquiry* 677–737.

Schwartz, Murray L. and Daniel J.B. Mitchell. 1970. "An Economic Analysis of the Contingent Fee in Personal-Injury Litigation." 22 *Stanford Law Review* 1125–1162.

See, Harold. 1984. "An Alternative to the Contingent Fee." 1984 *Utah Law Review* 485–509.

Selinger, Carl M. 1987. "Paralegals: The British Invasion." *National Law Journal* (November 16, 1987), 13–14.

Shanley, Michael G. and Mark A. Peterson. 1983. *Comparative Justice: Civil Jury Verdicts in San Francisco and Cook Counties, 1959–1980*. Santa Monica, Calif.: The Rand Corporation.

Sikes, Bette H., Clara N. Carson, and Patricia Gorai (eds.). 1972. *The 1971 Lawyer Statistical Report*. Chicago: American Bar Foundation.

Silver, Harry. 1981. "Going for Brokers: Political Innovation and Structural Integration in a Changing Ashanti Community." 14 *Comparative Political Studies* 233–263.

Simon, William H. 1978. "The Ideology of Advocacy: Procedural Justice and Professional Ethics." 1978 *Wisconsin Law Review* 29–144.

———. 1984. "Visions of Practice in Legal Thought." 36 *Stanford Law Review* 469–507.

———. 1985. "Babbitt v. Brandeis: The Decline of the Professional Idea." 37 *Stanford Law Review* 565–587.

Slovak, Jeffrey S. 1979. "Working for Corporate Actors: Social Change and Elite Attorneys in Chicago." 1979 *American Bar Foundation Research Journal* 465–500.

———. 1980. "Giving and Getting Respect: Prestige and Stratification in a Legal Elite." 1980 *American Bar Foundation Research Journal* 31–68.

———. 1981a. "Influence and Issues in the Legal Community: The Role of a Legal Elite." 1981 *American Bar Foundation Research Journal* 141–194.

———. 1981b. "The Ethics of Corporate Lawyers: A Sociological Approach." 1981 *American Bar Foundation Research Journal* 753–794.

Smigel, Erwin O. 1964. *The Wall Street Lawyer*. New York: Free Press.

Spangler, Eve. 1986. *Lawyers for Hire: Salaried Professionals at Work*. New Haven, Conn.: Yale University Press.

Spevack, Martin. 1973. *The Harvard Concordance to Shakespeare*. Cambridge, Mass.: Belknap Press of Harvard University Press.

Stern, Gerald M. 1976. *The Buffalo Creek Disaster*. New York: Random House.

Steven, Mark. 1987. *Power of Attorney: The Rise of the Giant Law Firms*. New York: McGraw-Hill.

Stevenson, Michael, Garry Watson, and Edward Weissman. 1977. "The Impact of Pretrial Conferences: An Interim Report on the Ontario Pretrial Conference Experiment." 15 *Osgoode Hall Law Journal* 591–615.

Stewart, James B. 1983. *The Partners: Inside America's Most Powerful Law Firms*. New York: Simon and Schuster.

Stover, Robert V. 1989. *Making It and Breaking It: The Fate of Public Interest Commitment During Law School*. Urbana: University of Illinois Press.

Sudnow, David. 1965. "Normal Crimes: Sociological Features of the Penal Code in a Public Defender Office." 12 *Social Problems* 255–276.

Suleiman, Ezra N. 1987. *Private Power and Centralization in France: The Notaires and the State*. Princeton, N.J.: Princeton University Press.

Szanton, Peter L. 1973. "Public Policy and the Law: Legal Training as 'Perverse' Preparation for Policymaking Role in Government." 6(3) *Antitrust Law & Economics Review* 51–66.

Title, Julius M. 1979. "New Settlement Techniques for the Trial Judge." 18 *The Judges' Journal* 42–49.

Trubek, David M., Joel B. Grossman, William L.F. Felstiner, Herbert M. Kritzer, and Austin Sarat. 1983a. *Civil Litigation Research Project Final Report*. Madison, Wisc.: University of Wisconsin Law School.

Trubek, David M., Austin Sarat, William L.F. Felstiner, Herbert M. Kritzer, and Joel B. Grossman. 1983b. "The Costs of Ordinary Litigation." 31 *UCLA Law Review* 72–127.

Trubek, David M., Herbert M. Kritzer, Karen Holst, and William L.F. Felstiner. 1984. "Costs, Processes, and Outcomes: Lawyers' Attitudes Towards Courts and Other Dispute Processing Options" [Report to the National Institute for Dispute Resolution]. Madison, Wisc.: Disputes Processing Research Program, University of Wisconsin Law School.

Tyler, Tom R. 1989. "The Quality of Dispute Resolution Processes and Outcomes: Measurement Problems and Possibilities." 66 *Denver University Law Review* 419–436.

Utz, Pamela. 1978. *Settling the Facts: Discretion and Negotiation in Criminal Courts*. Lexington, Mass.: Lexington Books.

Verkuil, Paul R. 1975. "The Ombudsman and the Limits of the Adversary System." 75 *Columbia Law Review* 845–861.

van den Haag, Ernest. 1975. *Publishing Criminals: Concerning a Very Old and Painful Question*. New York: Basic Books.

Vidmar, Neil. 1984. "The Small Claims Court: A Reconceptualization of Disputes and an Empirical Investigation." 18 *Law & Society Review* 515–550.

Viscusi, W. Kip. 1986. "The Determinants of the Disposition of Product Liability Claims and Compensation for Bodily Injury." 15 *Journal of Legal Studies* 321–346.

VUWLR. 1982. "Office of Ombudsman—Anniversary Issue." 12 *Victoria University of Wellington Law Review* 207–324.

Waldman, Sidney. 1972. *Foundations of Political Action: An Exchange Theory of Politics*. Boston: Little, Brown.

Wall, James and Lawrence Schiller. 1982. "Judicial Involvement in Pretrial Settlement: A Judge Is Not a Bump on a Log." 6 *American Journal of Trial Advocacy* 27–45.

Wanner, Craig. 1974. "The Public Ordering of Private Relations, Part One: Initiating Civil Cases in Urban Trial Courts." 8 *Law & Society Review* 421–440.

_____. 1975. "The Public Ordering of Private Relations, Part Two: Winning Civil Court Cases." 9 *Law & Society Review* 293–306.

Watson, R.A. and R.G. Downing. 1964. *The Politics of the Bench and Bar: Judicial Selection Under the Missouri Nonpartisan Plan*. New York: Wiley.

Wessel, Milton R. 1976. *The Rule of Reason: A New Approach to Corporate Litigation*. New York: Addison-Wesley.

Wheeler, Stanton, Bliss Cartwright, Robert A. Kagan, and Lawrence M. Friedman. 1987. "Do the 'Haves' Come Out Ahead? Winning and Losing in State Supreme Courts, 1870–1970." 21 *Law & Society Review* 403–446.

White, G. Edward. 1985. *Tort Law in America: An Intellectual History*. New York: Oxford University Press.

Will, Hubert L., Robert R. Merhige, and Alvin B. Rubin. 1977. "The Role of the Judge in the Settlement Process." 75 *Federal Rules Decisions* 203–236.

Williams, Gerald R. 1983. *Legal Negotiation and Settlement*. St. Paul, Minn.: West Publishing.

Wittman, Donald. 1985. "Is the Selection of Cases for Trial Biased?" 14 *Journal of Legal Studies* 185–214.

Wolf, Eric. 1956. "Aspects of Group Relations in a Complex Society: Mexico." 58 *American Anthropologist* 1065–1078.

Wolf, Jacob M. 1985. "Nonlawyer Practice Before the Social Security Administration." 37 *Administrative Law Review* 413–415.

Wraith, R.E. and P.G. Hutchesson. 1973. *Administrative Tribunals*. London: George Allen & Unwin.

Zander, Michael. 1978. *Legal Services for the Community*. London: Temple Smith.

Zemans, Francis Kahn and Victor G. Rosenblum. 1981. *The Making of a Public Profession*. Chicago: American Bar Foundation.

Zemans, Frederick H. 1986. "Recent Trends in the Organization of Legal Services." 11 *Queen's Law Journal* 26–89.

Cases Cited

Gideon v. *Wainwright*, 372 U.S. 335 (1963).

National Association of Radiation Survivors v. *Walters*, 589 F.Supp 1302 (1984).

Oertel v. *Williams*, 214 Wisc. 68 (1934).

Walters v. *National Association of Radiation Survivors*, 473 U.S. 305 (1985).

Index